P9-EDZ-622

The World of
Michelangelo

TIME LIFE BOOKS

TIME-LIFE LIBRARY OF ART

GREAT AGES OF MAN

THE LIFE HISTORY OF THE UNITED STATES

LIFE WORLD LIBRARY

LIFE NATURE LIBRARY

LIFE SCIENCE LIBRARY

TIME READING PROGRAM

INTERNATIONAL BOOK SOCIETY

LIFE Pictorial Atlas of the World

The Epic of Man

The Wonders of Life on Earth

The World We Live In

The World's Great Religions

The LIFE Book of Christmas

LIFE's Picture History of Western Man

The LIFE Treasury of American Folklore

America's Arts and Skills

300 Years of American Painting

The Second World War

LIFE's Picture History of World War II

Picture Cook Book

LIFE Guide to Paris

TIME-LIFE LIBRARY OF ART

The World of Michelangelo

1475-1564

By Robert Coughlan
and
The Editors of TIME-LIFE BOOKS

Time Incorporated, New York

About the Author:

Robert Coughlan, a reporter and editor for Time Inc. for more than 25 years, is the author of biographies of William Faulkner and Maurice Utrillo. His interest in Michelangelo grew out of his research into Renaissance Florence and the House of Medici, in preparation for a book on Lorenzo. In 15 years of collecting material on the Renaissance he has traveled widely in Italy and Europe, and for two years lived in Rome.

The Consulting Editor:

H. W. Janson is Professor of Fine Arts at New York University, where he is also Chairman of the Department of Fine Arts at Washington Square College. Among his numerous books and publications are his definitive *History of Art,* which ranges from prehistory to the present day, *The Sculpture of Donatello* and *The Story of Painting for Young People,* which he co-authored with his wife.

On the Cover:

The Hebrew prophet Isaiah, who foretold the coming of Christ, is shown in a detail from Michelangelo's Sistine Chapel ceiling.

End Sheets:

The Temptation and the Expulsion on the Sistine Chapel ceiling show Adam and Eve in a barren Garden of Eden—a rejection of nature in keeping with Michelangelo's profound conviction that the proper subject of art is man.

TIME-LIFE BOOKS

EDITOR
Norman P. Ross
EXECUTIVE EDITOR
Maitland A. Edey
TEXT DIRECTOR   ART DIRECTOR
Jerry Korn   Edward A. Hamilton
CHIEF OF RESEARCH
Beatrice T. Dobie
Assistant Text Director: Harold C. Field
Assistant Art Director: Arnold C. Holeywell
Assistant Chiefs of Research:
Monica O. Horne, Martha Turner

PUBLISHER
Rhett Austell
General Manager: Joseph C. Hazen Jr.
Planning Director: Frank M. White
Business Manager: John D. McSweeney
Circulation Manager: Joan D. Manley
Publishing Board: Nicholas Benton, Louis Bronzo,
James Wendell Forbes, John S. Wiseman

TIME-LIFE LIBRARY OF ART

SERIES EDITOR: Percy Knauth
Editorial Staff for *The World of Michelangelo:*
Associate Editor: Robert Morton
Text Editor: Diana Hirsh
Picture Editor: Kathleen Shortall
Designer: Paul Jensen
Assistant Designer: Leonard Wolfe
Staff Writer: Dale Brown
Chief Researcher: Martha Turner
Researchers: Jane Alexander, Peggy Bushong,
Carol Phillippe, Marjorie Pickens, Ruth Silva,
Patricia Skinner, Iris Unger

EDITORIAL PRODUCTION
Color Director: Robert L. Young
Copy Staff: Marian Gordon Goldman,
Muriel Kotselas, Dolores A. Littles
Picture Researchers: Margaret K. Goldsmith, Patricia Maye
Art Assistants: Douglas B. Graham, Mark A. Binn

The picture essays for this book were written by Dale Brown.
The following individuals and departments of Time Inc. helped to produce the book:
Doris O'Neil, Chief, LIFE Picture Library; Peter Draz, Chief, Time Inc. Bureau of
Editorial Reference; Richard M. Clurman, Chief, TIME-LIFE News Service; and
Correspondents Ann Natanson and Erik Amfitheatrof [Rome], Victor Velen [Florence],
Katharine Sachs [London], Elisabeth Kraemer [Bonn], Maria Vincenza Aloisi [Paris].

The World of Michelangelo © 1966 Time Inc.
All rights reserved. Published simultaneously in Canada.
Library of Congress catalogue card number 66-16540.
School and library distribution by Silver Burdett Company.

Contents

AUGUSTANA UNIVERSITY COLLEGE
LIBRARY

Introduction

Michelangelo was probably the greatest artistic genius who ever lived. He has left imperishable work in sculpture, painting, architecture and poetry: no one else has mastered at his level of attainment all four means of esthetic communication.

The sheer brilliance and uniqueness of his accomplishment explain the fascination he has always exerted. But he appeals to us for a further reason. In temperament he belongs to our modern world. We live in an age of nervous tension. Michelangelo, too, was tense, neurotic, always restlessly searching for a deeper significance. Everything he created reveals an inner conflict, an unreconciled struggle. Each masterpiece of his maturity is pushed close to the limit of expression. His opposed emotions generate an intensity of feeling unequaled in the history of art.

Though he was preoccupied with the beauty of the human form, he was tormented by awareness of the body's corruption and decay. His eyes were filled with the splendor of antique art; but his spirit was enthralled by the asceticism of the Middle Ages. His mind belonged half to the Greeks and half to Savonarola.

This dichotomy brought about the despair he constantly refers to in his poetry. His life was spent in creating the noblest works of art, which in the end he rejected. William Wordsworth's translation of one of his most famous sonnets conveys this anguish:

> Well-nigh the voyage now is overpast,
> And my frail bark, through troubled seas and rude,
> Draws near that common haven where at last
> Of every action, be it evil or good,
> Must due account be rendered. Well I know
> How vain will then appear that favoured art,
> Sole Idol long and Monarch of my heart,
> For all is vain that man desires below.
> And now remorseful thoughts the past upbraid,
> And fear of twofold death my soul alarms,
> That which must come, and that beyond the grave:
> Picture and Sculpture lose their feeble charms,
> And to that Love Divine I turn for aid,
> Who from the Cross extends his arms to save.

Much has been made of Michelangelo's belief in the theory—absorbed in his early formative years from the tutors in the Medici house-

hold of which he was a part—that the contemplation of physical beauty will lead to spiritual revelation. Less has been said of his ultimate disillusionment with Neoplatonism, as this doctrine was called. But his late sculpture and his late poems are evidence of his disenchantment. There is nothing of physical beauty left in the *Rondanini Pietà* and little in the *Deposition,* or popularly called *Pietà* of Florence. Compare these with the Vatican *Pietà* of Michelangelo's youth, presented in such hauntingly beautiful detail in the pages of this book, and a complete transformation of feeling in the sculptor is apparent: to the untutored eye the earlier work could almost be the creation of a different man.

His tormented preoccupation with the human predicament—age and death—is described in one of his most remarkable poems, which closes with these stanzas:

> What use to want to make so many puppets,
> If they have made me in the end like him
> Who crossed the water, and then drowned in slops?
>
> My honored art, wherein I was for a time
> In such esteem, has brought me down to this:
> Poor and old, under another's thumb,
>
> I am undone if I do not die fast.

In this dark pessimism lies the central quality of Michelangelo's genius. Triumphant as so many of his works appear to us—the young *David,* sublimely confident of his own faith and strength, the glorious *Creation* on the Sistine ceiling, from which emanates all the power of Divinity—for Michelangelo they still failed of the perfection which he felt he must attain. To this, in later years, were added the frustrations of being at the whims of patrons, of the ambivalence of his own feeling for the life of the senses, and finally of the ultimate limit set by Time itself.

The reputations of other artists have risen and fallen with the tides of fashion. Michelangelo's work has been recognized unvaryingly as a limit of artistic achievement. It is fitting therefore that this book, the first of a distinguished new series on Western art, should be devoted to this tragic and embittered human being—the wonder of his time and ours.

JOHN WALKER
Director, National Gallery of Art

I

The Roots
of Genius

"While the artists . . . were doing their best to imitate and to understand nature, bending every faculty to increase that high comprehension sometimes called intelligence"—so, around 1550, looking back over the growth and flowering of the Italian Renaissance, wrote the painter-biographer Giorgio Vasari in his *Lives of the Painters, Sculptors and Architects* —"the Almighty Creator took pity on their often fruitless labor. He resolved to send to earth a spirit capable of supreme expression in all the arts, one able to give form to painting, perfection to sculpture, and grandeur to architecture. The Almighty Creator also graciously endowed this chosen one with an understanding of philosophy and with the grace of poetry. . . . In the Casentino, therefore, in 1475, a son was born to Signor Lodovico di Lionardo di Buonarroti Simoni. . . .

"Moved by compelling impulse, he named the boy Michelangelo."

Michelangelo was in his seventies when Vasari wrote. Ahead of him, old as he was, still lay some of his noblest works, including that literal and symbolic pinnacle of Renaissance art, the dome of St. Peter's. But behind him were such works of genius—to mention only the most important ones—as, in sculpture, the *Pietà* of St. Peter's, the giant *David* that stood guard at the entrance to Florence's city hall, the overpowering *Moses* on the tomb of Pope Julius II in Rome, and the eloquent figures of *Day* and *Night, Dawn* and *Dusk* in the Medici Chapel in Florence; in architecture, the Medici Chapel itself and that marvel of civic planning, the redesign of the Capitoline Hill in Rome; in painting, the tremendous frescoes on the ceiling of the Sistine Chapel and, on its north wall, the far different but equally stirring sequel, the *Last Judgment.* It is an awesome list, to be sure, and for Vasari it furnished the whole theme of his book: that the greatest triumph and even the divinely destined purpose of the new era of the arts—what he called *la rinascita,* "rebirth," from which the term Renaissance comes—had been to nurture the sublime talents of Michelangelo, the consummate artist of all time.

What makes Vasari's attitude important instead of merely interesting and quaint is that it was shared by almost everyone of his time—and this in an age that had invented the concept of the "Universal Man," that

Michelangelo, in a bronze bust by his pupil Daniele da Volterra, betrays the loneliness of a man whose life was his work. And yet he was never satisfied: "Painting and sculpture," he said at the peak of his fame, "have ruined me. . . . It would have been better if in my youth I had hired myself out to make sulfur matches."

Daniele da Volterra:
Michelangelo Buonarroti, 1565

Giorgio Vasari, Michelangelo's friend and biographer, was a painter and architect in his own right, as attested by this contemporary engraving. Today, however, he is chiefly remembered for his *Lives of the Painters, Sculptors and Architects,* a work spanning some 300 years of Italian art history. Vasari's intimate knowledge and lifelong admiration for Michelangelo began when he was a boy of 13 and studied for a few months under the great artist. The devotion this brief apprenticeship instilled in him was responsible a few years later for his saving from permanent mutilation one of Michelangelo's most famous works, the *David,* whose arm was broken off during the melee after the expulsion of the Medici from Florence in 1527. As Vasari relates it, he and a friend "went to the piazza and picked up the pieces fearlessly in the midst of the guard."

made versatility in performance and breadth of interests the chief aim of education, that took for granted that a first-rate artist should be able to create fluently in several different media. Even so, when Michelangelo's contemporaries in the arts compared their own work with his, and their fondest expectations of what they might do someday with what he had already done, he seemed to them to belong to a different realm of being. They called him "The Divine Michelangelo." By the time he died in his 90th year, the apotheosis was complete. Benedetto Varchi, an eminent historian, delivered the funeral oration, and after describing Michelangelo's gifts and achievements seems to have been staggered by his own recital, exclaiming: "This is a phenomenon so new, so unusual, so unheard of in all times, in all countries, in all history that . . . I am not only full of admiration, not only amazed, not only astonished and startled and like one reborn—but my pulse flutters, my blood runs cold, my mind reels, and my hair stands on end, so moved am I by . . . trepidations."

Il Divino Michelangelo . . . the impression of the Holy Spirit at work in a mortal frame remained so strong that as late as 1905 the French novelist and man-of-arts Romain Rolland could write: "Nothing like Michelangelo had ever appeared before. He . . . captured painting, sculpture, architecture and poetry, all at once; he breathed into them the frenzy of his vigor and of his overwhelming idealism. . . . Every one of his great works . . . dominated generations of artists and enslaved them. From every one of these creations radiated despotic power, a power that came above all from Michelangelo's personality."

In our own more skeptical times one might expect to find critical judgments of Michelangelo's art and his contributions to the arts rather more reserved—and indeed they are. But any intelligent discussion of this subject must encompass a good deal of information: not only what Michelangelo did but what he was trying to do—and what he was prevented by others from doing; the conditions of the arts as he found them and as he left them; and the circumstances not only of his own long, tempestuous and often irrational life but of the tempestuous, often irrational and incredibly fertile and fascinating world of the Italian Quattrocento and Cinquecento—the 15th and 16th Centuries—in which he acted, and which reacted to him. These matters will be dealt with later. Here it is enough to make some short, simple, unqualified assertions:

Michelangelo was one of the greatest artistic geniuses who ever lived, and, if one were forced to choose one among all others, it still is he who would be "the greatest." He is also the most famous: the one, that is, whose name is immediately familiar to the most people in the parts of the world that have some link with Western civilization. Indeed, although his patent of divinity has lapsed, something else has happened that would have amazed, somewhat discomfited but also surely gratified him: for many people he has in effect lost connection with flesh-and-blood reality and become instead a figure of myth and symbol, a sort of heavenly archetype of The Artist, the template of perfection representing their generalized notion of what an artist is or could and probably should be.

How does one account for such a man? As for the ultimate question, the explanation of his genius, it may as well be faced first and answered

plainly: there really is no accounting for it. Certainly there was little in Michelangelo's background to suggest any potentiality for producing an artist of any caliber whatever. The Buonarroti Simoni were an eminently respectable Florentine family who could trace their lineage back some 250 years to a remote ancestor, Bernardo, who had founded the family fortune in trade and money-changing, the usual Florentine avenues to wealth. The family was both able and public-spirited; for generations its men served on the governing councils of the city or of the Santa Croce quarter where they lived. But their artistic interests seem to have been casual or less; at a time when Florence was developing into the artistic center of Italy, the Buonarroti Simoni never seem to have bought, or contributed anything to the creation of, any work of art.

In later generations, moreover, there were signs that the family vigor and initiative were becoming atrophied. The comfortable wealth shrank until all that Michelangelo's father, Lodovico, and his uncle Francesco inherited was a joint interest in a house in Florence (with a contested title) and a modest farm northeast of the city near the village of Settignano. Their pride, however, was retained by the brothers in full measure. Both were, after all, still landowners, with the habits and credentials of landed gentry, and accordingly could not stoop to work except in certain traditionally respectable positions, such as public office. Otherwise they preferred to suffer in genteel poverty, and, mainly, they did.

Michelangelo's father was a man filled with vanity, self-pity, mean-mindedness and complete indifference to the needs and dreams of others. Michelangelo's mother, Francesca di Neri di Miniato del Sera, was a dim and pathetic figure who married early, served her husband's wishes and died young. She bore Lodovico five sons, four of whom were quite ordinary. If she had any influence in forming the character of her exotic second-born, Michelangelo, he seems to have been unaware of it. He never really knew her, and in all the voluminous correspondence that he carried on later with his father and brothers, she never is mentioned.

A popinjay father, an anonymous mother, a set of featureless brothers, a heritage of "good family" gone hollow—why, then, Michelangelo? The more one puzzles over the mystery and examines the sequence of events of his life, the more one is compelled to think that in a general sense Vasari was right. His attribution of the phenomenon of Michelangelo to an "Almighty Creator"—the anthropomorphic patriarchal God whose portrait was set for all time by Michelangelo in his Sistine frescoes —is one way of dealing with a universally felt fact: that there is, indeed, "a destiny that shapes our ends." By itself, Michelangelo's genius would have remained only a set of potentialities which, to become realized, would need a whole conspiracy of favoring circumstances. And these did occur, all in proper order, as if moved by the finger of God.

In the autumn of 1474 Lodovico had the gratifying news that he was appointed to a term of six months as *Podestà* (governor) of Chiusi and Caprese, two small towns that lay 40 miles or so east and south of Florence. He was then 30 years old and had yet to work at a paying job, since nothing suitable to his station had been offered him. But as *Podestà* he would wear the dignity of authority, dear to his heart; so he set off on

horseback from Florence with Francesca, who was then 19, and their first and still only son, Lionardo, an infant of about a year and a half. Already she was some three months pregnant with the child who would be Michelangelo. It was a long journey, traversing much rugged country with mountains nearly 4,000 feet high. One day her horse stumbled and she had a bruising fall; but there was no miscarriage, and with a little rest she went on until they reached their official residence in Caprese. It was an old, partially ruined castle set among trees on a great, high rock; below on one side lay a deep, dark, narrow gorge cut by a small but swift river, rushing noisily to its far-off destination; this was the Tiber.

The Casentino, as this part of Italy is called, is a beautiful region, though with a sense of wild and somehow rather somber isolation. Chiusi, at the northern end of the district, perhaps an hour's ride from Caprese, was a traditional locus of government and trade for a scattering of farms and small villages. Here, too, Lodovico presided in a crumbling castle, and during some of his stays must have been accompanied by Francesca to see to his comforts. The massive ridge of rock on which Chiusi stands is, as it happens, in the watershed between the Tiber and the Arno, and the position of the castle puts it at the headwaters of the Arno. The latter river, of course, goes on to flow through Florence, and is as specifically Florentine in all its familiar associations as the Tiber is inseparable from Rome. Michelangelo was destined to spend his life in these two cities, passing like a vagrant force of nature from one to the other, so that his talents enriched both and helped inspire each in turn to a profuse artistic flowering unmatched since.

That Lodovico became *Podestà* when and where he did, that Michelangelo was nurtured in the womb and born in this particular region, that the nature of the place was a symbolic prefiguration of the pattern his life would take, are coincidences, of course. But they were only the first of many such coincidences.

Thus it happened that Lodovico wrote in his journal near the end of the winter of 1475: "Today this sixth of March . . . there was born to me a male child; I named him Michelangelo and he was born Monday morning before four or five o'clock and he was born when I was Podestà at Caprese . . . I had him baptized on the eighth of the same month, in the Church of Santo Giovanni di Caprese."

A few weeks later Lodovico's term of office ended and the family, with its very new addition, returned home. But the Caprese-Chiusi adventure had a sequel that was to be among the decisive influences in Michelangelo's life. Francesca found herself unable to nurse the baby, who consequently was sent to Settignano to stay with a wet nurse. There were many stone quarries in the area and, like most of the men there, the nurse's husband made his living as a quarryworker. In the household as well as in the neighborhood generally, stonecutting was not merely a livelihood but the normal way of life. And it was this life that Michelangelo absorbed, drawing it all in, as he once said, "with my nurse's milk."

He never really returned to the household of Lodovico and Francesca. His stays there were always tentative and insecure. The reason was Fran-

cesca's continued frail health, inexorably drained by Lodovico's endless demands and complaints and by the birth every year or so of a new baby to care for. When Michelangelo was six years old, she died. Afterward, for four years, he lived as the son of the stonecutter and his wife, visiting Lodovico only occasionally. He could not read or write, but he learned how to handle a hammer and chisel.

Then Lodovico remarried, and brought his new wife into the house in the Via dei Bentacordi in Florence. Michelangelo's country idyll among the stonecutters ended. At the age of 10, four years later than Florentine families of substance normally began the formal education of their sons, he was confronted for the first time by a school.

I t was an unhappy encounter, and a largely unsuccessful one. In three years under the tutelage of one Francesco da Urbino the young Michelangelo learned to read and write his own language, but little else. To his own later great regret, he absorbed only a smattering of Greek and Latin, the property of all educated men at that time. But more important, he had begun to feel an almost irresistible attraction to the arts. He loved to draw, and frequently stole time from his studies to do so, sketching from the life around him and from the statues and paintings abundant in Florence's churches and official buildings. He cultivated friendships among the boys apprenticed to painters and sculptors and became especially intimate with Francesco Granacci, an apprentice in the workshop of Domenico Ghirlandaio, at that time the city's most popular artist and a draftsman of consummate skill. Granacci was strongly enthusiastic about the work and urged Michelangelo to join him. Michelangelo hesitated for a time, but the urgings from without and within were too much: he decided to leave school and become an artist, and so informed his father.

For Lodovico the entire realm of art appears to have been a hopeless riddle. In the way that some people are tone-deaf or color-blind, he was deaf and blind to aesthetic messages from all sources. He remained totally uncomprehending of Michelangelo's work even when it was famous and kings and popes exclaimed over its beauty, although by then he could understand it very well in terms of the money it might bring into the family. Money and family: these were the intertwined fixations that ruled his thoughts—to protect and use every shred of status the Buonarroti Simoni still had, and to improve that status, and of course his own personal prestige and comfort, by somehow replenishing their wealth. The role he foresaw for his sons was that they would go into trade and provide the makings of a new mercantile fortune and a new dynasty.

Understandably, Michelangelo's announcement of his plans was received by Lodovico with shock and outrage. Ascanio Condivi, a favorite pupil and close friend of Michelangelo's, wrote a biography of him three years after Vasari's, and since Michelangelo supplied a great many of the personal details in the book it can be assumed that he was also the source for this account of the matter:

"Francesco's influence [i.e., Granacci's], combined with the continual craving of his nature, made him at last abandon his literary studies. This brought the boy into disfavor with his father and uncles, who often used

FRANC. GRANACCI PITTORE FIORINTINO.

Francesco Granacci, who recognized and encouraged the talent of the young Michelangelo, apparently had not enough of his own to become anything more than a secondary master. Even so, relates Vasari, Michelangelo "could not help loving him more than all his other friends, and confided to him more readily than to any other, his knowledge of art." Michelangelo went so far as to provide the design for a high altar and painting, now lost, which Granacci executed.

Of a happy and agreeable disposition, Granacci looked upon painting as a pastime rather than a necessity—which may be why so few of his works are known today. One, the *Holy Family,* is in the National Gallery of Art in Washington, D.C.

to beat him severely; for, being insensible to the excellence and nobility of Art, they thought it shameful to give her shelter in their house."

But Lodovico and the uncles had collided with a quality in Michelangelo that one day would frustrate stronger, shrewder men than they, driving princes to despair and cardinals and popes to the sin of anger—which in the strong-willed Pope Julius II, his greatest patron, stopped barely short of apoplexy. The quality was obdurate stubbornness—not in all things, of course, but commonly in matters that involved his art.

The outcome of Michelangelo's struggle with his elders is recorded in the ledger at the Ghirlandaio studio, where Granacci had long since introduced Michelangelo to Domenico and his younger brother David. The year was 1488; Michelangelo was 13. The ledger entry reads:

"I record this first of April how I, Lodovico . . . bind my son Michelangelo to Domenico and David de Tommaso di Currado for the next three ensuing years, under these conditions and contracts: to wit, that the said Michelangelo shall stay with the above-named masters during this time, to learn the art of painting, and to practice the same, and to be at the orders of the above-named; and they, for their part, shall give to him in the course of these three years twenty-four florins: to wit, six florins in the first year, eight in the second, ten in the third; making in all the sum of ninety-six lire."

With these words, written in the vocabulary of a bill-of-sale and with what bad grace one may imagine, Michelangelo was granted entry into his career—and his world.

It is surely true, as the American educator John W. Gardner reminds us in *Excellence,* his study of human achievement, that "responsibility for learning and growth rests finally with the individual. We can reshape the environment to remove obstacles. We can stimulate and challenge. But in the last analysis, the individual must foster his own development. At any age, the chief resource must be the individual's own interest, drive and enthusiasm." Yet this resource must operate within a set of historical circumstances which the individual had no part in making but which, like an enormous lottery, assigns a certain potential maximum value to his personal talents and qualities. There is a time to be born. As the 17th Century philosopher Baltasar Gracián observed: "It is not everyone that finds the age he deserves. . . . Some men have been worthy of a better century, for every species of good does not triumph. Things have their period; even excellences are subject to fashion."

The Destiny that gave Michelangelo his genius, and that brought him along the path to the profession in which his genius could be used, decreed also that he live in the age he deserved and, moreover, in the place and circumstances that could best allow his excellences to triumph. The World of Michelangelo, where he took up residence on April 1, 1488 after the necessary preliminaries of birth and childhood, was a world which was defined physically by the city and territories of Florence but which, because of the special character of this city at this time in history, was intellectually and artistically boundless. For Florence was a miraculous place; and what contributed to and sustained the miracle was that its citizens (leaving aside such as Lodovico) knew that they were living in a

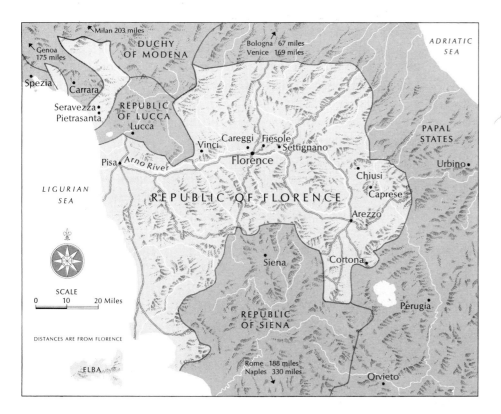

miracle. They compared their city and its place in the arts and learning of their era with the place of Athens in ancient Greece—and they were right. As Athens had led the way among the Greek city-states to the glory that was Greece, so Florence had led the way among the Italian city-states in "the revival of learning," the Renaissance. The Athenians had had their Golden Age, presided over by Pericles. The Florentines of the later 15th Century strongly sensed—and again rightly—that they were living in the Golden Age of their city and that the Periclean equivalent was at hand in Lorenzo de' Medici, "Lorenzo the Magnificent," the contemporary head of the family that for four generations had had the leading role in the city's affairs.

To understand the Florentines' fierce pride in their city, it must be recalled that at the time Italy itself was barely even a geographical expression. The inhabitants of the peninsula spoke more or less the same language, shared enough social institutions and cultural traits to enable a man to travel from his own region to almost any other without feeling completely foreign, and shared also an awareness of common origins in the old Roman Empire. Yet their sense of kinship from such things was vague and trifling compared with their sense of loyalty to their own place. The city and its surrounding territory—the city-state—this was a man's country, the locus of all his patriotic feelings. Inside the city a man's identity rested chiefly on his family. Outside it, unless he happened to be of a particularly notable family, he wore the identity of his city to such a degree that, for example, some of the artists became known not only by their family names but by their place-names, and have come down to us still carrying identities such as Perugino (Pietro Vanucci, from Perugia) and Mino da Fiesole (Mino di Giovanni, from Fiesole).

By the time of the Quattrocento, the map of Italy was a patchwork of more than a score of states of various sizes, shapes and governments. The

In the Italy of Michelangelo's boyhood—a collection of 14 fiercely competitive states and kingdoms—his native Republic of Florence occupied a strategic position, roughly halfway between Rome and Venice. The city of Florence itself lay practically at the center of the republic—in a long valley near several passes through the Apennine Mountains. The Arno River gave it access to the sea, and it was up this river that Michelangelo used to ship the marble blocks he quarried at Carrara, only a few miles from the coast. Spotted on the map are the names of some of the other towns and places associated with Michelangelo.

Kingdom of Naples ruled the south. In the center, from Rome, the Pope ruled a clutch of small territories known as the Papal States. In the north lay the great Republic of Venice, the big Duchy of Milan, a number of medium-size and smaller principalities and republics such as Genoa, Mantua, Ferrara and Modena, and the Republic of Florence, which ruled over a good part of the region called Tuscany.

A special spirit of individualism, adventure and sophistication set Florence apart from the rest. Many things had contributed to the creation of this spirit. The accident of geography had made the city a major land avenue of trade between the north and south of Europe. Trade breeds initiative, industry and ideas—and all these the Florentines developed in abundance. Importing wool and silk and flax, manufacturing and dyeing cloth, Florence became a leading European center of the textile industry and in time the financial capital of the West. Out of the money-changing activities spurred by trade, Florentine banks grew and thrived; they were the moneylenders to princes and the financial agents of the Church.

Along with economic vitality, Florence had great political verve. It lay in a part of Italy that had never been highly feudalized, and the traditions of republican Rome had survived there. At a time when despots flourished elsewhere without challenge, Florence remained a republic in which there was room for brawling political factions and outspoken public opinion. It was, in sum, an open society with unlimited horizons for the ingenious and ambitious. The impact on the city's intellectual and artistic life was profound and far-reaching. As wealth spread, so did opportunities for leisure, for gracious living and for cultivation of the arts. Riches began to pour into the building of fine homes and palaces, into the beautification of churches and public structures and into the advancement of learning.

Interested in the rewards of life in the here-and-now, the new materialists felt the need for an ethos not supplied by the Church, with its primary concern for the hereafter. Increasingly, they turned to the distant past, to the philosophy of the "good life" expounded by the Greeks and Romans. The fascination with antiquity deepened. The impressive mementos of Greece and Rome were looked at with fresh interest by architects; antique coins and fragments of statues with awakening admiration by artists; old Latin and Greek texts with new absorption by scholars. This was the beginning of the Renaissance.

The Renaissance was already well advanced in Florence and had spread in varying degrees to the other Italian city-states by the time the Medici began to take the leading role in Florentine affairs. Nevertheless they supplied the cachet of high approval and a good deal of the money that nourished it to magnificent full bloom in the city. In decisive ways they helped make it what it became, and their personalities are so inextricably interwoven in the great events of the times that the word Renaissance immediately evokes the name Medici.

The founder of the family fortune was Giovanni di Bicci de' Medici, a trader and banker who at the turn of the 15th Century rose from obscurity to become one of the richest men in Florence, with branch banks in Rome, Venice and Naples. He held several high offices in the republic

and in 1421 was elected to its highest as *gonfaloniere* (standard-bearer) of justice, executor of the laws; and he employed Filippo Brunelleschi, who was later to become architect of the dome of the cathedral of Santa Maria del Fiore, to build the Foundling Hospital and to rebuild the sacristy of San Lorenzo, the Medici family church. His son Cosimo, succeeding him as head of the family at his death in 1429, expanded the business until he was far and away the pre-eminent banker in Florence and accordingly in the world. Except for one term as *gonfaloniere* he avoided public office, but as banker to the republic and leader of its dominant political party he exercised unofficial but thoroughly effective control over government politics. Under his wise guidance, the city flourished in peace, and he grew so in general esteem that when he died in 1464 at the age of 75 there was inscribed on his tomb, by common consent, the title *Pater Patriae,* father of his country.

As for art and architecture, Cosimo spent on a scale both lavish and unprecedented. He commissioned Brunelleschi to rebuild the church of San Lorenzo, and the architect Michelozzo to rebuild the Dominican monastery and cloister of San Marco. Michelozzo also designed the Medici family palace, which became a repository for statuary and paintings by the foremost Florentine artists. In addition, Cosimo amassed a great collection of ancient manuscripts, hiring scholars to scour the libraries of monasteries and other likely sources all over the Mediterranean world. His fascination with the learning of the past, and especially with the works of Plato—hitherto known only in fragmentary form—caused him to bring leading Platonic scholars to Florence and maintain them at his own expense. From this group grew the celebrated "Platonic Academy," which made Florence the lodestone of Renaissance learning.

Cosimo's son Piero found that such huge and diverse outlays were no longer possible; business reverses had cut into the Medici fortune. Even so, Piero managed to continue the tradition of artistic patronage; it was he who commissioned the marvelous fresco the *Journey of the Magi,* by Benozzo Gozzoli, for the chapel of the Medici Palace. But Piero was a semi-invalid afflicted with severe gout, and he survived Cosimo by less than five years. His own oldest son, Lorenzo, was then only 20 years old. Yet so thoroughly had the habit of looking to the Medici for leadership been ingrained that 600 leading Florentines met and asked Lorenzo to take over his father's and grandfather's role as the first citizen and effective head of the state.

Thus, in December of 1469, began the climactic phase of Florentine history, an era in which the city reached its peak as the center of European culture, an era since called, by Lorenzo's name, the Laurentian Age. It was into this Age that Michelangelo was born, and it was in Lorenzo's Florence that he found his vocation and passed the formative years of his youth. In fact, as we will see, his future was shaped to a large degree by his life in Lorenzo's own household. But if Lorenzo inherited the opportunity that he used to lead the Florentine Renaissance to its climax, Michelangelo inherited all the artistic and spiritual values that his predecessors had created in Florence and thus, in some measure, the opportunity to bring the art of the whole Italian Renaissance to its climax.

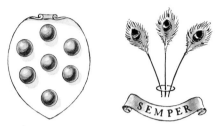

Cosimo de' Medici 1389-1464

Piero de' Medici 1416-1469

Lorenzo de' Medici 1449-1492

One way students of Renaissance art can give approximate dates to otherwise undatable Florentine works is to identify the Medici coats of arms and crests that often appear in them. During Cosimo's time, the coat of arms contained seven red balls, or *palle,* on a gold field, while Cosimo's personal crest was made up of three peacock feathers, signifying the cardinal virtues Cosimo most admired—prudence, temperance and fortitude. During Piero's reign, King Louis XI of France honored the family by allowing one *palla* to be emblazoned with three golden *fleurs-de-lis.* Piero's crest consisted of a falcon with a diamond ring, the ring probably symbolizing strength and eternity. Lorenzo the Magnificent reduced the number of *palle* to six, and adopted as his own device interlocking diamond rings, to which Michelangelo's stonemason's mark of three circles bears a strong resemblance.

Backdrop for a Giant

Born into an age of giants, Michelangelo was to become a giant himself—the greatest artist of his day and perhaps of all time. But, despite his achievements, he never won ease or happiness, nor could fame shake his feeling that he had been born to wretchedness —"predestined when I in the cradle lay" to darkness. What experiences, what influences in his childhood so affected him? Why did he grow up to be a tormented, suspicious, melancholy man who felt himself "a slave in others' power," a consort of princes and popes who seemed to prefer the company of stonecutters and mediocre artists? Why did he, so quick to call himself "a Florentine citizen, noble and son of a gentleman, and not a nobody. . . ." see even his most prestigious work as bringing him only "pain and grief"? One answer must lie in his quest for perfection, which made it possible for him to set figures free from "the living stone," but never his soul from its "earthly prison."

"If I am good for anything," he once told his friend Vasari, "it is because I was born in the good mountain air of your Arezzo and suckled among the chisels and hammers of the stonecutters." And, he should have added, because he had the rare fortune to grow up in Florence at a time when the city had become the intellectual center of the western world, under the leadership of its most influential citizen, Lorenzo de' Medici, *Il Magnifico.*

Unchanged in the four centuries since Michelangelo saw them as a boy, Brunelleschi's cathedral dome and the tower of the Palazzo della Signoria dominate Florence's skyline. Remembering this dome when planning his own for St. Peter's, Michelangelo said humbly, "I am going to make its sister, bigger, yes, but not more beautiful."

1. S. Maria Novella   2. S. Marco   3. S. Lorenzo   4. SS. Annunziata   5. Medici Palace   6. The Baptistery   7. Duomo (Cathedral)

A City of Monuments

The Florence familiar to Michelangelo as a boy looked as it does above—a squat walled town of heavy stone, traversed by the muddy Arno. From where the young apprentice painter lived in the unfashionable but respectable Santa Croce quarter near the river, it was but a short walk to some of the city's greatest monuments—the fortresslike Palazzo della Signoria, seat of the city government; the church of Or San Michele, shrine of the arts and crafts guilds; the octagonal Baptistery; the cathedral with Brunelleschi's enormous dome and, beside it, the slender stalk of Giotto's bell tower. Across

8. Giotto's Campanile (Bell Tower)   9. Bargello   10. Or San Michele   11. Palazzo della Signoria   12. Loggia dei Lanzi   13. S. Croce   14. Ponte Vecchio

the city stood the churches of Santa Maria Novella, San Marco and San Lorenzo, the last virtually the personal temple of the ruling Medici, for which Michelangelo would one day provide a chapel. And close by San Lorenzo was the massive, three-story palace of the Medici into which he would soon move.

Within its five miles of walls Florence counted 70,000 souls. Its narrow streets wound in and out between some 50 squares. Catering to spiritual and physical needs were more than 100 monasteries and convents, four hospitals and 66 doctors. Four bridges spanned the Arno—the most famous of them, the Ponte Vecchio, carrying some 40 shops. In the two dozen years or so before Michelangelo's birth, 30 palaces had gone up, and new ones were being erected all the time. Apart from such progress, however, Florence remained a city without sewers or public garbage collections and, not surprisingly, it fell frequent victim to pestilences— as well as to fires, floods and famines. Yet, in spite of such disasters, it was a gay place, famous for its street life and festivals, and even the moody young Michelangelo must have found welcome relief from the somber atmosphere of his father's crowded home in the city's uninhibited revelries.

The social and political center of Florence in Michelangelo's day was the Piazza della Signoria, shown under a shadow cast by the *palazzo* from which it got its name. In this broad square only a few blocks from the artist's home, the populace gathered for ceremonies, tournaments, debate and, on occasion, to view events reflecting the darker side of the Florentine character. Here, for example, where a stone lion still stands, real lions were set loose to attack stags and buffaloes, goaded with lances by men safe inside wooden "tortoises." If this was brutal sport, it was as nothing compared to the inhumanity of the mobs that frequently crowded the square during Michelangelo's lifetime to see justice done (or undone), often to

hysterical cries of *Libertà!* Such a mob, when Michelangelo was just three years old, hacked to pieces the captured conspirators in the abortive Pazzi rebellion against the Medici; a priest who had already been hanged was decapitated and "quarters of his body with one arm" were borne through the streets. And here, when Michelangelo was 23, the Dominican monk and prophet Savanarola, whom he admired and whom the Florentines had at first embraced and then violently rejected, was strung up with two followers and burned. Perhaps the recollection of events like these prompted Michelangelo years later to write bitterly of his fellow citizens, "Never have I associated with more ungrateful and arrogant people than the Florentines."

In the Piazza della Signoria stands a replica of Michelangelo's *David*, seen here under the belly of a Roman lion.

Sandro Botticelli: *Adoration of the Magi*, c. 1475

The Amiable Tyrant

The dominant figure in the city of Michelangelo's youth was Lorenzo de' Medici. Of medium height, nearsighted, with no sense of smell and "a voice and pronunciation harsh and unpleasing, because he spoke through his nose," he nevertheless profoundly affected everyone with whom he had dealings. "Before he begins to speak," a Venetian envoy wrote, "his eyes speak for him."

Lorenzo was educated by humanists and became one himself. He took pleasure in enlarging his collections of books, carved gems and antique statuary, and as an accomplished musician and poet he gave support to artists of all kinds. In this he was not only indulging a personal whim but maintaining the tradition of patronage started by his great-grandfather, founder of the family fortune. By his father's time, the name Medici had become so indelibly associated with the arts that when a friend of the family sought a way to please its members, he commissioned Botticelli to execute the *Adoration of the Magi* reproduced above. The Three Wise Men are supposedly none other than Lorenzo's grandfather, father and uncle. Two of the more conspicuous worshipers are believed to be the scions of the family: Lorenzo, the proud figure at extreme left, and his brother Giuliano (who three years later would be struck down by assassins' daggers), the thoughtful youth standing at right behind the younger Magi.

Of the countless art treasures that the Medici themselves commissioned and lived with, only one remains today in the Medici palace. It is Benozzo Gozzoli's *Journey of the Magi*, painted in 1459 on the walls of a private chapel for the delectation of the family and permanent house guests among whom, 30 years later, would be Michelangelo.

Though religious in theme, the fresco is actually a very topical painting which constitutes an elaborate tribute to the Medici for all they had done to enrich Florence. One of the events it commemorates is the Great Council of 1439, convoked in Ferrara by Pope Eugene IV but lured away to Florence by Cosimo, Lorenzo's grandfather. This prestigious meeting between the Roman and Greek Orthodox Churches brought to the city a dazzling array of important people. Not only did the Pope come but also the Patriarch of Constantinople and one of the last Byzantine emperors. The gorgeousness of their retinues, matched by the splendor of the Medici, is recalled in Gozzoli's fresco. Shown prominently on a white horse in this portion is a youth traditionally identified as Lorenzo. Straight-backed and solemn-faced, he seems already to have taken to heart his father's advice "to be old before your time; to behave as a man and not as a boy."

Less directly, the fresco also recalls the Fall of Constantinople 14 years after the Great Council. At that time, many of the most brilliant men of the East remembered the Medici hospitality and took refuge in Florence, making that city an even greater center of learning. Some of their faces appear in this detail, along with those of leading Florentine scholars and literati, many of whom Michelangelo would come to know in the Medici household. Gozzoli's own portrait looks out from between the heads of two bearded Greek scholars on the left, his signature in Latin on his cap.

Benozzo Gozzoli: *Journey of the Magi*, detail, 1459

Giotto: *The Ascension of John the Evangelist*, detail, c.1330

Drawing after Giotto, *The Ascension of John the Evangelist*, c.1489

First Works

While Lorenzo busied himself furthering the Medici reputation as patrons of the arts, the young Michelangelo, in a precocious display of talent that would soon catch *Il Magnifico's* eye, was sketching the works of art around him. But rather than concentrate on the paintings of older contemporaries like Botticelli, Filippino Lippi, or even his own teacher Domenico Ghirlandaio, he turned back to Masaccio and the still earlier Giotto. What did these men, long since dead, offer him? What caught his eye in their frescoes? Both had painted figures that were heavy, substantial, real. To a boy brought up among stonecutters, these must have seemed sculptural. And, as a comparison between his copies and details from the originals shows, Michelangelo even added to their massiveness by defining more clearly the relationship between body and clothing.

In his rendition of the Giotto *(left)*, the belt of the upright figure does more than simply

Masaccio: *The Tribute Money*, detail, c. 1427

delineate the waist: it blouses the upper portion of
the garment. The furrowed sleeve and the slight
bulge at the knees suggest the very stuff of which
the robe is made, while the hand thrusting from the
sleeve has a boniness that gives conviction to its
grip. Michelangelo treated the Masaccio similarly
(right). His St. Peter, minus a halo, is wrapped in a
garment of many folds that produces an effect of
enclosed bulk and weight, yet suggests the muscular
frame underneath.

Although these pen-and-ink drawings,
particularly in their cross-hatching technique, show
the influence of Michelangelo's teacher Ghirlandaio,
a painter, they are in the truest sense the studies of a
budding sculptor. Recalling these first lessons in
drawing, which were invaluable to him, the adult
Michelangelo could give no finer advice to aspiring
artists than to draw. "Draw, Antonio," he
commanded one of his assistants. "Draw, Antonio,
draw—and don't waste time!"

Drawing after Masaccio, *The Tribute Money*, c. 1493

Battle of the Centaurs, 1492

Madonna of the Stairs, 1491

From Ghirlandaio's workshop Michelangelo was soon to move on to the school for sculptors set up by Lorenzo—and it was here that he carved his first true works in stone, the *Madonna of the Stairs* and the *Battle of the Centaurs.* Recalling the fluid style and low reliefs of Donatello, the greatest Florentine sculptor of the Early Renaissance, the *Madonna of the Stairs* shows an astonishing mastery of marble techniques for a boy not yet even 17. Vasari enthusiastically described it as being "so exactly in Donatello's manner that it really looks like a Donatello, except that it is more graceful and better designed."

The second relief, the *Battle of the Centaurs,* was executed a year later and demonstrates a startling rate of growth. Michelangelo found the theme for it in a Greek legend recounted by the humanist Poliziano, tutor of the Medici children; he drew his inspiration from Roman sarcophagi and a bronze *Battle of the Horsemen* carved by his aging teacher Bertoldo. And yet whatever it may have owed to others, the *Battle of the Centaurs* bears the unmistakable stamp of Michelangelo's genius. Here, for the first time, he used the plasticity of the human body to express conflict in dramatically compelling terms. In its pulse and thrust and in the very way in which he attacked the marble, the *Battle of the Centaurs* is a preview of the great works to come. Apparently Michelangelo regarded this early essay in stone with special fondness; he kept it all his life.

Pitti Madonna, c. 1504-1505

How greatly Michelangelo was to mature as a sculptor can be demonstrated by leaping ahead a dozen years to the only other reliefs he did, the *Pitti Madonna* and the *Taddei Madonna*. They show him still preoccupied with the theme of Virgin and Child, but now much freer in his treatment of it. Neither was actually finished, and it is tempting to suppose that the reason is that he liked them that way: their unworked details give them a suggestive power which might have been lost in a more polished version. In the *Pitti Madonna* Michelangelo set the focus of his composition in the center of the circle: all the contours gently curve away from it. In the *Taddei Madonna,* he boldly placed the Virgin to one side, with the Child rushing away from the center, frightened by the fluttering goldfinch in the hands of John the Baptist—the symbol, according to Renaissance belief, of Christ's passion.

II

Il Magnifico's Pleasure

All that was revolutionary in art at the beginning of the 15th Century is revealed in this detail from a fresco by Masaccio, the founder of Renaissance painting. Here is space rendered for the first time through the application of perspective, while light emanating from its natural source gently models the figures.

Masaccio: *St. Peter and the Death of Ananias,* detail, 1426-1428

By the time the thirteen-year-old Michelangelo began his career at the workshop of Domenico Ghirlandaio in April 1488, Florence had become a museum of the arts—a living museum, in which art was an integral part of everyday life. Painters were at least as common as physicians and apothecaries, with whom in fact they were lumped in one of the numerous guilds. Because there was as yet no clear distinction between "artists" and "artisans," a studio such as Ghirlandaio's might easily be busy with a score of projects of all sorts, from the fashioning of jeweled brooches to the building and gilding of picture frames, from cabinet-making to the construction and painting of great altarpieces. Ghirlandaio himself, one of the finest fresco painters of his day, was equally at home in goldwork, having started out as a goldsmith. His place was a *bottega,* a workshop for the creation of aesthetically pleasing objects. There were at least a score of these *botteghe* around the city—differing in size and in their amount of specialization and of course in the quality of their work, but basically similar—where the Florentines ordered beauty according to their means and particular fancies and needs.

Perhaps a dozen very rich families bought and built on a scale comparable to that of the Medici, and dozens less rich did so in proportion. But private wealth was only one source of custom. Others were the government, the churches and religious organizations, and the guilds into which all the professions and trades were grouped, so that one way or another, through their taxes, offerings and dues, all but the proletarian poor were patrons of the arts.

Thus, for example, it was the Signory, the executive branch of the government, together with the cloth merchants' guild, that at the opening of the 15th Century had commissioned Lorenzo Ghiberti to create a pair of sculptured bronze doors for the Baptistery. By the time the doors were finished 22 years later they had cost 22,000 florins; the enormity of this sum can be gauged by the fact that a man could live in style—with a fine house, servants and a horse—on an income of about 200 florins a year. Ghiberti's doors so pleased the sponsors that they commissioned him to do another pair. These took 23 years and were received with even

greater enthusiasm. Ghiberti was elected to the Signory and given a bonus. Michelangelo, when he himself had become famous and his remarks were being remembered, once called the second set of doors—now on the east side of the Baptistery—"so fine that it would grace the entrance of paradise." The metaphor took hold: the doors have been known ever since as the *Gates of Paradise.*

It was this broadly based support, which in turn was based on the city's republicanism and prosperity, that had nourished the individuality of Florentine artists and enabled them to be as venturesome in their explorations of form, content and artistic media as Florentine traders and bankers had been in their restless explorations of the possibilities of the world-at-large. At Ferrara, Urbino, Mantua, Bologna and many other cities, great works had been and were being created, but more often than not under the patronage of local reigning dukes and princes and their attendant corps of nobles and rich retainers at court, where life was centered and taste was set. Local artists worked within the limits of that taste or not at all; those from other cities were invited because their styles were admired, and they would repeat for the prince-patron work of the kind they had already done.

The effect was to make Florence "the school of the world" for artists, and the main source of supply for the prince-patrons. Young artists flocked from many parts of Italy to learn, to seek work and eventually to be sought after—first by patrons and, in due course, by fresh generations of apprentices eager to learn in turn. As a result, the history of Quattrocento art resembles a combination genealogical table and chronicle of the comings and goings and notable deeds of some very large, peripatetic Florentine family, with numerous cousins continually arriving from elsewhere, especially from the Tuscan countryside.

It is remarkable how often the lines of descent lead to Michelangelo. In fact, they form such a web that one might begin at any of a number of places and arrive at the same destination. But a logical starting point is the first year of the Quattrocento, 1401, the year the Signory and cloth merchants' guild invited artists to submit designs for the Baptistery doors. Ghiberti, who up to then had been mainly a goldsmith and painter, won against a field that included Brunelleschi and the sculptor Jacopo della Quercia. Brunelleschi, too proud to bear the imputation of being second-rate (a spirit typical of the Renaissance), quit sculpture and became the great architect whose supreme achievement was the dome of the cathedral: this dome, which dominates the Florentine skyline and was an ever-present part of Michelangelo's consciousness from the time he first saw the city, was the inspiration and principal model for the dome he created long afterward for St. Peter's. Della Quercia remained a sculptor and produced masterpieces in his own Siena and in Bologna; when Michelangelo was 19, he spent almost a year in Bologna, and della Quercia's influence is clearly evident in some of his early works.

The year 1401 also saw the birth in Florence of Tommaso di Ser Giovanni di Mono, who became known by his nickname "Masaccio," or "Hulking Tom." Though he died young, at 27, and left only a few works, Masaccio opened a whole new era in painting; he was the found-

er of what Vasari a century later called the "modern" style, what we know as Renaissance style. Masaccio synthesized all the lessons his own and earlier times could teach and then through his bold and imaginative genius evolved something altogether unique: a three-dimensional realism never before achieved on a two-dimensional surface. From the works of the early master he most admired, Giotto, he drew the inspiration for giving a sense of flesh-and-blood solidity to the human form, so long depicted by medieval painters in cardboard-cutout fashion; Giotto had used light and shadow to intensify the illusion of roundedness, and this technique—chiaroscuro—Masaccio developed with new subtlety and power. From his contemporary, Brunelleschi, he learned the then-new science of perspective to effect a sense of depth and provide a natural spatial setting for his figures. From Brunelleschi's close friend, the sculptor Donatello, and from the newly emerging influences of classical art, he learned to use the body to convey emotion, the tension of action captured at a moment in time, and the noble potentialities of mankind.

The sum of Masaccio's achievement is contained in his group of frescoes in the Brancacci chapel of the church of Santa Maria del Carmine, showing episodes in the life of St. Peter. This became a place of pilgrimage for all the painters of Florence then and forever after. Those who came to marvel and learn included Fra Angelico, Fra Filippo Lippi, Paolo Uccello, Andrea del Castagno, Sandro Botticelli, Andrea del Verrocchio, Andrea del Sarto, Leonardo da Vinci (who pronounced the frescoes "perfect works"), Perugino, Ghirlandaio and many others. But none studied the Masaccio frescoes with more profit than Michelangelo; his drawings of them are among the first known works of his boyhood, and what he learned is apparent in his own Sistine Chapel frescoes.

There was another fruitful source for Michelangelo through a collateral line of artistic descent. Domenico Veneziano, who arrived in Florence from Perugia in about 1439 to paint some frescoes in the church of Sant'Egidio, was so enthralled by the possibilities revealed by Masaccio's chiaroscuro that for the rest of his life his particular interest was the mutation of color by light. At Sant'Egidio he had a young assistant, Piero della Francesca, a native of the small Tuscan town of Borgo San Sepolcro. Piero, who matured into one of the enduring giants of art, advanced the science of perspective to near-perfection and eventually gave up painting to write treatises on its complex mathematical harmonies. One of his disciples was Perugino (who also worked at Verrocchio's *bottega*, where a fellow-assistant was Leonardo da Vinci, and who later, when he had his own *bottega*, was the teacher of Raphael).

Another disciple of Piero was Luca Signorelli, a fellow Tuscan from Cortona. Signorelli combined skill at perspective with superb draftsmanship, and an interest in antique classical perfection of form with an acutely perceptive interest in the living human form in all its range of expressive movements and attitudes; he became one of the early great masters of the nude. His prodigious set of frescoes of the *Last Judgment,* in the cathedral at Orvieto, is intensely alive with the writhing naked forms of the damned being driven into hell by muscular demons, while the pure and saved, also naked, rise sublimely toward heaven. In its general

The creation of Adam was a popular theme with Renaissance artists, and in this marble relief by Jacopo della Quercia it found one of its most potent expressions until Michelangelo tackled the same subject in the Sistine Chapel ceiling three quarters of a century later. Michelangelo knew this revolutionary work which, in its bold treatment of the nude, seems to point the way to his own preoccupation with the human form. It influenced his conception of Adam, who reclines in much the same pose on the ceiling but is more inert, more languid, as he awaits the animating spark of life.

conception, and especially in its use of the nude body to express deep emotion, it presaged Michelangelo's *Last Judgment* and preceded it by more than 40 years. Vasari, in his chapter on Signorelli, commented: "This work was a source of enlightenment to all who came after him. Nor am I surprised that the works of Signorelli were ever praised by Michelangelo or that for the divine *Last Judgment* in the Sistine Chapel Michelangelo should have courteously availed himself to a certain extent of the inventions of Signorelli . . . as everyone may see for himself." This would seem to be both a fair statement of the facts and a graceful balancing of two loyalties, for Signorelli was Vasari's great-uncle.

With Michelangelo's abiding love for sculpture, any review of his artistic genealogy must take in at least his direct line of descent in that art. This again goes back to the time of Ghiberti. During the 45 years Ghiberti spent on the two sets of doors of the Baptistery he trained several generations of artists in his shop. Among his earliest apprentices was the young Donato di Niccolò di Betto Bardi: Donatello. After three years Donatello left to execute his own first commission, one of the numerous statues being carved for the cathedral of Florence, and from there he went on to become a brilliant innovator, combining a love for classicism with a devotion to realism. He was one of the triumvirate of founding geniuses of Quattrocento art: what Masaccio was to painting and Brunelleschi to architecture, Donatello was to sculpture. One of his pupils, who helped complete the work he had left unfinished at his death—two bronze pulpits, facing across the nave of the Medici church of San Lorenzo—was Bertoldo di Giovanni. And Bertoldo, in his later years, became the teacher of Michelangelo.

There was a great deal else in Michelangelo's inheritance: so many artistic riches not only from the Quattrocento but from the century preceding that it would take part of a lifetime really to see and savor it all. The 13-year-old apprentice had only to use his legs to encounter a treasure around every other curve in the city's labyrinthine streets.

Nearly all of the architectural landmarks of present-day Florence already existed, and some had begun to seem quite old. The tall, battlemented government palace, the Palazzo della Signoria (now usually called the Palazzo Vecchio, "the old palace") with its soaring 308-foot tower, the enormous cathedral, and the large and beautiful church of Santa Croce—all had been started in the 1290s. The Piazza della Signoria, the great plaza on which the government palace fronted, had been laid out and paved with finely joined cobblestone in the 1300s. On one side of this, abutting on the palace, an arcaded portico for public ceremonials had been built in the 1370s—the Loggia della Signoria, now known as the Loggia dei Lanzi. The Baptistery, of course, existed with its Ghiberti doors and a handsome earlier set on the south side, completed in 1336 by Andrea Pisano. The 276-foot bell tower which adjoined the Baptistery and cathedral, and which like them had outer walls decorated by multicolored marble paneling, had been begun in 1334 by Giotto—commissioned by the Signory, which explicitly requested a structure that would "exceed in magnificence, height, and excellence of workmanship everything of the kind achieved of old by the Greeks and

Romans when at the zenith of their progress." Giotto was then in his late sixties, and when he died three years later, was buried in the cathedral in the corner closest to the tower.

The Bargello, a fortress-palace that had been the seat of government until the Signory outgrew it; the Foundling Hospital, with Brunelleschi's graceful arcade and Andrea della Robbia's charming blue and white terra-cotta medallions between the arches; the Benedictine monastery that was known simply as La Badia, "the abbey"; the Dominican monastery of San Marco; the churches of Santa Maria Novella, San Lorenzo, Santo Spirito, Santissima Annunziata, Santa Maria del Carmine, Or San Michele and a score or more of other notable churches and residences of religious orders; numbers of small shrines and tabernacles set into the walls and corners of buildings everywhere in the city; even the shop-lined Ponte Vecchio, completed in 1345, and most of the other bridges that spanned the Arno—all of these were there and filled with life, filled with art that was available to the people of Florence, including properly behaved 13-year-old apprentices.

And for anyone as intensely interested in art as Michelangelo, merely to live and move among these places was a continual and mainly effortless process of learning. Indeed, on a single 15-minute stroll along the axis of the city, from the center of its spiritual and cultural life at the Cathedral-Campanile-Baptistery complex to the center of its social and political life at the Piazza-Palazzo-Loggia della Signoria, he would have seen (and quite certainly often did see) four works which, if set apart from the great many others he would have encountered, could fairly well have described and summarized the course of sculpture for the past 150 years.

One, a set of marble reliefs representing the physical, intellectual and moral progress of human history, lay on the east side of the Campanile near eye-level; these had been carved by Andrea Pisano in about 1335. Another was Ghiberti's *Gates of Paradise* for the Baptistery. Another was at Or San Michele, the special church of the guilds where each had a shrine-niche in the outer wall containing or awaiting a figure of its particular patron saint. For the Guild of Flax Merchants, Donatello in 1411 and 1412 had made a marble free-standing statue of St. Mark—his first fully mature work, in which he achieved that balance of the heroic and mundane, of man ennobled yet filled with the breath and emotions of mortal life, which so influenced later sculptors. It was among the works Michelangelo most admired; he once said of this St. Mark, "It would have been impossible to reject the Gospel preached by such a straightforward man as this."

Ending this imagined stroll, Michelangelo would have encountered the last summarizing work by entering the Signory's porticoed courtyard, newly remodeled by Michelozzo. Here, atop a fountain in the center of the courtyard, he would have seen a small, free-standing bronze statue of a child holding a dolphin—a work with all the anatomical precision of Donatello's but with a new sense of movement and vitality that was to become the hallmark of Renaissance sculpture. Verrocchio, a follower of Donatello, had completed this appealing figure about 1475, the

year Michelangelo was born; Verrocchio died in this year of 1488, when Michelangelo became an apprentice.

As for painting, no brief stroll would have sufficed. From Giovanni Cimabue, the medieval painter to whom Giotto may have been apprenticed, to Masaccio and onward, almost every significant Italian painter for 225 years had contributed something and usually much to the enormous picture gallery Florence had become. Generation to generation, they directed their efforts to work out and master the *means* of their art—perspective, chiaroscuro, and all the rest—that would enable them to imitate nature. They strove to "understand nature," too, as Vasari noted, and to present it with more than merely a mirror-image veracity; yet the advancement of methods and materials and devices necessarily remained a major preoccupation. The long trail from Cimabue and Giotto and Masaccio led straight toward Ghirlandaio, for in him all the lessons converged, were absorbed and applied with the greatest of ease. And so the strangely attentive Destiny that seemed present even at Michelangelo's conception seemed now to have brought him to precisely the right place at the right time.

For even geniuses need mastery of the tools of their trade, and this mastery comes only through learning and repeated application. Undoubtedly Michelangelo learned a great deal at Ghirlandaio's that was useful to him later, because this was the most diversified *bottega* in the city, filled with Ghirlandaio's own eclectic spirit of welcome for whatever (and nearly whoever) came along that was different and promising or simply for some reason interesting.

Like most master painters, Ghirlandaio did only the designs and the more demanding parts of a picture—in a portrait, for example, only the face, or even only certain features—and let his apprentices do the rest under his supervision. This system gave them the chance to apply what knowledge they had quickly and on a high level of professionalism. In 1488 and 1489 Ghirlandaio was engaged in the biggest commission of his career, frescoes of the life of the Virgin and of St. John the Baptist in the choir of Santa Maria Novella, for Giovanni Tornabuoni, a maternal uncle of Lorenzo the Magnificent and the head of the Rome branch of the Medici bank. Ghirlandaio involved his numerous assistants in the work, including Michelangelo, who was thus, although not yet 14, actually painting part of what it was assumed would be a masterpiece for the ages, in one of the major churches of Florence, for one of its most prestigious citizens. Moreover, Ghirlandaio excelled at drawing: the use of hard, exact, fluent line to capture movement and express emotion—a Florentine specialty. He emphasized and incessantly demonstrated this to his pupils, and evidently to Michelangelo's benefit. In later years Michelangelo himself always stressed the primary importance of drawing, and his own habitual use of strong, fluid line is seen in all his pictures. As careful an authority as Bernard Berenson declared that the hand of the teacher always remained discernible in Michelangelo's work in this regard.

Even as he learned from Ghirlandaio, however, Michelangelo displayed signs of the individuality that would forever set him apart. Apprentices, by definition, are a docile lot, always mindful of their master's

dictates, but two episodes recounted by Vasari illustrate Michelangelo's unwillingness to conform to the pattern. One day a fellow pupil showed him a pen sketch he had made, from Ghirlandaio's own design, of a group of draped female figures. Michelangelo seized a pen with a thicker nib and, without concern for what the master might think, reworked the outlines of one of the women to improve the sketch to his own liking. Another time, during the fresco project at Santa Maria Novella, while Ghirlandaio was absent Michelangelo took the opportunity to pause in his assigned labors and sketch the other apprentices at work on the scaffolding. Instead of being angry when he returned and saw the drawing, Vasari relates, Ghirlandaio was so "amazed at the power and originality of the lad's work" that he could only exclaim, "This boy knows more than I do."

Ghirlandaio's general reaction to the restless and assertive youth in his employ seems to have been an uneasy one. Vasari says that he was "dismayed" by Michelangelo's tendency to innovate. Condivi suspects him of jealousy. At any rate he seems to have been Destiny's more than willing accomplice in opening the next—and decisive—period of Michelangelo's life. The time was the summer of 1489; Michelangelo was a few months past his 14th birthday, and had completed only one year of his three-year contract with Ghirlandaio. Vasari describes in detail what happened, and it is well to quote him directly:

"Lorenzo the Magnificent at about this time engaged the sculptor Bertoldo not so much to be curator of his great collection of antiquities in the Medici gardens, as to form a school for sculptors. It is true that Bertoldo was old and could no longer work, but he was an excellent craftsman, especially in bronze. Lorenzo was concerned because there were no sculptors comparable to the many able painters of the day. He asked Ghirlandaio to recommend and bring to the school any promising young sculptors.

"Michelangelo and Granacci, among others, were sent to the Medici gardens. Torrigiano was already there working on some terra-cotta figures in high relief. Michelangelo, with great enthusiasm, tried his hand at it, and was so successful that he was given a piece of marble to work on. He began to copy the head of a marble faun, a Roman work. He changed it, opening the mouth wider to show all the teeth. The Magnificent [Lorenzo] was delighted with it. He said that he did not think a faun as old as that would have such a perfect set of teeth. Michelangelo, in his simplicity, took him seriously and set to work again. He broke out a tooth and even filed down the gum to make it look shrunken. Lorenzo was much amused.

"Lorenzo sent for Lodovico, Michelangelo's father, and formally arranged to receive Michelangelo into his princely household. The lad stayed there . . . until the death of Lorenzo, receiving for himself an allowance of money and a purple cloak to wear, while his father, Lodovico, was made an official of the customs."

Vasari's account of this crucial juncture in Michelangelo's life requires some amplification.

The Medici gardens that he mentions were a fairly small private park,

leafy and walled, on the Via Larga. They were better known as the Gardens of San Marco because of their proximity to the monastery of San Marco (although they had no connection with it). The antiquities assembled in the gardens represented the accumulation of three Medici generations: Cosimo, Piero, and Lorenzo. All were avid collectors, and theirs was certainly a "great collection" by the standards of the time. The sculptured pieces—the ones Vasari means—included sarcophagi and funerary urns and tomb portraits, some portrait busts, medallions, statues, columns, capitals, votive vessels, wall inscriptions and carvings, and other odds and ends, in marble, bronze, and terra-cotta. These various works were mainly Roman, and mainly in a damaged or fragmented condition. The earth of Italy and Greece and Asia Minor still concealed most of the classic masterpieces we now know of, such as the *Venus de Milo* and the *Laocoön*. The search was going on full tilt, however; new finds were being made and causing vast excitement.

Simultaneously, the past was also being rediscovered through the medium of ancient texts. Because they were portable, easily hidden if need be, and because there always had been men who cherished learning and tried to preserve it, the old manuscripts came in rather steadily. In this branch of antiquities the Medici collection was indeed great.

Lorenzo's concern about the imbalance between sculptors and painters was acutely justified. The distinguished line that had begun with Andrea Pisano and Ghiberti (and included many other splendid sculptors) had been reproducing itself at a steadily diminishing rate and finally, with the death of Verrocchio, had simply stopped. Antonio del Pollaiuolo, a younger contemporary of Verrocchio, had moved to Rome to work on the tombs of Popes Sixtus IV and Innocent VIII. Bertoldo, as Vasari notes, was too old; Florence no longer had any first-rate talents engaged in this art which had been among its chief glories. As leader of the city, as head of the Medici family, and above all as himself, Lorenzo viewed this as a serious problem worthy of serious effort on his own part. Scholars tend to doubt the story Vasari tells about Michelangelo and the faun's teeth and Lorenzo's on-the-spot decision to send for Lodovico; and no doubt things were neither that fast nor that simple. However, considering the parlous state of sculpture, Lorenzo's obvious interest, his extraordinarily keen eye for talent and his congenial custom of inviting people of outstanding gifts to be his permanent guests at the Medici Palace, the general sense of the story is not only plausible but probable.

Pietro Torrigiano, the sculptor who broke Michelangelo's nose, never did live down the deed. Vasari reserved for him epithets like "violent and overbearing," "proud, thoughtless and ungoverned," and Cellini could not even "bear to look at him." After leaving Italy to work among "the brutes of the Englishmen," Torrigiano went to Spain. There he became so enraged over payment for a *Madonna and Child* that he smashed the sculpture, only to be accused of heresy by his patron and brought before the Inquisition. He was imprisoned, and, Vasari recounts, fell "into such . . . melancholy that he remained several days without food, and becoming gradually weaker, he died."

The Torrigiano mentioned by Vasari turned out to be the traditional school bully. He had some talent and a hot temper, and has only one important claim on posterity's attention. In the church of Santa Maria del Carmine, when the Bertoldo class was there one day sketching the Masaccios, he and Michelangelo got into an argument that erupted into a fight. Torrigiano landed a heavy blow full on the bridge of Michelangelo's nose and broke it, marking him for the rest of his life with that sad and battered face that is so familiar from his portraits, and marking him also with what may well have been the beginnings of his lifelong feelings of dissatisfaction with himself, with the hard world of reality and even in part with life itself.

Finally, as for Lorenzo's encounter with Lodovico Buonarroti concerning his son, a more detailed version than Vasari's has been supplied by his fellow-historian Condivi: "When Lorenzo saw how cleverly he [Michelangelo] had performed the task, he resolved to provide for the boy's future and to take him into his own household. So, having heard whose son he was, 'Go,' he said, 'and tell your father that I wish to speak with him.' Michelangelo accordingly went home, and delivered the message of the Magnificent. His father, guessing probably what he was wanted for, could be persuaded only by the urgent prayers of Granacci and other friends to obey the summons. Indeed, he complained loudly that Lorenzo wanted to lead his son astray, abiding firmly by the principle that he would never permit a son of his to be a stonecutter. Vainly did Granacci explain the difference between a sculptor and a stonecutter: all his arguments seemed thrown away. Nevertheless, when Lodovico appeared before the Magnificent, and was asked if he would consent to give his son up to the great man's guardianship, he did not know how to refuse. 'In faith,' he added, 'not Michelangelo alone, but all of us, with our lives and all our abilities, are at the pleasure of your Magnificence.'"

Who was this man Lorenzo? What was so admirable that he brought to Florence? What warranted the homage given him by the Florentines, who were not easy to impress and who had irreverently dubbed his father *Il Gottoso,* Piero the Gouty?

Lorenzo's magnificence did not lie in mere wealth, nor in lavish displays, nor even in his patronage of arts and learning. To be sure, he spent amply in these ways, but with well-calculated purpose and within restraints imposed by his own taste. He conducted himself in princely style, but this, after all, was an age of princes, and as first citizen of Florence he had status to maintain. He had to live above the scale of other great financial barons of the city (but not so far above as to arouse their active jealousy), and he had to guard his own prestige, as well as that of his family and of Florence, among the other leading personages and families and states of Italy and Europe. Besides the Medici Palace he had half a dozen country houses; and he entertained in a way that was designed to stagger distinguished visitors, and did.

His grandfather Cosimo had set the precedent in 1439 when he persuaded his good friend Pope Eugenius IV to choose Florence as the new site of the Great Council he had called to heal the 400-year-old schism between the Western and Eastern branches of Christianity—the Church of Rome and the Greek Orthodox Church led by the Patriarch of Constantinople. Ferrara, the original meeting place, had been struck by a plague, and Cosimo succeeded in having the Council transferred to his city. For months Florence was iridescent with the pomp and pageantry befitting the presence of the two leaders of Christendom and their galaxies of cardinals, bishops, theologians and functionaries, as well as the presence, for a time, of the Byzantine Emperor and his resplendent retinue. Cosimo, in his dual role as personal host and de facto head of the city, paid a large part of the expenses from his own pocket.

Again, when Lorenzo was married in 1469 to Clarice Orsini, daughter of the aristocratic and politically powerful Orsini of Rome, his father

Giovanni Pico,
Count of Mirandola (1463-1494)

Pico della Mirandola, the most brilliant of the intellectuals to sit at Lorenzo's table, is commemorated by a medallion cast in Florence sometime around 1493. By his early twenties Pico had mastered 22 languages and "ranged through all the masters of philosophy, investigated all books, and come to know all schools." Out of his fund of knowledge he compounded 900 theses or propositions, which he was prepared to debate singlehandedly with all comers at a congress of scholars and intellectuals. But before the gathering could take place, the Church intervened, disturbed by the heretical and suspect nature of 13 of the theses. From a man-oriented view of the world, Pico later shifted to a God-centered one and, only a day before his death at 31, took the vows of a monk.

Piero had held a three-day fete of unexampled splendor for the hundreds of wedding guests and the city at large. As his part of this affair, Lorenzo staged a jousting tournament and entered the lists himself. He rode first a prancing horse sent by the King of Naples and then a charger sent by the Duke of Ferrara; he wore, along with the necessary armor, a velvet cap spattered with pearls, a velvet jacket spangled with gold and jewels, and a silk scarf embroidered with pearls; he carried a shield set with a famous diamond, *Il Libro*. He wrote in his diary: "In order to do as others, I held a joust on the Piazza of Santa Croce, at great expense and with much pomp, on which I find about 10,000 ducats were spent. Although neither my years nor my blows were very great, the first prize was awarded to me, a silver helmet with Mars as its crest."

All this ostentation was part of the politics of the time. When not on public view, however, Lorenzo lived, if not in austerity, at least with simplicity—so much so that when Franceschetto Cibò, Pope Innocent VIII's illegitimate son, married Lorenzo's daughter Maddalena and first stayed at the Medici Palace, he was audibly surprised at the plain style of his new in-laws' private life. Lorenzo explained that although nothing was too good for guests, the family itself preferred the simple comforts of home, and that they were making Franceschetto welcome by treating him as one of the family.

Lorenzo's greatness lay in qualities that money—wonderfully useful though it was—could not buy or express. He combined modesty with self-confidence, cool realism with warm personal charm, and contemplativeness with a capacity for decision and action. The result made him a leader who was not only obeyed but admired and respected.

With his broad-ranging and acute intelligence, and with nearly as broad a span of personal talents, he was absorbed in the entire panorama of major events and developments of his time and participated directly in many of them. His interests extended all the way from the intricacies of Italian statecraft to the harmonies of the Petrarchan sonnet. He was a greatly admired poet and certainly the greatest statesman of his era, keeping Italy comparatively at peace for decades through his personal diplomacy. As a young man, before the family affliction of gout overtook him, he was an athlete; and with his robust, life-loving, outgoing nature he and his brother Giuliano, four years younger, had kept Florence bubbling with gaiety and excitement. He not only sponsored and organized and paid for feasts and carnivals for the pleasure of the whole city but led the revelry, joined the street dances, and even wrote many of the *carnevale* songs. His tunes and verses became popular classics, as skilled on their level as his sonnets were on theirs. One of them is well known in an English translation:

> *How fair is youth,*
> *That flies away!*
> *Then be happy, you who may;*
> *Of tomorrow who can say?*

Yet he was a serious student of philosophy, too, deeply interested and informed in the Platonism that Cosimo had done so much to revive. He

had grown up in it; his tutor had been Marsilio Ficino, Cosimo's protégé and the leading Platonist of the time. At Marsilio's villa outside Florence, Lorenzo and his friends met regularly for philosophic discussion. This group, a number of whom lived or were long-term visitors at the Medici Palace, included Cristoforo Landino, a great Latinist and authority on Dante; Pico della Mirandola, a philosopher-theologian who had one of the most brilliant and wide-ranging minds of his time; Gentile Becchi, Lorenzo's first tutor and later Bishop of Arezzo, who was an authority on classical studies; and the classicist Angelo Poliziano, who was Lorenzo's closest friend, the tutor of his seven children and, in the opinion of the times, his only superior as a poet.

It was into this house and family and vibrant assembly of guests and friends that Michelangelo came to live—to live, as Romain Rolland has said, "at the very heart of the Renaissance." Lorenzo treated him like a foster son, giving him fine clothes, an allowance of five ducats a month, and, according to Condivi, "a good room in the palace, together with all the conveniences he desired." For all his tender years, he was made to feel at home and at ease in the glittering company of his elders. Condivi notes: "All these illustrious men paid him particular attention, and encouraged him in the honorable art which he had chosen. But the chief to do so was the Magnificent himself, who sent for him oftentimes in a day, in order that he might show him jewels, cornelians, medals and suchlike objects of great rarity, as knowing him to be of excellent parts and judgment in these things."

Michelangelo shared in Poliziano's classes with the young Medici, and indeed shared the life of this brood—among whom were two future Popes. Giovanni de' Medici, Lorenzo's second son, was only eight months younger than Michelangelo, an intelligent and witty and energetic boy of such manifest promise that Lorenzo, thinking ahead toward the family's future security and power, settled on the Church as his best career. In the same year that Michelangelo entered the sculpture school, the 14-year-old Giovanni was promised a cardinalate through the Medici influence with the reigning Pope and in due course fulfilled his father's dreams by ascending to the papacy himself as Pope Leo X. Lorenzo did not live to see that, but his early pride in Giovanni is memorialized on the back of the first letter the boy wrote to him after going to Rome several years later to be invested with the insignia of his high office. Before putting the letter carefully away, Lorenzo wrote on it: "From my son, the Cardinal."

The other boy, a bit younger, was Giulio de' Medici, the illegitimate son of Lorenzo's dead brother Giuliano: Lorenzo had taken the child to raise as one of his own. He was the future Pope Clement VII. A few decades from this time the paths of these three boys—Giovanni, Giulio and Michelangelo—would cross and recross, with profound effects on Michelangelo's life and works.

But now he learned and worked, always under the attentive paternal eye of Lorenzo, who guided and encouraged the flowering of his genius. He learned avidly, with an electric new interest in knowledge, from Poliziano and from the whole brilliant circle, especially from Landino, who

Marsilio Ficino (1433-1499)

Angelo Poliziano (1454-1494)

Chief among the members of the Platonic Academy—that loosely constructed association of intellectuals devoted to Plato's philosophy—were Marsilio Ficino (top), its founder and president, and Angelo Poliziano. Ficino was a puny man, possessed of a gentle and melancholy nature. He became a priest in 1473, but still began his discourses by addressing "My very dear ones in Plato," rather than "My very dear brethren in Jesus Christ." Poliziano was still an impoverished student when discovered by Lorenzo. A poet and translator of the first rank, he rose to prominence in the Medici household as tutor, but left after a quarrel with Lorenzo's wife. Lorenzo, however, cajoled him into coming back, and this time he remained until his benefactor's death.

instilled in him such love for the poetry of Dante that with the passing years he committed much of *The Divine Comedy* to memory; half a century later, the vivid imagery of Dante's *Inferno* would be reflected in Michelangelo's *Last Judgment*. At the same time he became almost equally devoted to Petrarch. In this house, which contained two of the leading poets of the time, and where a favorite after-dinner diversion was to improvise verses to the accompaniment of a lute, he absorbed poetry as naturally as, at Settignano, he had acquired his love of sculpture when he "suckled among the chisels and hammers of the stonecutters." It was at this time, probably, that he began to try his hand at sonnets and madrigals and formed his lifelong habit of confiding his personal emotions and private thoughts to verse. He never considered himself more than an amateur poet, and the poems that have survived are only a small fraction of those he wrote—he destroyed the rest as unworthy to be seen.

Meanwhile, he worked under Bertoldo, who, besides being curator and master-teacher at the sculpture gardens of San Marco, was a permanent guest at the Medici Palace. How much he owed to Bertoldo's instruction is a moot question among scholars. For Bertoldo was by then quite decrepit; further, he had devoted most of his career not to carving marble but to modeling for bronze—work which required a quite different set of skills and which Michelangelo heartily disliked. From Michelangelo's addiction to working with marble and his rapid mastery of his art, it could be deduced that somewhere along the line he had already acquired some of the basic technical skills.

Recent research has nominated as the hypothetical unknown instructor Benedetto da Maiano, a sculptor much respected at the time. A possible clue is found in a marble altar he completed in 1488, the year before Michelangelo came to the Medici Gardens. The altar's sculpture includes two *putti*—those plump cherubs that were such a staple of Italian art— holding a garland. One *putto* is Benedetto's beyond a doubt; but the other is so far superior to it that it must have been done by a greater artist— just possibly the very young Michelangelo. Further: it was quite unusual for apprentices to be paid anything their first year, yet Ghirlandaio, in the contract with Lodovico cited above, had for some reason agreed to pay Michelangelo six florins that year. Did this mean he had already had some instruction in artistic techniques? It is a mystery—worth noting here because it is one of the earliest of the numerous, indeed nearly innumerable, mysteries that one encounters in the life of Michelangelo, a source of endless fascination to scholars and of endless frustration to his biographers.

But of one thing there is no doubt. He did, in the year 1489, transfer from Ghirlandaio's *bottega* to Bertoldo's school at the Medici Gardens, and there he produced sculptures that evolved from promise to excellence and toward mastery. Probably he did a number of practice-pieces such as the faun mask that had caught Lorenzo's eye, but apparently his first important venture, in which he felt ready to try out his new skills in a work demanding a large measure of real professionalism, was a rectangular marble plaque, carved in low relief, showing the Virgin holding the infant Jesus to her breast and seated at the bottom of a flight of

CANZONE A BALLO COMPOSTE DAL
MAGNIFICO LORENZO DE MEDICI
et da M. Agnolo Politiano, & altri autori.
infieme con la
Nencia da Barberino,& la Beca da Dicomano
Compofte dal medefimo Lorenzo.
NVOVAMENTE RICORRETTE.

The title page from a book of popular dancing songs composed by Lorenzo de' Medici, Poliziano and others, shows what may be *Il Magnifico* himself accepting a gift from a kneeling girl, while in the background chorusing maidens dance under the Medici coat of arms. A composer of light, sometimes bawdy, verse as well as serious sonnets in Italian, Lorenzo excelled at ballads that expressed his musician's sense of rhythm and his humanistic appreciation of life. One of his carnival songs, which puts girls and gossips at each others' throats, gives the girls the upper hand in the last stanza—"Long live love and long live courtesy; death to envy and the Tattlers; say then, ye who would speak evil, we will do it and ye shall say it."

steps. This *Madonna of the Stairs* was done about 1491 and thus possibly under at least the preliminary supervision of Bertoldo, who died during that year, and under the strong influence of Bertoldo's old teacher and hero, Donatello. Vasari declared that it is "so exactly in Donatello's manner that it really looks like a Donatello, except that it is more graceful and better designed," but this is flagrant hyperbole and shows how numbed Vasari's judgment could become in matters involving Michelangelo. Nevertheless, it is a work of enormous promise.

His next undertaking was also a relief, this time on a classical theme probably suggested to him by Poliziano: the struggle of fair young heroes to rescue a lovely maiden from the assault of a band of centaurs. *The Battle of the Centaurs* is interesting for several reasons, but initially and not least because it directly followed the *Madonna of the Stairs.* Renaissance art had at first been almost entirely devoted to religious subjects (as of course medieval art had been), and it was only gradually that classical themes had come into fashion—really not until the middle of the 15th Century. Thus it was only with the time of Lorenzo and his circle (and primarily through their influence) that an artist might easily find himself working on, say, a Risen Christ and an Apollo in succession for the same patron. The most popular religious subject was the Madonna and Child; the most characteristic classical themes were from Greek and Roman mythology, with the mythological characters presented in some imagined situation and scene, very often allegorical.

Thus Michelangelo, with his *Madonna* and his *Centaurs,* was flexing his talents in the two most familiar—but also most demanding—regions of art. But the *Centaurs* was by far the more difficult. He loaded the battle scene, in fact overloaded it, with naked male forms in violent, tangled action, which put great tests on his skill at composition and even more on his knowledge of anatomy. And his success was much greater than with the *Madonna.* It is not a triumphant work, not a masterpiece, but in its great vigor, its uninhibited use of the expressive nude and its venturesome handling of composition—all betokening originality, daring and skill developing at high speed—the *Centaurs* pointed to the greatness that lay not very far off.

The miracle of living and working and learning in the Medici circle lasted almost three years, until Lorenzo's death at 43 in the year 1492. He died on the night of Sunday, April 8, at Careggi, near Florence, in a country house where he had spent some of the happiest times of his boyhood and youth. Death came from a combination of gout, rheumatic fever and an excruciating stomach disorder, perhaps perforated ulcers, complicated by the mixture of ground pearls and precious gems that his physicians fed him as their final life-giving elixir.

With Lorenzo's passing, an era ended not only for Michelangelo but for Florence and for Italy. A time of dark troubles and tragedies lay ahead. But these three years had molded Michelangelo's mind, his character, his philosophy and his art. What he received from Lorenzo, who in truth was one of the most remarkable men of his own or any time, was a gift that would grow with the years and last all his life, and, through his art, last forever.

The death mask of Lorenzo, with accompanying inscription to the effect that the world fell apart at his passing, recalls the chilling incidents that heralded the event. As *Il Magnifico* lay dying, lightning struck the dome of the cathedral and sent marble blocks tumbling in the direction of his palace. A comet flared in the sky and wolves howled. In the city's menagerie, lions kept as symbols of the republic began to fight and one was killed; a hysterical woman at worship in church had a vision of a bull with flaming horns setting fire to the city. And as the climax to all these events, the morning after Lorenzo died, the body of his doctor was found in a well. Some said that he had hurled himself in out of despair, others that he had been thrown in.

The School of Florence

Though trained in Ghirlandaio's workshop and Bertoldo's sculpture gardens, Michelangelo acknowledged no master—he was too independent a spirit for that. Nonetheless, he recognized himself as the product of a time and a place, and his works as the fulfillment of both. "There are to be found in Italy," he wrote later in life, "cities which are nearly all painted . . . inside and out." And Florence, the city he called his nest, was the chief of these. It was here, only 75 years before his birth, that a new style in art had emerged that led Florentine painters to some of the boldest creative experiments of the century. The laws of linear perspective, the interplay of color and light to define form, the representation of real people showing real emotions—all these enabled the artists to create a three-dimensional world on the two-dimensional surfaces of wood panels or walls, in a dramatic break with the flat and highly symbolic style of the Middle Ages.

By Michelangelo's day, the fruits of these experiments were everywhere to be seen—in frescoes and panel paintings, in sculpture and in large new buildings, all bespeaking the new interest in man and the world around him. And so it was that the dynamic school of Florence became quite literally Michelangelo's own school—and Michelangelo, in turn, its master.

Fra Filippo Lippi was among the first of the Florentine artists to use local models, like these children, in his paintings. But then he was a worldly man, this monk: he ran off with a nun, and out of their union came another painter, Filippino Lippi.

Fra Filippo Lippi:
Madonna and Child, c. 1452

ECCE VIRGO CONCIPIET 7 PARIET FILIVM 7 VOCABIT NOMEN EIVS EMANVL. YSA.VI.C

ECCE CONCIPIES INVTERO 7 PARIES FILIVM 7 VOCABIS NOMEN EI IHESVM .LVCE . I . C .

Fra Angelico: *The Annunciation,* c. 1450

Fra Angelico, who gave the angel in this
Annunciation the colorful wings of an outsize butterfly,
was a far more saintly friar than Fra Filippo Lippi.
He was a Dominican who spent much of his time
painting for his fellow monks in the convent of San
Marco, and his art had its roots far back in the Middle
Ages. Still, for all this spirituality, he did not ignore

the artistic trends of the day. Here, for example,
Fra Angelico shows a thorough understanding of
the laws of linear perspective, and has placed
the Virgin and angel in a contemporary setting—
a Renaissance courtyard whose capitals, columns and
round arches tell of the new Florentine fascination with
architectural motifs taken over from classical Rome.

Domenico Veneziano: *St. Lucy Altarpiece*, c. 1445

An innovator in a different sense from his contemporaries Masaccio and Fra Filippo Lippi, Domenico Veneziano was the first painter of the Renaissance to attempt to capture outdoor light in his works. In his *St. Lucy Altarpiece* (one of only two paintings that can be definitely attributed to him today), the realistically portrayed saints, Virgin and Child are defined as much by the sunlight streaming in from the right side and the strong shadow it creates, as they are by the meticulously worked-out perspective. Domenico achieved this luminous effect through the judicious use of color, with light pink, green and white predominating—and the entire scheme electrified by patches of intense red, blue and yellow.

Sandro Botticelli: *Primavera*, 1487

Sandro Botticelli, whose poetic *Primavera* is reproduced at left, cared little for perspective: a sinuous line was his chief mode of expression. In this allegory of spring, in which a wistful Venus is attended by Mercury, the Three Graces, Flora, Cupid and two amorous zephyrs, the linear contours of flesh and clothing create gentle rhythms that animate the entire composition. The scene takes place on a flowered plain, backed by a forest where trees bloom and bear fruit at the same time; the picture space is only a few feet deep, yet the figures in the foreground, light, floating, attenuated, have a voluptuousness that speaks of living bodies.

Despite its paganism, the *Primavera* is a Christian painting. It is, in fact, a visual statement of Neoplatonism, that rationalizing philosophy of the Renaissance which attempted, among other things, to fuse the myths and figures of antiquity with the stories and characters of the Bible. Thus Botticelli intended his Venus to represent divine beauty and divine love; to devout Neoplatonists like those in the circle of the Medici, this demure woman, with delicately raised hand, could even represent the Virgin.

Andrea del Castagno: *Youthful David*, c. 1450-1457

Paolo Uccello, more than any other Florentine painter of the 15th Century, was obsessed with perspective. His *Battle of San Romano*, a detail of which is shown at left, reveals the extreme limits to which he stretched it: knights and horses are so drastically foreshortened that they seem photographed through a telephoto lens. The total effect is strange and unreal, with figures that have volume but no life, and with action crowded into an area of little depth. Despite Uccello's insistence upon having his lines converge on a vanishing point, the picture is united more by surface patterns than by spatial construction.

Andrea del Castagno, who painted the *David* on the decorative leather shield above, also became concerned with perspective and used it to initiate a mood of stark dramatic realism in Florentine painting. But unlike Uccello, he did not spend a lifetime exploring it. As he matured, his work began to show linear tendencies. The figure of David, in spite of the dramatically foreshortened left arm, seems to dwell less in three-dimensional space than to exist on the surface of the shield, almost as though it had been carved there in relief. Rather than modeling in chiaroscuro, the play of light and shadow, Castagno defined David in terms of a strong outline, which combines with the lines of his windblown hair and swirling jerkin to achieve an effect of immense energy.

Paolo Uccello: *Battle of San Romano*, detail, 1456

Of the many 15th Century painters who contributed to Michelangelo's education, only a few can actually be shown to have had a direct influence on him. Not surprisingly, one of the most important of these was Ghirlandaio, who taught him drawing and fresco painting. A precise exponent of visual realism, Ghirlandaio excelled at portraiture and flattered rich Florentines by inserting them into his religious scenes. Below, for example, in addition to the man who commissioned the fresco (shown bald, on the right, surrounded by his family), he included Lorenzo de' Medici, with hand outstretched; Poliziano, the tutor of Lorenzo's children; and the children themselves—Giovanni, Piero and Giuliano.

Far more powerful was the Umbrian Luca Signorelli, whose use of the body to express drama made a lasting impression on Michelangelo. A master of human anatomy, Signorelli filled his paintings with nude people in violent action, their gestures fraught with emotion. His epic fresco *The Damned Cast into Hell (opposite)* remained vivid in Michelangelo's mind for more than three decades: there are strong echoes of it in the *Last Judgment*.

Domenico Ghirlandaio: *Pope Honorius III Confirming the Rule of the Order of St. Francis,* 1485

Luca Signorelli: *The Damned Cast into Hell,* detail, 1499-1502

Filippo Brunelleschi: Old Sacristy, San Lorenzo, c. 1421-1429

In Pursuit of Perfection

Like the painters, the architects and sculptors of
15th Century Florence sought in many ways to achieve
perfection in their art. Chief among the experimenters
were Brunelleschi, whose Old Sacristy *(above)* was
a source of Michelangelo's design for the New Sacristy;
Lorenzo Ghiberti, who labored 23 years to produce
the set of bronze doors which, after Michelangelo's
phrase, became known as the *Gates of Paradise (opposite);*
and Donatello, who, as the next pages will show,
advanced sculpture into new realms.

Brunelleschi found his inspiration in the ancient
past; he even discovered the laws of linear perspective
while drawing Roman ruins to scale. But he was not an
imitator. He took the various elements of classical
architecture—the column, the capital, the rounded arch—
and recombined them, with a mathematician's regard
for proportion, in such a fresh way that a completely new

style emerged. The Gothic emphasis on soaring lines
disappeared, and the solid awesomeness of old buildings
like the Palazzo della Signoria was superseded by
an elegant lightness. Here, in the Old Sacristy, balance
reigns, with horizontals and verticals harmoniously
and symmetrically disposed, and windows, doors
and medallions quietly echoing one another.

Just as Brunelleschi made proportion the foundation
of his art, so Ghiberti attempted to make perspective
the basis of his. "I have ever striven," he wrote in
his autobiography, ". . . to examine the ways of nature,
to discover how pictures are conceived, how the sense
of sight works." His *Gates of Paradise,* illustrating
10 stories from the Old Testament, are the measure of
his achievement: no panel is deeper than four inches,
and yet perspective is so precisely handled the figures
seem, as Ghiberti proudly stated, "sculpture in the round."

AUGUSTANA UNIVERSITY COLLEGE LIBRARY

Lorenzo Ghiberti: *Gates of Paradise,* c. 1429-1452

Donatello: *David*, c. 1430-1432

Sculpture was Michelangelo's chosen art, and the greatest of sculptors in the world into which he was born was Donatello. It was he who created living people out of stone by imparting to them the weight and balance and psychological depth of human beings. Donatello viewed the body as an articulated structure, to be treated as such in art, and not as a dummy on which fanciful draperies could be superimposed. Thus his early *St. Mark (opposite)*, a revolutionary work that deeply moved Michelangelo, did not depend upon its setting for its existence or effect as did the statues of the Middle Ages; it could be taken down from its niche and left to stand by itself. His saint appears in a natural pose, a figure of great authority, with the weight of the body descending through one leg and dimpling the pillow underfoot. Donatello's somewhat later *David (above)* goes still further in its articulation of the body— it dispenses with clothes to become the first life-sized free-standing nude since classic antiquity. In the still later *Judith and Holofernes (left)*, a new, harsh realism takes over, and in Judith's withdrawn, anxious expression there is moving evidence that man no longer looked solely to God for an explanation of his condition, but inside himself as well.

Donatello: *Judith and Holofernes*, c. 1460

Donatello: *St. Mark*, 1411-1413

III

The Making of a Sculptor

A sculptor first, a painter second, Michelangelo gave his *Doni Tondo* the hard edges and polished look of carved marble. "The more relief a painting shows," he wrote, "the more it approaches and assumes lifelike quality."

Doni Tondo, c. 1504

Guarda e passa . . . look and pass on: such was Virgil's advice to Dante when, in the vestibule of the Inferno, they came upon a scene of indescribable din and tumult. The viewer of the Florentine political scene in the Quattrocento may well be guided by this counsel, for even in the hindsight of history its complexities are incalculable and perhaps infinite. In passing, however, a few general points need to be made about the peculiarities of the Republic of Florence and the correspondingly peculiar methods by which the Medici ruled it. For it was the breakdown of this apparatus soon after Lorenzo's death that changed the city, converted the Medici from the most respected citizens into the "most wanted," wrecked and scattered the Medici circle and drastically altered the lives of all its members, including Michelangelo.

First, it must be understood that Florence was not even remotely a democracy as we understand the term today. Of its population of some 70,000, only about 3,000 were eligible to vote. Essentially, this imbalance derived from the city's economic history, for it was the venturesome traders and bankers and processors of goods who had made the city rich and vigorous. They and their descendants, establishing great families such as the Medici, had taken over the governing power from the feudal nobility as a matter of manifest right. The trade associations—the so-called *Arti Maggiori*, or Greater Guilds—into which they had grouped themselves became their vehicles for political expression.

In the course of time, the butchers, bakers and others on the same economic level began to form guilds of their own. Finally there were 14 of these Lesser Guilds, or *Arti Minori*, double the number of the old established Greater Guilds, and exceeding them in membership by a far greater ratio. But although the Lesser Guilds demanded voting rights for their members and got them, the terms were so rigged by the Greater Guilds that the latter generally managed to keep effective control of the government. As for the proletarian masses, they were shut out entirely.

Thus Florence created a republic: a government elected by, and responsible to, those select citizens who by virtue of wealth, industry, intelligence and other elevated characteristics were deemed suited to run

Giuliano de' Medici

Lorenzo de' Medici

Murder and a narrow escape in Florence's cathedral are commemorated by two medallions cast after the Pazzi family's failure to overthrow the Medici. At top, the handsome murder victim, Giuliano de' Medici, darling of all Florence, is shown in profile; he also appears among the smaller figures, sprawled out in death before the choir rail, pierced 19 times by daggers. In the medal at bottom, Lorenzo is being attacked by his would-be assassins—two priests who were so inept at wielding weapons that they bungled the job, enabling him to leap over the rail to safety. For their part in the murder plot, they had their ears and noses chopped off before being hanged.

the best possible government; and best not merely for themselves, so the theory went, but for everyone else. In principle it was not unlike the republican form of government in the United States in the first few decades after 1789, satisfying John Adams' notion that rule ought to be by "the rich, the wise, and the wellborn."

In the bracing commercial atmosphere of the city the built-in social and economic distinctions of the Florentine constitution were bound to cause trouble. New men kept making good and seeking equality with those whose wealth they had equaled or surpassed; the older established families, not unexpectedly, preferred the status quo. This struggle became a fixture of Florentine life; it passed through endless permutations and brought all manner of chicanery, corruption and violence.

At the pinnacle were the *popolo grasso,* the "big people," with the connotation of "well-fed, big-stomached people." Their life appeared from below to be glorious—and frequently was. Yet, envied as these few score wealthy families were, in fact they suffered from a gnawing anxiety and an urgent dissatisfaction. The main source of their nervousness was not the lower orders but their own. For it was a striking characteristic of members of this class—not merely in Florence but everywhere in Renaissance Italy—that they were ravenous for great affluence, great deeds, great acclaim and great power with all its visible appurtenances: what they already had, whatever it might be, was almost never enough. Nor was their discontent just the product of gluttonous ego. In considerable part it grew from the most fundamental, stimulating and, for that matter, inspiring idea of the Renaissance: the idea that man has in him the capacity to achieve almost anything he wants, to master the earth and all the riches thereof. On the one hand the Florentines believed passionately in equality and were quick to resent any airs of superiority toward their own family by any other; on the other hand, as the contemporary historian Francesco Guicciardini said of his fellow citizens, "There are few so in love with liberty that they would not seize the opportunity of ruling and lording it." In short, every wealthy Florentine family would have liked to be in the shoes of the Medici and every such family entertained the pleasant, covert thought that somehow, sometime it would be—a corollary, of course, being the disappearance of the Medici.

This raises the interesting question of how Cosimo, Piero and Lorenzo had managed to maintain for nearly 60 continuous years their rule of this cauldron of unruly ambitions, old grudges and factionalism—a city so politically volatile that in the pre-Medici era, as one fugitive from the fray wryly estimated, there usually were enough Florentines in exile to populate another whole city the same size. Actually, each of the three men in his own time had been the very-near-victim of a plot to dispose of him, so part of the answer would have to be that the Medici were not only talented but lucky. Most notably, in 1478, in a plot organized by members of the Pazzi family, then the most powerful rivals of the Medici, assassins attacked Lorenzo and his younger brother Giuliano during Mass in the cathedral. Giuliano was killed; Lorenzo narrowly escaped by fleeing through a sacristy.

Accordingly, from the most vivid kind of personal experience, the

Medici learned something that helped them stay lucky: that the price of liberty and of life itself is eternal vigilance. Their intelligence network spread through Italy and Europe and grew famous for its efficiency.

Luck, vigilance, and of course a great deal else helped entrench the Medici—above all, perhaps, two rules that have always been instinctive with really first-rate political leaders. Rule One: Nothing beats the personal touch. Rule Two: Build loyal alliances.

Lorenzo, like his father and grandfather before him, avoided public office for the most part, preferring to work quietly from his *palazzo* to strengthen and maintain the loyalty of a majority of members of the governing bodies of Florence. He was very much like a modern city boss, and, like a modern boss, he always had to reckon with an opposition and with public opinion. Because of his breadth of knowledge, and because of his empathy and warm personality, Lorenzo not only could talk with almost anyone about that person's own interests but could cultivate an easy, natural relationship, whether the person happened to be a rich fellow-oligarch, young Michelangelo, or a shoemaker, oil vendor, gold-thread spinner, pastry cook, melon and cucumber peddler, rag-picker or street beggar—these last being some of the categories of people for whom, in fact, he wrote his carnival songs. As the historian C. M. Ady has said, "Perhaps his greatest gift is best expressed in the word *civiltà*, the capacity to live as a citizen among citizens."

This ability to communicate with people obviously had its uses in Lorenzo's diplomacy. For example, in the early years of his rule, when King Ferrante of Naples and Pope Sixtus IV had combined against Florence, and their armies were closing in, Lorenzo visited Ferrante, talked him out of the alliance with Sixtus and made him a loyal friend—thus saving the city in one of the legendary virtuoso performances in diplomatic history. But as Cosimo had once remarked when reproached for hardheartedness in banishing 80 members of the hostile Albizzi political faction, "States are not built on Paternosters"; and neither are dependable alliances built on friendly feelings alone. At home and abroad, Lorenzo buttressed the perishable effects of his own charm with every pillar he could find, and wound it all round with everything from solid chains of gold, represented by loans from the Medici banks, to gossamer threads of flattery and loving kindness. During his campaign to win Pope Innocent VIII, for example, his agents in Rome discovered and reported the Pope's weakness for the small European table bird called the ortolan, and henceforth every courier from Lorenzo to His Holiness carried a box of ortolans.

In the spirit of his times, Lorenzo also used his own children to further his political ends. The most brilliant marriage in the family, that of his daughter Maddalena, at the age of 14, to Pope Innocent VIII's 40-year-old son, was directly instrumental in securing what Lorenzo happily called "the greatest honor that has come to our house," the cardinalate for young Giovanni. Piero, the oldest of Lorenzo's three sons, married Alfonsina Orsini, a distant cousin of his mother's in the powerful Orsini clan of Rome. Lucrezia, Lorenzo's oldest daughter, married Jacopo Salviati, thereby healing the breach that had occurred between the Medici

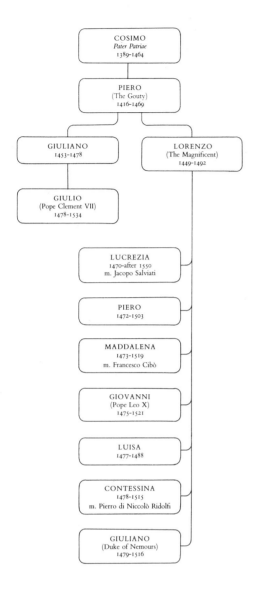

```
COSIMO
Pater Patriae
1389-1464

PIERO
(The Gouty)
1416-1469

GIULIANO          LORENZO
1453-1478        (The Magnificent)
                  1449-1492

GIULIO
(Pope Clement VII)
1478-1534

LUCREZIA
1470-after 1550
m. Jacopo Salviati

PIERO
1472-1503

MADDALENA
1473-1519
m. Francesco Cibò

GIOVANNI
(Pope Leo X)
1475-1521

LUISA
1477-1488

CONTESSINA
1478-1515
m. Pierro di Niccolò Ridolfi

GIULIANO
(Duke of Nemours)
1479-1516
```

Four generations of the fast-rising Florentine Medici are traced in this family tree from Cosimo through the children of his grandsons, Lorenzo the Magnificent and Giuliano. Lorenzo saw to it that the family name flourished by seeking positions of social prominence for its members. When his brother Giuliano was murdered in the Pazzi conspiracy, he adopted Giuliano's only child, a posthumous son, born of a woman to whom the father had been betrothed, and perhaps secretly married. In part because of Lorenzo, the boy was assured a brilliant future; he grew up to become Pope Clement VII.

and this influential Florentine family at the time of the Pazzi conspiracy. Contessina, the youngest daughter, was betrothed at the age of 11 to Niccolò Ridolfi, the scion of another of the great families of the city. The web of useful alliances would keep growing—and Michelangelo, as a surrogate member of the family, would in the years ahead often find himself encountering, with mixed consequences, the strands of this far-spreading network.

Important as marriages were in shaping the future of the Medici, what counted even more, in this age of strong individualism, were the personal qualities of the new generation of Medici males, Lorenzo's sons. In the part of his mind that he necessarily kept barricaded against private emotions, where the needs of the House of Medici and of the Florentine state were unceasingly calculated, he judged his boys coolly and objectively. One day he summarized his findings in one sentence in his private journal, distilling the predominant characteristics of each boy in a single word: one was foolish, one was clever, and one was good.

The clever one was Giovanni, the boy-Cardinal and future Pope Leo X.

The good boy was the youngest, Giuliano, named for Lorenzo's murdered brother. He was only 13 when Lorenzo died, too soon to have decided how to turn this goodness to best account, but it will suffice for now to note that Giuliano remained good, just as Giovanni remained clever, and that he too had a part to play in Michelangelo's later life.

The foolish boy was the firstborn, Piero. Lorenzo must have come to this opinion painfully, and with prayerful hope that maturity and experience would make him wiser, for by the custom of primogeniture Piero would succeed him as head of the House of Medici, and at least presumably as first citizen of Florence, just as he had succeeded his own father, Piero *Il Gottoso*. But sadly, disastrously, young Piero remained foolish.

A few days after Lorenzo's burial in the sacristy of the family church of San Lorenzo, in the presence of a host of grief-stunned mourners among whom surely was young Michelangelo, the Signory of Florence declared by an overwhelming majority that Lorenzo's position of leadership should be vested in Piero. After nearly six decades of Medici rule this seemed natural enough, but it was also, as the official decree stated, "a public testimony of gratitude" to the dead leader.

Piero and Michelangelo had never been on close terms. Piero was three years older, had different interests and a different temperament and may also have resented the attention his father paid Michelangelo. It seems likely that Michelangelo lacked both any invitation from Piero to stay on at the Palace and any inclination to do so; and so, in Vasari's words, "in great sorrow for the loss of his patron, he returned to his father's house."

For a while he seems to have been too disheartened to do much work. But through a friendship he had formed with the prior of the Monastery of Santo Spirito, he was able to secure an extremely valuable part of his education, an accurate knowledge of anatomy. Santo Spirito housed one of the city's important hospitals and hence contained a morgue. Although dissection of human bodies, except when expressly

approved by civil authorities, was illegal and in fact punishable by death, the prior allowed Michelangelo to come there and explore the secrets beneath the skin—the way muscles truly looked, and how they joined with each other and with the bones to produce the unity of all the parts in all the nuances of action of the living body.

Perhaps encouraged by his increasing sureness of anatomy, Michelangelo began working on his first figure in the round, a standing, larger-than-life-sized marble sculpture of Hercules. He sold it to the Strozzi family and it stood in the Strozzi Palace for years. Later, in the 1530s, it was sent to France as a gift to King Henry IV and was placed in the gardens of the Palace at Fontainebleau. Still later it was lost; the only visual record of it is a rear view in a French engraving of the gardens. The *Hercules* in turn may well have helped bring Michelangelo's first actual commission—which was from Piero, of all people, and, of all things, was a snow-giant. On January 20, 1494, Florence had a tremendous snowfall. Piero, in the carnival spirit of his father, decided that such a remarkable event needed a suitable memorial. He sent for Michelangelo and asked him to create a colossus of snow in the Medici Palace courtyard. The result pleased Piero so much that he urged Michelangelo to come back and live in the Palace again, in his old room. Michelangelo accepted and stayed for some months.

Piero was an athlete, a dancer, a horseman, a robust pleasure-seeker—as Lorenzo himself had been. But Lorenzo had had a sense of the appropriate, of tact and taste and innate style; above all he had been careful not to offend the touchy republicanism of the Florentines. Piero's maladroitness matched his father's adroitness. He galloped his stable of fine horses around the city for everyone to admire—and envy. He condescended to the masses; he was assertive and rather patronizing to the upper classes. Lorenzo had been homely but more than made up for it by charm: Piero was handsome but more than offset it by arrogance. Where Lorenzo was subtle and profound, his son was brash, with the untroubled self-confidence given only to the truly foolish. Hence whenever he tried to duplicate one of Lorenzo's achievements—a carnival or a diplomatic coup—the result was apt to be distorted and sometimes was a grotesque failure. The Florentines, watching his performance with mounting disfavor, decided that there was not much Medici in him and that he had taken after his mother's side, the Orsini, who were notorious for their proud ways and rude predilection for using their powerful private armies to dispose of arguments. *Orso* is the Italian for "bear," so the Florentines, never ones to overlook a pun, decided they were being led by a bear—a strong, awkward and rather dangerous young bear.

This was bad enough, but there was something far worse: Piero was unlucky. Like Michelangelo he seems almost to have been a child of Destiny but in a reverse way, as dogged by malign coincidences as Michelangelo was attended by benign ones. He came to power when two vastly disturbing historical forces, in the persons of a Dominican monk named Girolamo Savonarola and King Charles VIII of France, were threatening the peace of Florence and of Italy.

Savonarola has been called a harbinger of the Reformation and a

Girolamo Savonarola, the Dominican friar whose preaching instilled in the hedonistic Florentines a fearful, at times even hysterical, awareness of their sins, is shown in a portrait by Fra Bartolommeo. The Latin inscription underneath proclaims him to be a prophet sent by God—a view with which Savonarola seemed to concur. "I shall no longer . . . relate things that are past," he boldly asserted, "but shall tell of things to be." So great a hold did his oracular gifts give him over the Florentine imagination that at the peak of his power he was drawing crowds of up to 14,000 people to his sermons. Among the many events he predicted with eerie accuracy were the deaths of Lorenzo de' Medici, Pope Innocent VIII and the King of Naples.

throwback to medievalism who "rejected the Renaissance"; a demagogue and a democratic champion of the people; a genius and a madman; a scholar well-versed in the knowledge of his time and a narrow bigot. There is a good deal of truth in all of these descriptions. It was, in fact, this very complexity that enabled him to appeal to such an extraordinary range of people, from illiterate day laborers to the exquisite Pico della Mirandola, who had undertaken as his personal responsibility to reconcile Judaism, Christianity, Islam and Platonism. Savonarola held men spellbound—many appeared literally hypnotized—by the peculiar inner incandescence of the zealot-mystic who believes himself privy to God's plans and appointed as His messenger, and by the sheer overpowering drama of his verbal imagery and his way of preaching and his voice, which was like the Voice of Doom itself. Even as a youth in Ferrara—where his grandfather, a doctor, was attached to the ducal court—he had become increasingly obsessed with sin: the innumerable sins that he saw people committing all around him, and the stealthy urgings of his own flesh. He fled the world at 22 to enter a Dominican monastery in Bologna, and for the next seven years immersed himself in study and in chastising the devil within.

The Dominicans are preaching friars. After a lame start in Florence, where his superiors had posted him to the Monastery of San Marco, Savonarola was sent out to preach in other cities. In time he found his pace and style, and his confidence in himself and in his mission grew. So did his reputation, until at last in 1490—ironically, at the request of Lorenzo himself, acting on the suggestion of Pico—he was re-posted to San Marco. Soon the monastery church could not hold his audiences, and after a time neither could the vast cathedral of Florence.

He had two themes, the wickedness of public morals and the wickedness of the Church, and two aims, the reform of both. He was completely fearless. In denouncing Rome, he left no doubt that the source of Church corruption was the Pope himself and his cardinals and higher clergy. As for Florence, it was not a new Athens but a new wicked Babylon. Savonarola viewed the public leaders who modeled themselves on Cicero, the philosophers with their Neoplatonism, the writers who aped Virgil and Aristophanes, the artists who glorified the nude human form, as contributors less to a revival of learning than to a revival of paganism, antithetical to Christianity; and he regarded the worldly, pleasure-seeking interests of the Florentines as antithetical to what should be the true concern of Christians, the salvation of their souls. The chief culprits, Savonarola made clear, were Lorenzo, a tyrant and corrupter of youth, and his fellow financial oligarchs and his circle of friends. Disasters were about to befall both Church and state, Savonarola warned, in apocalyptic imagery so gruesome that even the sophisticated Pico, by his own report, found himself chilled to the marrow of his bones.

Among the rapt listeners of this fateful monk was young Michelangelo. Much—probably too much—has been made of the influence this had on his later great works; while it is difficult to exaggerate the significance of Michelangelo's religious philosophy in his art, his beliefs, as they developed, were far more profound than Savonarola's essentially

simplistic hellfire-and-damnation approach. However, for a youth as vulnerable as Michelangelo—rather shy and inward, acutely sensitive to the feel and look of life but inclined to a morbid view of it—Savonarola's dread prophecies were bound to rouse feelings of tragic foreboding: a vision of man snared and perhaps doomed by his imperfections, his mortality, and by the follies and ironies of the human condition. And so, as Sir Kenneth Clark has remarked, "two essential ingredients of Michelangelo's art, a passion for anatomy and a consciousness of sin, were, so to say, poured into his mind" at about the same time.

Lorenzo had been fascinated, disturbed and puzzled by this swarthy, hook-nosed, awesome angel of destruction that he had inadvertently loosed inside his citadel. In 1491, when the friars of San Marco elected Savonarola as prior, the monk refused to pay the customary courtesy call on Lorenzo on the grounds that he had no obligations except to God. Lorenzo made overtures to him but without success, and then gave up. He left his hapless heir, Piero, to face a critic who now became increasingly unbridled and disruptive, and a citizenry that responded to him with mounting signs of hysteria.

For the nerves of the Florentines, never calm, were already being jangled by troubles abroad. English and French cloth processors and dyers were learning to duplicate the fine Florentine workmanship and were offering stiff competition in domestic and world markets. A recent war between the Venetians and the Turks had blocked some of Florence's best channels of trade; the effects were felt in a number of Florentine bankruptcies and in a general economic depression. Taxes had been increased. The Medici fortune had been reduced when the family banks in London, Bruges and Lyons successively lost vast amounts on political loans that turned out to be uncollectable.

Far worse, there was mounting evidence that France was about to invade Italy. The French threat was an old one, involving dynastic claims to both the Kingdom of Naples and the Duchy of Milan. The French King, Charles VIII, decided to move on Naples (egged on by Milan, which was currently quarreling with Naples and hoping to use Charles to demolish its foe). Florence was an ally of both France and Naples. Keeping the French out of Italy and the jealous Italian states from major fratricide had been the cornerstone of Lorenzo's foreign policy. The foolish Piero now fed the flames by declaring Florence on the side of Naples and against France. This further exasperated the Florentines, for France had been their biggest customer and now boycotted them.

The whole situation lifted Savonarola to even more petrifying heights of apocalyptic prophecy. He became intoxicated with the potency of his own words, which went clamoring through the dark cathedral vastness like God's own lightning bolts. As Pico wrote of one of these sermons, it "caused such terror, alarm, sobbing, and tears that everyone went about the city bewildered, speechless, more dead than alive." Nearly 60 years later Michelangelo told Condivi that he could still hear the terrible voice resounding in his ears. Savonarola had predicted to his brother friars at San Marco that Lorenzo and Pope Innocent VIII both would die in 1492. And both did. He had also predicted that Charles VIII would

invade the country, and welcomed him as the Scourge of God sent to punish the Church, the Florentines and all the cities and men of Italy for their abominations.

In the late summer of 1494, Charles crossed the Alps with an army of more than 30,000 splendidly trained and equipped troops, and by early fall was bearing through Tuscany toward Florence. Piero, in a panic, suffered a change of heart. One October day he left secretly to visit the enemy leader and persuade him to desist; he hoped thereby to follow the model that Lorenzo had set almost exactly 15 years earlier when Florence was about to go down before the armies of Naples and the papacy. But Piero then showed how truly foolish he could be. Instead of negotiating he reversed himself completely: he allied Florence with France against Naples, and as earnest handed over all of the Republic's key fortresses to French garrisons. When he returned to Florence on November 9 and went to the Palazzo della Signoria, the assembled Signory barred the door to him. That evening he rode hurriedly away to safety and exile. He never saw Florence again.

The next day mobs looted the Medici Palace from top to bottom, dispersing in a few hours the accumulated treasures of four generations. Not long afterward Donatello's great bronze *Judith and Holofernes,* celebrating the Biblical heroine's murder of the enemy Assyrian general, was moved from the Palace courtyard through the city to a place by the entrance of the Palazzo della Signoria, to stay there as a reminder to all men that Florence hated tyrants.

Michelangelo had not waited to see the fall of the House of Medici. He had left the city with two companions a few weeks earlier, even before Piero's abortive mission to Charles VIII. His nerves were already raw from the abrasions of Savonarola; further, as Vasari says, "he feared evil consequences from Piero's arrogance and bad government, for he was a member of the household." It was almost as if Michelangelo's solicitous Destiny, weighing the unreliability of humans and especially of the Florentines in an excitable situation, had decided to take no chances with his safety; for although there was little blood spilled on November 9, there had been a strong probability of civil war which would most likely have ended in a massacre of Medici adherents and friends.

The measure of Michelangelo's dread was that he fled across the Apennines to Venice, which was about as far north as he could feasibly go while remaining in Italian-speaking territory, and which had remained neutral in the Charles VIII imbroglio. He and his companions looked for work, found none and headed south again for Bologna. Unknown to them, that city had a new decree requiring foreigners to register at the gates and receive a red wax seal on the thumbnail. They had hardly arrived, therefore, when they were arrested for violating this law, fined 50 lire and held in custody at the customs office because they had not enough money to pay.

Here was a predicament indeed. Or, rather, it would have been except for the timely presence on the scene of Gianfrancesco Aldovrandi, who was a city councilor of Bologna, a nobleman and an enthusiast of the arts. Learning from Michelangelo that he was a sculptor and pro-

tégé of Lorenzo, Aldovrandi not only had the three Florentines released but urged Michelangelo to come and live at his house.

Michelangelo stayed with Aldovrandi more than a year, vastly pleasing his new patron with his Medicean table-talk of art, philosophy and literature. "Every evening," Condivi writes, "he [Aldovrandi] made Michelangelo read aloud to him out of Dante or Petrarch, and sometimes Boccaccio, until he went to sleep." Through Aldovrandi's influence, Michelangelo was commissioned to work on Bologna's most cherished sculptural project, the tomb of St. Dominic, founder of the Dominican order. Begun in 1265, the tomb still lacked some final touches, and Michelangelo supplied them by finishing an uncompleted small statue of St. Petronius and adding a companion figure of St. Proculus and a kneeling angel holding a candle. It was now, too, that he encountered the sculpture of Jacopo della Quercia, who, as noted earlier, was to have an important influence on Michelangelo's work; he spent many of his spare hours studying della Quercia's Bolognese masterpiece, a series of marble reliefs on the exterior of the church of San Petronio.

But he was homesick for Florence. Much of the news from there was saddening: Pico had died in the winter of 1494, Ficino was seriously ill, the whole circle of Lorenzo's friends had been scattered to the winds. Other tidings were somewhat more reassuring. Charles VIII had come and gone and marched south to humiliate the Pope and conquer Naples; now, betrayed by his erstwhile ally Milan and with his lines of supply threatened, he was retreating northward through Tuscany and back home to France. Florence itself had a new and more democratic constitution. The first election under it, in December of 1494, had been won overwhelmingly by the *Popolari,* or People's Party, which Savonarola ran *ex cathedra,* or more precisely *ex monasterio,* from San Marco. Its members accordingly were known to their opponents, in typical Florentine shorthand, as *Frateschi* (Friarists) or *Piagnoni* (Weepers). Order and peace prevailed in the city. And so, at the end of 1495, Michelangelo, aged 20 now, went home again.

He was received without rancor and in fact with some flattering signs of favor. Since part of the new democratic apparatus was a Grand Council of 1,000 members, a vast new hall had to be constructed in the Palazzo della Signoria. Michelangelo, as a rising young artist of some reputation, was invited by Peoples-Friars-Weepers officials to serve on the committee of consultants. Soon he also received a paying commission from a wealthy patron who found it prudent to go by the name Lorenzo Popolano, but whose real name was Lorenzo di Pierfrancesco de' Medici. He was the third cousin of Lorenzo the Magnificent and the current head of what was known as "the junior branch" of the Medici family, descended from a younger son of the family patriarch, Giovanni. Because the junior Medici had helped effect the ouster of their foolish cousin Piero they were tolerated by Florence's new regime. Nevertheless, so hated had the name Medici become that they dropped it (until such time as the wind changed) in favor of the more congenial, though improbable, alias of Popolano, meaning "of the people."

Lorenzo Popolano commissioned Michelangelo to carve a young St.

John the Baptist, the city's patron saint; it served nicely to advertise in Savonarola's purified Florence both the piety and patriotism of the Popolano-Medici. This statue later joined the ranks of Michelangelo's lost works: several times during the past century it purportedly has been found, but none of these discoveries so far has been authenticated.

After this commission there were no others. What happened next is still debated by scholars. But Condivi tells a story that merits retelling. According to this account, the junior-grade Lorenzo now put forward a suggestion so rich in its consequences that in the end he must be reckoned among Michelangelo's most helpful patrons, however inadvertent. The suggestion was this: in view of the great vogue for antique sculpture and the high prices it fetched, Michelangelo should carve a figure from classical mythology, contrive to give it a suitably age-worn neglected look, and ship it off to Rome, the largest center of the antique market, as an authentic classical relic. Lorenzo even knew the right unreliable dealer there to handle the sale and offered to arrange the whole transaction with him.

Accordingly, Michelangelo carved a sleeping Cupid, gave it a properly weathered look and sent it off to Rome and the shady agent awaiting it, one Baldassare del Milanese. Before long he received the welcome sum of 30 ducats in payment, followed by word from Baldassare that he had managed to sell it—with a profit for himself that he considered satisfactory—to a rich collector, Cardinal Raffaello Riario. What Baldassare neglected to mention was that the selling price had been 200 ducats.

However, before long the Cardinal became suspicious and demanded his money back. Baldassare steadfastly refused, insisting that the Cupid was everything he had claimed. The Cardinal, reasoning that if it was in fact a fraud the artist skillful enough to have created it must be a Florentine, sent an agent to Florence to find him and persuade him to come to Rome and confront Baldassare. Condivi tells what happened then:

"This gentleman, pretending to be on the lookout for a sculptor capable of executing certain works in Rome, after visiting several, was directed to Michelangelo. When he saw the young artist, he begged him to show some proof of his ability; whereupon Michelangelo took a pen . . . and drew a hand with such grace that the gentleman was stupefied. Afterward, he asked if he had ever worked in marble, and when Michelangelo said yes, and mentioned among other things a Cupid of such height and in such an attitude, the man knew that he had found the right person." Learning of the 200-ducat sale price, Michelangelo agreed to join the Cardinal's cause.

And thus it came about that in June 1496, at the age of 21, Michelangelo first saw the city that was to become his other home and the other arena of his genius.

The affair of the *Sleeping Cupid* ended to the satisfaction of the Cardinal, at least, when the discomfited Baldassare gave up the 200 ducats and took back the statue. However, to Michelangelo's demand that the sequence continue so that he could reclaim his statue for 30 ducats, Baldassare replied indignantly that it was his property and that he could not part with such a valuable work for such an absurd price. Nor did he.

Through channels unknown, the *Cupid* was acquired in 1496 by Caesar Borgia (son of the reigning Pope, Alexander VI) who later presented it as a gift to the Duke of Urbino. Still later it disappeared without a trace.

Michelangelo's visit to Rome stretched out to almost five years. Relatively little is known of how he spent this time. According to Vasari he stayed more than a year as the guest of Cardinal Riario. There is an indication in one of three letters by Michelangelo preserved from this period that he may have done a piece of sculpture for his host, but there is nothing to show for it. But his presiding Destiny was still watchful. A friend from Florence worked in the bank of a rich Roman named Jacopo Galli. By early 1498 or thereabouts, Jacopo had taken over the role of patron and was filling it splendidly, thereby attaining immortality for himself and adding two distinguished works to Michelangelo's list. One of these—larger-than-life-sized, nude and thoroughly pagan in spirit—is the *Bacchus,* "the form and aspect of which," Condivi writes, "correspond in all parts to the meaning of ancient authors. The face of the youth is jocund, the eyes wandering and wanton, as is the wont with those who are too much addicted to a taste for wine." The second sculpture, later lost, was a life-sized figure apparently also inspired by "the ancient authors"; it is believed to have been either an Apollo or a Cupid.

Jacopo, model patron that he was, wanted to share his joy in Michelangelo's work with other men of sensibility. One day he introduced Michelangelo to his friend the French Cardinal Jean de Villiers de la Groslaye. The Cardinal, after years as special emissary to the Papal Court, was planning to retire and return home, and he wanted to leave for posterity some worthy souvenir of himself and his country in the Chapel of the Kings of France at the old basilica of St. Peter. He had in mind a *pietà*, and Jacopo brought Michelangelo to him as just the sculptor to handle this theme to perfection.

The historic contract for the *Pietà*, dated August 26, 1498, says: "Let it be known . . . that the most Reverend Cardinal of San Donigi [the name of his titular church] has thus agreed with the master Michelangelo, sculptor of Florence, to wit, that the said master shall make a *pietà* of marble at his own cost; that is to say, a Virgin Mary clothed, with the dead Christ in her arms, of the size of a proper man, for the price of 450 golden ducats of the papal mint, within the term of one year from the day of the commencement of the work." At the end of the contract came a guarantee from Galli: "And I, Jacopo Galli, pledge my word to his most Reverend Lordship that the said Michelangelo will finish the said work within one year, and that it shall be the finest work in marble which Rome today can show, and that no master of our days shall be able to produce a better. . . ."

On behalf of a sculptor still so young and so little known, Galli's pledge was bold indeed. Michelangelo not only fulfilled but far exceeded it. He created a work so glorious that to this day the term *pietà* evokes, for most people, only one image: the *Pietà* of St. Peter's. It made Michelangelo famous immediately. More than merely famous, he was seen to be, without dissent, one of the surpassing artists of his time. He was 24 years old then, and the divine nimbus had begun to glow.

The Heart's Image

The masterpiece of Michelangelo's youth was the *Pietà,* today a treasure of St. Peter's in Rome. Living up to the claim that no other sculptor could produce a better work, he was able to take a block of white marble, wider than it was tall, and carve from it, in pyramidal form, a statue of marvelous compactness and monumentality, in which Mary betrays her sorrow with a single gesture—an outstretched hand.

Pursuing what he called "the heart's image," Michelangelo disregarded conventional reality and substituted for it in the *Pietà* a set of strange and compelling paradoxes that build into a super-reality. The Christ, though dead, is still alive, His veins distended by the pulse of life, His body limp with sleep, His torso flowing into the mold of His mother's arm and lap. The Virgin, traditionally represented as a woman disfigured by grief, is here much younger than her Son—the personification of "perpetual purity." And while the Christ is life-sized, in keeping with Michelangelo's obligation to provide a figure as big as a well-proportioned man, the Virgin is bigger than life. Were she to stand, she would be seven feet tall. And yet her head is the same size as Christ's. One of the wonders of the *Pietà* is that aberrant proportions like these in no way disturb the viewer. "It is necessary to keep one's compass in one's eyes," Michelangelo said, "and not in the hand, for the hands execute, but the eye judges."

A work of deep Christian piety, the *Pietà* also expresses Michelangelo's Neoplatonic belief that physical beauty is the manifestation of a noble spirit. To critics who carped at the youthfulness of his Virgin, the sculptor had a ready reply— "Do you know that chaste women maintain their freshness longer than those who are not?"

Pietà, c. 1499

Until the 15th Century, the theme of the *pietà*
belonged almost exclusively to the artists of
northern Europe, whose gruesome figures of Jesus
and Mary, mainly of wood, seemed designed to
shock worshipers into awareness of Christ's sacrifice.
Michelangelo, already the master of all he had
learned in Florence about line, design, perspective
and anatomy, took this alien and difficult subject,
stripped it of its horror and bent it to marble,
a resisting medium for so demanding a composition.
By emphasizing not the Virgin's grief, but her
acceptance of fate, he sought to stir the beholder to
philosophic reflection. "If life pleases us," he once
wrote, "death, being made by the hands of the same
creator, should not displease us." Gently encircling
Mary's face with the delicately carved ripples of her
robe, he gave to her features a look of spiritual and
physical beauty new to his work. And drawing upon
his extensive knowledge of anatomy, he turned
the nude figure of Christ into the very quintessence
of man—a figure in which there was no need, as he
put it, "to make the human disappear behind the divine."

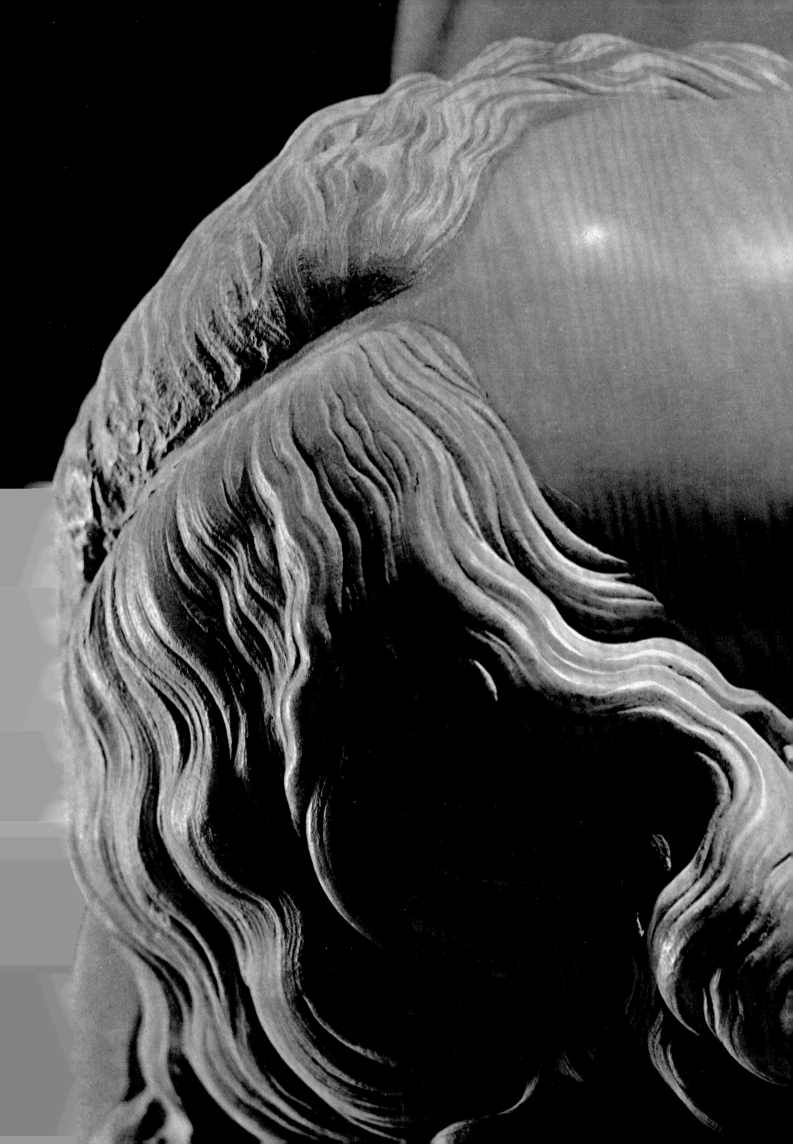

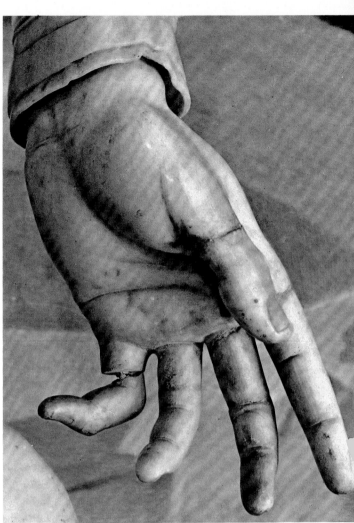

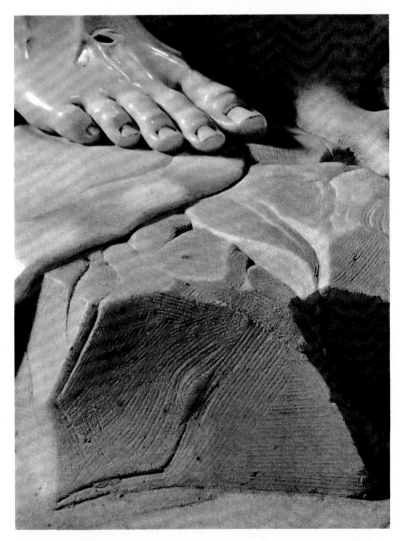

Michelangelo had agreed to carve "the finest work in marble which Rome today can show," and he saw to it that the *Pietà* was just that, in all its details. No other sculpture to come from his hand is more finished. Its surface gleams with many rubbings, its delicate modeling gives cold marble the warmth of living flesh and its intricately carved draperies impart a vibrant energy to the entire work. With each finger separate and gently curving inward, the Virgin's hand *(above)* is still a sculptor's miracle, despite an accident two centuries ago which robbed it of some of its free-floating grace.

Even the base—the rough earth under the Virgin's and Christ's feet—received Michelangelo's most careful attention. Here, as the details at right and left reveal, he used his chisel almost as a pencil to sketch rhythmic lines on the marble, or to "color" it with broad, coarse strokes; and where he wanted to punctuate a line, he drilled shadowed holes. Thus he achieved dramatic contrasts with the smooth, liquid ripple of Mary's hem, cut so daringly thin in places as to be translucent.

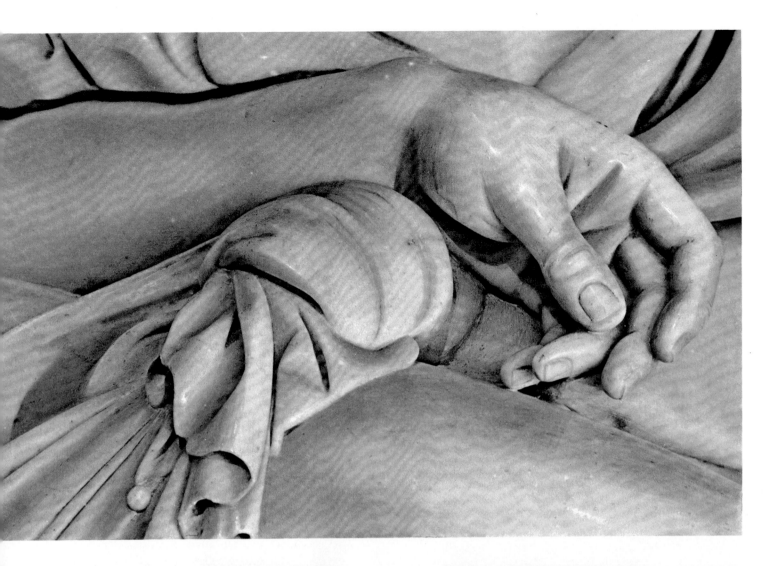

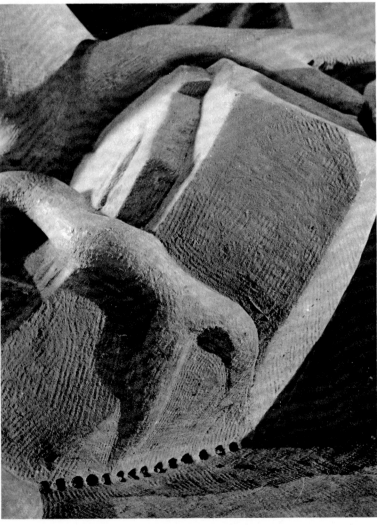

Madonna and Child

Two years after completing the *Pietà,* Michelangelo produced another great work, the *Bruges Madonna (left).* Here again the young sculptor sought to extract new and deeper meanings from a familiar theme. He carved no smiling, worldly Virgin with gently tilted head, as was so popular during the second half of the 15th Century. He harked back instead to an earlier type, the prescient Mary of a Donatello or a Jacopo della Quercia. There is even in his Madonna a strong echo of Donatello's Judith displaying the severed head of Holofernes *(page 60).* Her severe frontality and the very way in which her face is framed by the draperies covering her head recall the earlier group. Inward-staring, she sits ramrod straight on a pile of stones. She knows what is going to happen to her Son. And the Child in turn, although at first glance appearing to be a playful cherub, reveals upon closer examination a seriousness that betrays the role He will play as a man. In a departure from tradition, Michelangelo placed the young Jesus between Mary's knees, rather than on her lap. By doing so he was able not only to play off smooth flesh against the elaborate folds of the robes, as in the *Pietà,* but to increase the complexity and liveliness of the composition as a whole —the Virgin with her left knee raised higher than her right, the Christ Child with His right foot dangling in space as though He were about to step down from His perch into the waiting world.

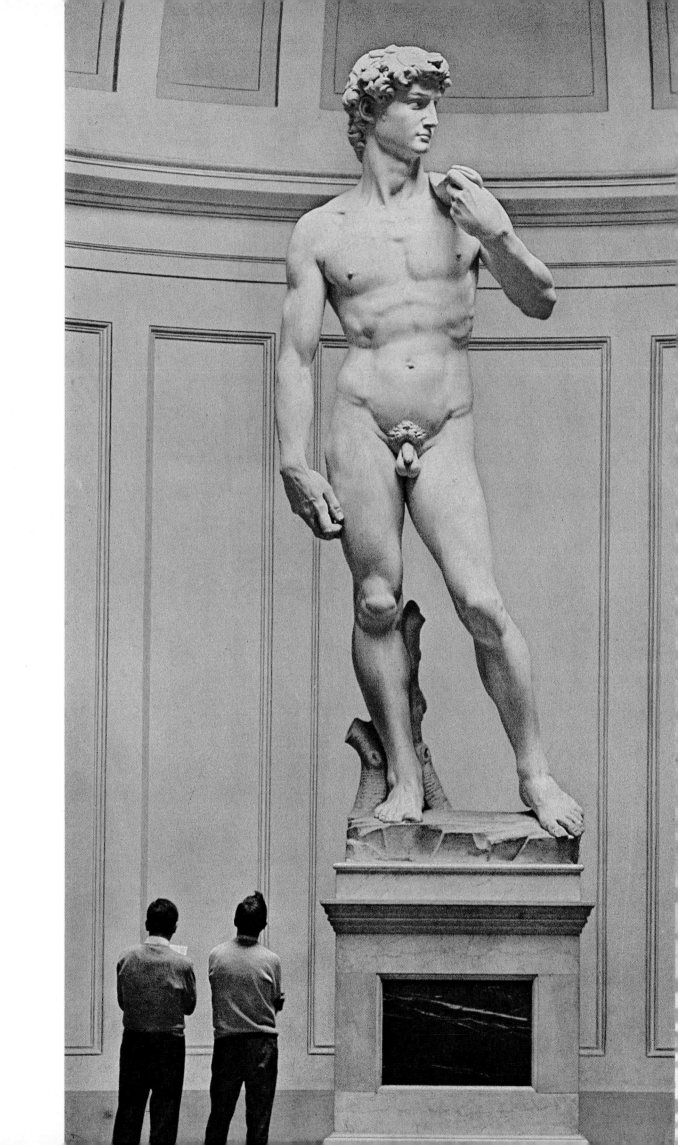

IV

The Giant Emerges

Almost 17 feet tall, Michelangelo's *David* epitomizes the Renaissance civic virtues of force and anger. Ready for action, the youth looks guardedly to the left, a reflection, perhaps, of the medieval belief that while the right side is protected by God, the left is open to evil.

David, 1501-1504

In the spring of 1501, Michelangelo left Rome and returned to his beloved Florence—his "nest," as he sometimes called it. He was homesick; his family needed him; and too, as Vasari recounts, he "now received letters from friends in Florence telling him that, if he came back, he might have the big piece of marble that Piero Soderini, then *gonfaloniere* of the city, had talked of giving to Leonardo da Vinci, but was now proposing to present to Andrea Sansovino, an excellent sculptor, who was making every effort to get it."

This prize was a huge oblong chunk of pure white unflawed Carrara marble—some 18 feet high and weighing several tons—that had been badly blocked out and then abandoned by an earlier sculptor, Agostino di Duccio. It had lain for 35 years in the cathedral's workyard, an awesome ghostly reminder to all young sculptors of the challenge of their craft. The stone remained a tantalizing enigma: no sculptor had been able to suggest a use for it that satisfied the cathedral's Board of Works.

Michelangelo's acquaintance with the "Giant," as the block was commonly called, probably went back at least a dozen years to his time at the Medici sculpture gardens. Obviously it had stirred his imagination. When he returned home, he found the cathedral Board cordial to an idea he presented for it; but the decision would take time.

In the interval Michelangelo went off to Siena to start work on a three-year project he had contracted for just before leaving Rome: a commission from Cardinal Francesco Piccolomini to carve 15 statues of saints for his family chapel in Siena's cathedral. He had just finished plotting and measuring the locations for the statues when, returning to Florence in mid-August, he learned that he had won the Giant.

With a contract (signed jointly by the cathedral Board and the Guild of Wool Merchants) that guaranteed him six golden florins a month for two years, he decided to put the Piccolomini saints aside until he had this new and stimulating project well in hand. And so it came about that at dawn on Monday, September 13, 1501, in a large shed that had been built near the cathedral for this purpose, he set to work wresting from the old form of the Giant his superb statue of the young David.

The date is important in history, for this was also the dawn of a new era in art. Together with the works that Leonardo da Vinci produced about the same time (the *Last Supper;* the *Virgin and Child and St. Anne;* the *Mona Lisa*), Michelangelo's *David* ushered in the Cinquecento and the period known as the High Renaissance, in which all the achievements of the Quattrocento came to fruition and art moved far beyond the "imitation of nature" to the noblest realms of the spirit. The *David* was Michelangelo's own first really characteristic, unmistakably personalized work: the one in which his technical prowess, his esthetic comprehension, his native imagination and daring, and his philosophies of art and of life and even of politics coalesced in a statement of his mature genius.

What manner of man was it who worked in the intense privacy of creation behind the high wooden enclosure? Although there are no existing portraits or detailed descriptions of him during this period, an account of his appearance written many years later by Condivi gives us a notion of what he must have looked like as a young man:

"Michelangelo is of good complexion; more muscular . . . than fat or fleshy in his person: healthy above all things, as well by reason of his natural constitution as of the exercise he takes, and habitual continence in food and sexual indulgence. . . . His countenance always shows a good and wholesome color. Of stature he is as follows: height middling; broad in the shoulders; the rest of the body somewhat slender in proportion. The shape of his face is oval. . . . The forehead, seen in front, is square; the nose, a little flattened. . . . The lips are thin. . . . The eyes may even be called small, of a color like horn, but speckled and stained with spots of bluish yellow . . . the hair of the head is black, as also the beard . . ."

As for his personality, he had already begun to exhibit, at the age of 26, many of those peculiarities of temperament, manner and habit that, as they became confirmed by the passing years, made him often seem strange and forbidding. These traits included both an excessive optimism and a deep strain of melancholy. The optimism showed itself in the grandeur of his artistic ambitions and conceptions (exemplified in the *David*) and in his willingness to take on the most challenging and time-consuming projects. He was full of confidence in his powers, full of eagerness to demonstrate them to his fellow artists, his city and the world (and, one may surmise, not least to his father). His appetite for fame and his belief that he could accomplish whatever he set his mind to do were normal attributes of Renaissance man. But in his case they were linked with an abnormal unwillingness or inability to face the fact that even he had only a certain amount of time and energy. So he was forever pressed, falling behind, failing his patrons, failing himself: and this was in turn one of the abiding sources of his melancholy. The first symptom of this dichotomy in his nature had been his acceptance of the Piccolomini and *David* assignments only two months apart, the combination requiring him to try to cram five years of work into three. And quite soon there would be a whole succession of these conflicting commissions, undertaken, as Romain Rolland has said, "in the first intoxication of his imagination."

The work, once begun, was an intoxicant of another sort; it afforded him a fierce if wholly private pleasure. He was transported to a realm far

removed from mundane realities, and was resentful when forced by circumstances to remember them. The normal creature comforts meant very little to him. Condivi wrote: "He has always been extremely temperate in living, using food more because it was necessary than for any pleasure he took in it; especially when he was engaged upon some great work; for then he usually confined himself to a piece of bread, which he ate in the middle of his labor. . . . And this abstemiousness in food he has practiced in sleep also; for sleep, according to his own account, rarely suits his constitution, since he continually suffers from pains in the head during slumber, and any excessive amount of sleep deranges his stomach. While he was in full vigor, he generally went to bed with his clothes on, even to the tall boots. . . . At certain seasons he kept these boots on for such a length of time, that when he drew them off the skin came away together with the leather, like that of a sloughing snake."

This anchoritic self-denial was in part, no doubt, a product of years of having to contribute every *picciolo* he could spare to his family's support. Yet despite the continual drain, his income was now large enough so that he could have lived in comfort. Thus it was not just need that accounted for his ascetic ways, and these suggest that there was something in his character that found satisfaction in suffering.

If we add that he tended to be suspicious and withdrawn in his relationships, that along with his shyness and a certain timidity he was nervous, quick-tempered and capable of violent rages, that he was sensitive to slights, real or imagined, while often sarcastic and blunt, it can be seen why he so often disconcerted people, so often seemed unapproachable and irascible and managed to make more than his share of enemies.

Yet these were only facets of his complex character. Among those whom he trusted he was humorous and companionable, generous and gentle. He was often surprised to learn that he was considered difficult. He had a number of devoted friends and he repaid them with equal affection. One was the *gonfaloniere,* Piero Soderini, who understood him well. Later, when Michelangelo had to leave Florence and work in Bologna for a time, Soderini gave him a letter of introduction to his brother Francesco Soderini, the Cardinal of Volterra: "We certify that he is an excellent young man, and in his own art without peer in Italy, perhaps also in the universe. We cannot recommend him more emphatically. His nature is such, that with good words and kindness, if these are given him, he will do everything; one has to show him love and treat him kindly, and he will perform things which will make the whole world wonder."

This, then, at least in his general attributes, was the young man who in 1501 had come home to Florence. And what sort of home city, *patria,* did he find?

Outwardly Florence was little changed: the banks, guilds, churches, works of art—nearly everything was intact save the Medici Palace, which lay silent, stripped of all furnishings, a great gray mausoleum of Lorenzo's Golden Age. Yet beneath the surface Florence and the Florentines had been badly hurt, and they would never recover. Too much had happened, both to the relationships of the Florentines to one another and to the relationships of the city to Tuscany, to Italy and to Europe.

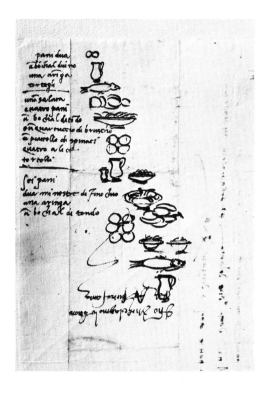

Although Michelangelo's frugality extended to the food he ate, he apparently was not averse to occasionally sharing his table with a friend or co-worker. Three menus in his own hand, with drawings, perhaps for the benefit of an illiterate servant, show what the artist ate when alone and when someone dined with him. The first, a bachelor's repast, consists of two breads, wine, a herring and *pasta.* The second menu includes a salad, four breads, two wines, a plate of spinach, four anchovies and *pasta*—a dinner probably intended for an honored guest. The third menu consists of six breads, two bowls of fennel soup, one herring and wine, in this case perhaps a meal to be eaten with a helper.

A sweet white wine called Trebbiano seems to have been one of Michelangelo's rare pleasures over the years—and one that he readily shared with friends in Rome whenever his nephew Lionardo sent him a shipment from Florence. But toward the end of his life, he confessed to not knowing what to do with the 36 flasks he had just received, "because all of my friends having disappeared, I have no one left to whom to give any."

It will be recalled that at the end of 1494, in the first election under the new constitution, Savonarola's party had overwhelmingly won control of the government. Neither then nor later did the friar take on any official position in the city's affairs or even in those of the party; but then neither had Lorenzo, and just as Lorenzo had nevertheless run Florentine affairs from his palace, Savonarola ran them from his monastery. Florence was his: of that there was not the faintest doubt. Some three and a half years later, however, his one-time followers hanged and burned him in the Piazza della Signoria and threw his ashes into the Arno.

Even for the Florentines, this was an extraordinary reversal, and it came about through an extraordinarily involved skein of circumstances. As noted earlier, Savonarola's two related aims were the reform of Church practices and the reform of public morals. He used as his model the primitive Christianity of early times: like the communities of saints, men should live together in selfless Christian love, preparing for eternity while striving to establish the Kingdom of God on earth. But the Florentines were among the most cosmopolitan people ever known, prone to a full catalogue of vices, and marked by a temperament noted for capriciousness and a lively sense of the absurd. It was this unpromising material that Savonarola resolved to convert into a model Christian community.

At his behest the Grand Council, dominated by his *Popolari* "weepers," formally declared Christ the King of Florence. Sin, in effect, was outlawed: horse racing, gambling, profanity, ribald songs, prostitution, lewd performances and provocative female dress were now severely penalized. Servants were encouraged to tattle on their masters and mistresses, and children on their parents. Disciplined bands of youths, pledged to clean living and clean thinking, roamed the city collecting alms, pouncing on gamblers and sending women whom they judged to be immodestly attired back to their homes to change their dress.

Many Florentines, employing a well-developed skill, merely swam along with the tides. But in others Savonarola's revival produced genuine conversions. Among them was the painter Baccio della Porta, who joined the Dominicans and is known to us as Fra Bartolommeo: after his ordination he painted a series of religious pictures at San Marco including a striking portrait (from memory) of Savonarola which still hangs in the prior's cell along with his hair shirt and other memorabilia.

One of Savonarola's particular targets was the pre-Lenten Carnival of Florence, with its semipagan delight in temporal joys. The prior converted the revel into a religious festival, and in 1497 added a dramatic new feature. The youth bands scoured the city door to door demanding from each inhabitant a contribution of a "vanity": some symbol of worldly pleasure such as cosmetics or a fancy item of adornment, or, better still, some souvenir of regretted wickedness—cards, dice, nude pictures, and spicy books such as the *Decameron*. These trophies the youngsters carried to the Piazza della Signoria where, as the days passed, the collection grew to a huge, many-tiered pyramid with a keg of gunpowder at its core. On the last night of Carnival, as church bells rang and long, golden ceremonial trumpets blared, the pyre was lit and the vanities were consumed in a towering pillar of flame. This ritual purifi-

cation was deemed so successful that a similar Burning of the Vanities was staged the next year.

Inevitably, there was a reaction. There were backsliders and dropouts, and more and more of them as ecstasy dimmed into dutifulness, boredom and finally resentment. The political opposition took heart. One part of it consisted of Medici adherents. Since overt declarations for the return of any of the family would have been dangerous these Medici partisans worked in a sort of political twilight zone and were known accordingly as the *Bigi,* or "grays." The much larger and more outspoken part of the opposition was led by the great anti-Medici families such as the Pazzi; to the Savonarolist weepers (also called *Stropiccioni,* or hypocrites; *Collitorti,* or wry-necks; and *Masticapaternostri,* or prayer-chewers) these vehement objectors were known as the *Arrabbiati,* or "mad dogs."

Opposition, as usual, only excited the prior to new heights of denunciation. With Florence still more or less under his control, he aimed his thunderbolts increasingly at Rome and the person of Pope Alexander VI. The latter was, indeed, as worthy a target as could be imagined. As the historian Ferdinand Schevill describes him, he "was addicted to all the lusts of the flesh . . . he had many children into whose laps he did not scruple to pour the riches of the Church . . . he purchased his elevation to the papacy by open . . . bribery . . . enthroned upon St. Peter's chair, he sold, as it were, under the hammer, all the dispensations, pardons, bishoprics and cardinalates at his disposal." In Savonarola's mind, the Pope emerged ever more clearly as that diabolical deceiver whose reign on earth would signal the approaching Day of Judgment—the Antichrist.

Whatever his moral shortcomings, Alexander was an excellent administrator and an intelligent man; and for a while he regarded Savonarola as a nuisance but a quite endurable one. Still, his forbearance had its limits, which the little prior seemed bent on finding; and Alexander finally resolved that something had to be done about him. He invited Savonarola to Rome for a fatherly chat about his visions and prophecies.

Savonarola suspected, quite properly, that a journey to Rome would bring a quick end to his career. He replied, therefore, that he must postpone the visit owing to ill health. Alexander then forbade him to preach, but Savonarola ignored the ban. Alexander responded by ordering San Marco to be absorbed into a new Tuscan-Roman Congregation, which meant that Savonarola could be transferred to some other place. The prior rejected the union and denounced Alexander in a Lenten sermon. Alexander excommunicated him; Savonarola completed the break by celebrating Mass and, in turn, anathematizing and "excommunicating" Alexander; the latter then threatened the city of Florence with an interdict unless the Signory forced Savonarola to stop preaching; the Signory so ordered and Savonarola obeyed; but he had already written to the rulers of Spain, France, Germany and Hungary, urging them to call a General Council of the Church to depose Alexander. One of Alexander's agents purloined a copy of the letter and sent it to him.

A few weeks later, on Palm Sunday, a mob of "mad dog" supporters stormed San Marco. Savonarola and his two closest associates were arrested by orders of the Signory, imprisoned for six weeks in the Palazzo

The hanging and burning of Savonarola and his two followers in the Piazza della Signoria is recorded in this detail of a painting by an unknown Florentine artist who showed them dangling from a gibbet, its arms lopped off to destroy its resemblance to the cross. Savonarola, the last to be hanged, had mercifully died only moments before the fire sprang up; his executioner, pausing to clown before the throng, neglected to light the pyre in time. As the flames rose, the dead man's right arm jerked up and the palm opened, two fingers extending in a gesture of blessing. Afterwards, the ashes of all three martyrs were tossed into the Arno—thereby fulfilling Savonarola's prophecy that the wicked "will take the just men and burn them in the center of the city; and that which the fire does not consume and the wind does not carry away, they will throw into the water."

della Signoria and examined under repeated torture. Finally he signed his name to a document in which—as edited by the Signory's notary—he confessed that all his revelations had been sham. On May 23, 1498, he and his two companions were led out along a specially built wooden causeway into the Piazza della Signoria, where they had so recently staged their Burnings of the Vanities. There they were duly hanged, stoned by youths—probably including some defectors from the once enthusiastic moral vigilantes—and then were committed to the flames.

The republic survived with its Grand Council and other democratic paraphernalia, but these proved so cumbersome that in 1502 the Council decided that for the salvation of the state there had to be executive strength and continuity and elected Piero Soderini *gonfaloniere* of justice for a life term. Soderini was head of one of the leading families, a patron of learning and the arts, a patriot—in short, at least in general outline, an acceptable facsimile of Lorenzo. For a while he even had a run of characteristically Laurentian good luck, beginning with two opportune deaths that freed Florence of two of its most worrisome sources of trouble.

The first to go was Alexander VI, in August 1503, in the 11th year of his pontificate, the 46th year of his less than selfless service to the Church, the 73rd year of his long, happy life. His successor was Pius III—the same Cardinal Piccolomini whose commission for 15 statues Michelangelo had put aside while he worked on his *David*. But within 26 days, Pius III was also dead, and was succeeded by Cardinal Giuliano della Rovere. The new Pope, who was as tough and shrewd as any Borgia but gifted with a conscience of distinguished purity by the standards of the time, took the name of Julius II. He reigned for nearly 10 years and, as we will see, was the most important and beneficent—as well as the most demanding, troublesome, and nerve-racking—patron in Michelangelo's life.

The second opportune fatality for Florence, following Alexander by only four months, was Piero de' Medici. For nine years that unhappy character had lurked in the wings conniving with various military and political leaders to arrange his re-entry into Florence. During one of these efforts, he aligned himself with the French, who had renewed their struggle for hegemony over the Italian peninsula. The French forces were routed in a battle on the banks of the Garigliano River. Piero, seeking to retreat across the river, was drowned. Luckless to the very end, he took his place in the iconography of history as Piero the Unfortunate.

Less than a month after his death, on January 25, 1504, a committee of Florence's most distinguished artists met at the cathedral to recommend where Michelangelo's *David* should be placed in the city. The members included Leonardo da Vinci, Botticelli, Andrea della Robbia, David Ghirlandaio, Perugino, Filippino Lippi and Michelangelo's old friend Francesco Granacci, as well as the architects Simone del Pollaiuolo and Giuliano and Antonio da Sangallo. The list of names is enough by itself to show that Michelangelo's patrons, on seeing the nearly finished *David*, recognized it as a work so important that the whole city must be concerned about it. Already it was a public treasure.

It will be useful, since the *David* presages so much that would be seen in Michelangelo's later works, to ask what this statue meant to him. Ob-

viously, there are dimensions of meaning that no one but he could ever know, but certain others can be reconstructed.

His choice of the subject matter itself was a natural one. The character of small, brave David-the-Giant-Killer had long appealed to Florence as a symbol of itself, a city willing to take on all comers in defense of its liberty. Along with a number of lesser versions, the city already possessed two famous *Davids* by two of Michelangelo's most famous predecessors, Donatello and Verrocchio. Thus the subject gave Michelangelo a chance to express his love for Florence in patriotic symbolism, and at the same time to prove his great mastery of his art by competing, in effect, with these two great masters of the past on a common theme. And it is precisely in his treatment of the theme, compared with theirs, that one finds revealed the essentials of his philosophy.

These other two *Davids* are more or less life-sized bronze portrayals of two boys in early adolescence, true to type in their undeveloped boyish frames and in their expressions. Michelangelo's *David,* in contrast, is a strapping specimen of early manhood at the peak of physical power and grace, superbly muscled and superbly spirited, filled with righteous anger and emanating intractable will and awesome force—a quality the Italians call *terribilità.* With the head of a beautiful Apollo and the body of a young Hercules, he is an apotheosis of all the most heroic qualities in all young heroes, a figure human in form but superhuman in his perfection of mind, body and soul. This *David,* in short, has only the most tenuous connection with the individual it purports to represent, or indeed with any individual. Instead it is a portrait of an Ideal for which the Biblical David was simply a convenient symbol. This *David* is not Hebraic but Greek, not scriptural but Platonic, not the son of Jesse the Bethlehemite but figuratively of Lorenzo the Florentine—and his godfathers were Poliziano, Pico and the rest of that great informal faculty at the Medici Palace where Michelangelo had acquired so much of his education.

Platonism—or more properly Neoplatonism, a term that includes various embellishments of the original teachings—was in fact the primary influence in Michelangelo's thinking about the nature of the world and of man, and about his own proper role as a man, a citizen and an artist. For years it was the primary influence in his religious outlook, too, though in time he veered toward a more orthodox Christianity. It was a comprehensive philosophy, but here our concern is with the way in which it influenced Michelangelo's art, and in that regard the principal element was the Platonic doctrine of "Ideal Forms."

Platonism held that the visible world and all the things thereof—whether as solid as mountains or as intangible as human emotions—represent imperfect copies of the Ideal Forms of these things which exist in the realm of pure spirit. The human soul came from this Ideal realm and still has memories of it, however dim, and hence is bound to be dissatisfied with earthly, imperfect existence. Death enables the soul to return to the Ideal realm—*if* the person has lived a life in pursuit of the good, the true and the beautiful. It is the love of these things, which are simply other names for the Ideal, that enables the soul to find its way back to God.

Love is awakened by beauty, in the first instance by the beauty of an-

Just how Michelangelo transferred the proportions of the full-sized models he sometimes used to blocks of marble is not known, but the device in the old print above suggests one method he may have employed. Known as a "definitor," it consisted of a disc marked off in degrees and pegged on the clay model, and a rotating ruler from which plumb lines could be hung. The sculptor wishing to measure the model would begin with the farthest extremity—here, the finger. First, he would swing the ruler from a fixed starting point on the disc to a position above the finger—noting the number of degrees the ruler traveled, as well as the distance from the center of the disc to the plumb line. Then he would measure the distance between ruler and finger. Such measurements as the width of the arm, for example, were determined by moving the line from one side of the arm to the other, and noting how many degrees the ruler had rotated in the process. After tabulating these measurements, the sculptor would then transfer them to the marble by means of a duplicate definitor set atop the block.

other person; but then it proceeds by stages to higher levels so that the soul appreciates beauty of character, of thought, of all goodness and all things perfect. Finally, having come so far, the virtuous person will find a supreme beauty, the source from which all other beauties flow. Love is thus the catalyst and binder of the universe: in a manner of speaking, Love is God. And since beauty is the visible initiator of love, it follows that those who create and encourage beauty, such as artists and philosophers, are acolytes in the divine mystery. By seeking beauty, they seek God. But also, in a phrase from a later age, "Beauty is Truth, Truth Beauty": to know truth, one must seek knowledge. Thus the pursuit of knowledge is a moral requirement, for it leads to the understanding of what is truly good and virtuous and sets one on the proper pathway to the Ideal realm.

In Neoplatonism Lorenzo and his circle could find room for nearly all their most cherished interests: their love of beauty, their pursuit of knowledge, and their fascination with classical antiquity. For the Greek and Roman sculptors, in portraying their gods and legendary heroes—and for that matter their actual kings and warriors and athletes—had given them a more than mortal nobility, endowing them with those ideal properties in which ordinary humans recognize their own best potentialities. For the same reasons, the antique divinities and heroes were left naked, to arouse not carnality but admiration; for by Platonic definition, a perfect human body is visible evidence of man's potential grandeur, his Ideal self.

All of this was absorbed into Michelangelo's thinking and much of it became manifest in the *David*. The scholar Charles de Tolnay has defined this thinking compactly: "He did not intend to represent things as the human eye sees them but as they are in essence. . . . Michelangelo treats form . . . as nature intends it, before it becomes marred by the vicissitudes of life. . . . It follows that the artistic *concetto* (the Idea) is the inner image that the artist creates for himself of nature's intentions."

In his earlier years Michelangelo had studied nature so intently that, according to Condivi, he often visited the fish stalls in the market to take notes on the exact color and shape of the varieties of scales, the exact opaqueness of the dead eyes. But he had mastered all the ways of showing visible reality; the discoveries and devices of the Quattrocento had become, for him, a mere bag of tools, the means toward a greater end. His eyes were fixed on the celestial regions of the Ideal, those noble mansions of Plato and Christ.

This was his path to lasting greatness—and to the divinity with which fellow artists clothed him. But it was bound to be a hard path and often a frustrating one. Condivi noted: "He has scarcely ever been satisfied with his creations and has belittled them." And Vasari: "His imagination was so perfect that he could not realize with his hands his great and sublime conceptions, and so he frequently abandoned his works and spoiled many." Thus the increasing success, fame and adulation that came to him did not relieve his melancholy, but often seemed to intensify it.

However, the penalties were not evident for a while. And meantime, he was happier than at any other time in his adult life. By early 1504 he

had put the finishing touches on the *David*. The distinguished committee in charge of placing it, having, in the manner of Florentine committees, dissolved into splinter groups, finally voted to accept Michelangelo's own preference. He favored the spot by the entrance of the Palazzo della Signoria that was occupied by Donatello's bronze of *Judith and Holofernes*. Whereas *Judith* told a story of gore and violence and revenge, *David* carried a far different message. Vasari summed up its meaning, probably paraphrasing words he had heard from Michelangelo, thus: "As David defended his people and governed with justice, so should this city be defended with courage and governed with justice."

In mid-May 1504 came the process, fraught with all sorts of possible disasters, of moving the *David* from its shed through the narrow, winding streets to the Piazza della Signoria. According to a contemporary description: "They broke the wall above the gateway enough to let it pass. That night some stones were thrown at the Colossus with intent to harm it. Watch had to be kept at night; and it made way very slowly, bound as it was upright, suspended in the air with enormous beams and intricate machinery of ropes. It took four days to reach the Piazza. . . . More than 40 men were employed to make it go; and there were 14 rollers joined beneath it, which were changed from hand to hand."

On September 8, the *David* was officially unveiled. Florence was dazzled. Michelangelo was already famous. At this point he became more: he was incontestably the greatest sculptor in Italy.

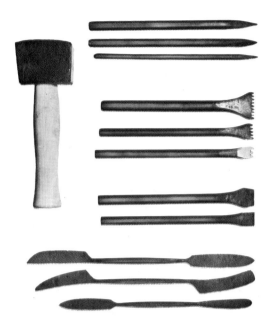

Although no tools for carving marble survive from the Renaissance, today's tools, illustrated above, probably differ little from those Michelangelo employed. In the initial stage, he would chip away at the marble with a mallet and pointed chisels (*first group*), which leave pockmarks like those on the beard of the *Captive* below. Next, he would utilize toothed chisels (*second group*) to bring out more detail, as in the *Captive's* face, preliminary to refining the surface further with smooth chisels (*third group*). The final smoothing was achieved with files and rasps (*fourth group*).

Meanwhile the city fathers, already anticipating the acclaim that would come and anxious to keep him working for the glory of Florence, had contracted with him to carve 12 larger-than-life-sized apostles for the cathedral, to be delivered at the rate of one a year. As extra inducement they built a dwelling and workshop which he was to occupy without charge and acquire as his own property at the rate of a twelfth part a year, in pace with his delivery of the statues. The arrangement gave him what he needed most: honor, privacy and financial security.

It also, of course, added to his backlog of existing commitments, but he had reason for confidence that he could handle them all. He had already proved his ability to manage a prodigious output of work. From the fall of 1501 to that of 1504, he had produced not only the giant *David* but had begun another one, almost life-sized, in bronze, modeled after Donatello's *David,* that Soderini needed as a gift for an influential official of the French court (since lost, this *David* is preserved only in a preparatory drawing). He had, moreover, produced a marble Madonna and Child for a rich merchant family from the Flemish city of Bruges, and three representations of the Madonna and Child in *tondo*—that is, in circular form like outsize medallions, a Florentine speciality. Two were of marble, carved in high relief, and the other was a painting; they were known by the names of the families that commissioned them, respectively, as the Taddei, the Pitti, and the Doni *tondi*.

Even so, with the first of the apostles soon due, the Piccolomini saints to deliver and the bronze *David* to finish, Michelangelo had enough work on hand to keep him fully occupied for the next several years. Yet it was at this point that he took on one of the major commissions of his

life—a project that by its very size was bound to absorb his creative energies completely. It was not imposed on him, yet it must have attracted him; for this time he had not only a great and difficult work of art to create but a personal rival to challenge and vanquish. The rival—the enemy, because Michelangelo did consider him that—was Leonardo da Vinci, the only artist whose prestige still exceeded Michelangelo's. In effect the prize at stake in their encounter, surely one of the most bizarre and dramatic personal confrontations in history, was the crowning of one of them as the supreme artist of the age.

At Soderini's initiative, it had been decided to decorate the Grand Council's hall in the Palazzo della Signoria with vast murals showing heroic scenes in Florence's history. Leonardo picked a subject that enabled him to display his encyclopedic knowledge of horses: the Battle of Anghiari, a wild cavalry melee of 1440 in which the Florentines routed a superior force of Milanese. Early in 1504 he began his cartoon—the full-scale, detailed drawing on paper of the scene that was to be painted. The *David* was still to be unveiled to the public. The full measure of fame and glory enjoyed by Leonardo lay just beyond Michelangelo's reach; and meantime he fretted.

A number of more or less rational reasons have been suggested for Michelangelo's envy, resentment and dislike of Leonardo. That the Florentine Leonardo had preferred living in Milan, serving a tyrant, Lodovico Sforza, whose unscrupulous double-dealings had brought endless troubles to Florence; that he then also served as chief military engineer to Caesar Borgia, another tyrant and potential military threat to Florence —these facts could have affronted Michelangelo's own intense patriotism and made him regard Leonardo as an unprincipled opportunist. That Leonardo had devoted a good deal of his time to directing festivals and weddings for the Milanese nobility and to designing pavilions and costumes for pageants and tournaments—this, to Michelangelo, could have made Leonardo seem more a sybaritic court favorite than a true artist. That Leonardo had declared painting superior to sculpture, and yet that before its destruction his equestrian statue of Lodovico Sforza's father had been hailed as a sculptural triumph of the age—this, to Michelangelo, may have seemed doubly insulting to his own art.

But beyond such seemingly cogent reasons was the matter of Leonardo's appearance and personality and mode of life. He was extraordinarily handsome. He compelled admiration by the subtlety and breadth of his mind, his refinement, his never-failing poise; he had all the social and physical graces and the power to transfix and charm. And in his work, as in all things, he gave the appearance of superb assurance.

In short, Leonardo was almost everything that Michelangelo was not, and it is a more than reasonable guess that Michelangelo felt the contrast painfully, and felt demeaned and challenged. With his broken nose and shyness and melancholy and yearning for affection, and with his seething sensitivity, he could nevertheless prove himself Leonardo's equal or superior in the one way that counted: by excelling in Leonardo's own chosen field of art, painting. It was well known that he had little liking for painting, and he had done very little of it since his apprentice days at

Ghirlandaio's. But he made it plain to his friend Soderini that he, too, wanted to paint a wall in the Grand Council hall.

In the fall of 1504, Michelangelo was given the commission and told to choose his own subject. He found one ideal for his purposes in the Battle of Cascina. This had occurred in 1364 when Sir John Hawkwood and his troop of English cavalry, employed by Pisa in one of its wars with Florence, surprised a force of 400 Florentine soldiers while the latter were bathing in the Arno. An alert sentry blew a warning and the naked Florentines struggled from the river, grabbed their armor and weapons, and managed to win the victory. With such a scene Michelangelo could make full use of his mastery of the nude form in every variety of tension, posture, and emotion-charged action.

Leonardo, proceeding with his usual contemplative care, took more than a year to get his cartoon finished and on the wall of the Grand Council hall. Michelangelo started some eight months later, but then attacked the work with such fury, driving himself to exhaustion, sleeping in his clothes and rising after a few hours to attack again, that he moved his project forward at a far faster pace than Leonardo. The Florentines were entranced by this battle of titans, and inevitably formed into vehement factions to applaud their respective champions.

But in the end, neither man won—and the whole world lost. The two great artists, possibly the two greatest the world has ever seen, shared triumph and tragedy. Each was a superlative draftsman, and each outdid himself in these monumental drawings. Artists came from all over Italy to see the two cartoons, old masters and young students alike. Among the admirers was Raphael, then a doe-eyed youth of 23, soon to emerge as the precocious third of the great trio of geniuses who dominated the High Renaissance. Benvenuto Cellini, a boy of six at the time both cartoons were displayed, had vivid memories of them and of the stream of pilgrims. In his *Autobiography* he wrote of the drawings: "So long as they remained intact, they were the school of the world."

The tragedy was that neither artist managed to produce a finished painting, and that ultimately both cartoons were destroyed and lost. Leonardo began to paint his fresco in the spring of 1505, and apparently did a considerable part of his large central scene, the *Battle of the Standard*. But, characteristically, he experimented with his materials and with methods to make the paint adhere to the wall. The result was that pigments changed color and some even melted, oozing down the surface in blobs and streams. There was no way to repair the damage, and by May of the next year, Leonardo had abandoned the project forever.

As for Michelangelo, he never had the chance to begin painting his fresco. Before he could do so the new Pope, the iron-willed Julius II, summoned him to Rome and embroiled him in new projects of such complexity that all other engagements—the saints and apostles as well as the Cascina fresco—had to be deferred and finally forsaken. He faced the most difficult years of his life, and the beginnings of a new tragedy that would haunt him for decades. Yet his peculiar Destiny had arranged that from these enormous difficulties would emerge his greatest triumph. He was, in fact, on the threshold of becoming The Divine Michelangelo.

The Observing Eye

What were Michelangelo's working methods? How did he go about freeing the figures he envisioned as lying locked inside their marble prisons? Was his art as effortless as he liked people to believe? One amazed eyewitness reported having watched the sculptor, already an old man, knock "more chips out of the hardest marble in a quarter of an hour than three young masons could have done in an hour. . . . With one blow he would remove chips as thick as three or four fingers, and his aim was so accurate that had he but chipped off a little more all might have been ruined." But this was Michelangelo in the fury of execution, the skilled craftsman realizing at last the idea that had tantalized him for so long. Only his intimates could know how much careful preliminary work actually went into his pieces. For almost any project, Michelangelo would produce dozens of sketches, often drawing from live models or turning out little clay or wax figures, *bozzetti,* or "buds," with which to study poses and proportions. The minutest details of anatomy were subject to the probing of his "observing eye"—veins, wrinkles, fingernails. But, however accomplished his sketches were, he destroyed all those in his possession before he died, so anxious was he that his works "give no other appearance than that of perfection." The relatively few that survive not only have the merit of being works of art in themselves but also show Michelangelo seized by an idea and struggling to bring it to the first stages of being.

Only in his later life did Michelangelo produce what he considered finished drawings, and this is one of them. A gift to his friend, the nobleman Tommaso dei Cavalieri, it shows the Fall of Phaëton: at top, Jupiter hurls a thunderbolt that upsets the chariot of the sun and panics the weeping Heliades below.

The Fall of Phaëton, 1533

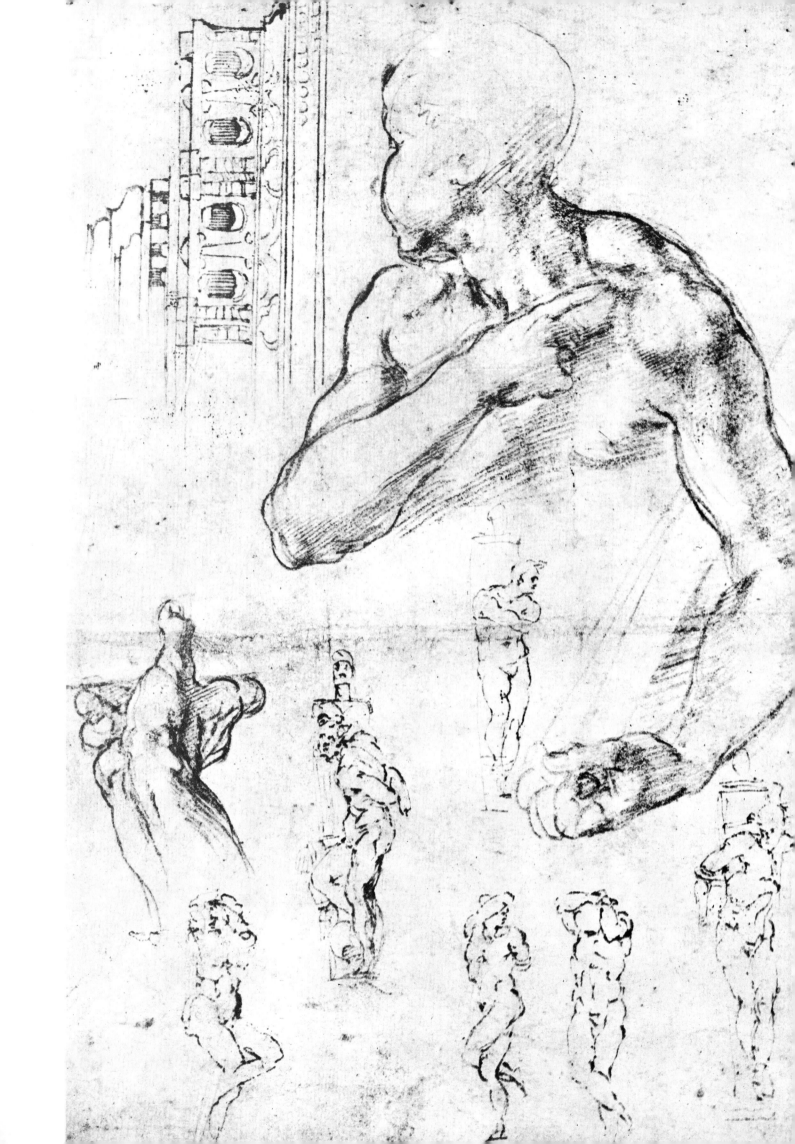

Here, with decisive strokes of pen and chalk, Michelangelo provides glimpses of himself at work. In the crowded sheet opposite, he is preoccupied; he has three projects on his mind —figures for the Sistine Chapel ceiling, sculptures for the tomb of Pope Julius II, and the architecture of the tomb itself. In the sketches for a river god below, he is the craftsman thinking ahead, indicating the dimensions of the marble he will need. But in the sketch at right, which combines the arm of the marble *David* with a design for a lost bronze *David,* he is being elusively autobiographical. For, in addition to his signature and a line from Petrarch ("Broken is the lofty column and the green"), he has included a verse of his own —"David with the sling, / and I with the bow."

Sketches for two Davids, 1501-1502

Sketches for a River God, c. 1525

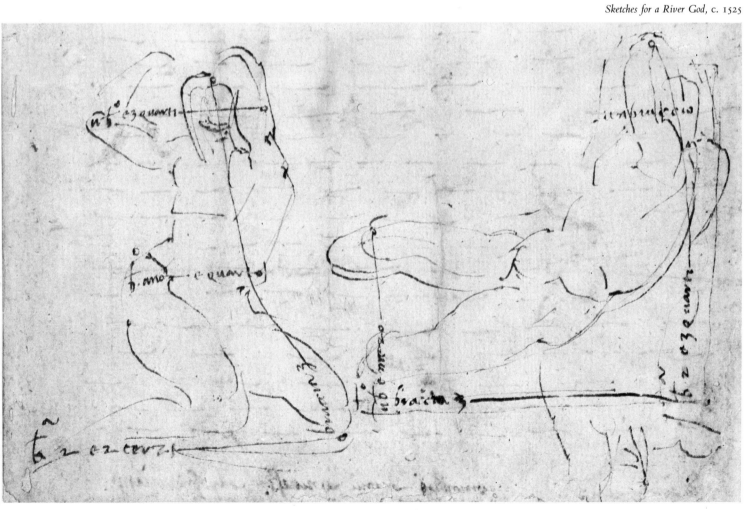

Sketches for Sistine Ceiling
and *Tomb of Julius II,* c. 1511-1513

99

A half century separates the drawing
reproduced on the opposite page from the
one on the right. In the intervening years,
not only Michelangelo's style changed
but also Michelangelo himself. When he
drew the face of the bearded man, he was
young, full of what he called
"impassioned fantasy." The sketch—
perhaps a study for the prophet Ezekiel on
the Sistine Chapel ceiling, or even a
portrait of Julius II, later to be idealized in
the face of the marble *Moses*—radiates the
young artist's confidence in his own
powers. Boldly modeled, it is done with
great economy of line.

By the time Michelangelo did the
drawing of the Virgin and Child, he was
an old man, his senses failing, convinced
that his impassioned fantasy—which had
made art "Sole Idol long and Monarch of
my heart"—was but an illusion. Here, he
has forsaken the strong modeling so
characteristic of earlier drawings, and is
pursuing instead what can only be termed
a vision. He seems to be looking ahead to
death ("Lord, in my latest hours, / Around
me let Thy pitying arms be thrown"),
and at the same time, to be turning
back to his childhood—perhaps to his own
mother, who died when he was six.
The Virgin encloses the Child with
her arms, and the Child reaches up to kiss
her cheek—and both figures, in a welter
of tiny black strokes, merge with each other.

V

God's
Terrible Vicar

Pope Julius II, Michelangelo's
self-willed and violent patron, is
shown at prayer in a Vatican fresco by
Raphael. His bushy white beard,
a memento of battle, was grown while
the "warrior-pope" campaigned
against the French.

Raphael: *Mass of Bolsena,* detail, 1512

It was Michelangelo's friend and fellow Florentine Giuliano da Sangallo who had recommended him to Pope Julius II. Sangallo was architect to the Pope and his principal adviser on all artistic matters, and Michelangelo saw him frequently after arriving in Rome early in 1505.
Years later Sangallo's son Francesco recalled:

"I was at that time a boy in Rome, when one day it was announced to
the Pope that some excellent statues had been dug out of the ground in a
vineyard near the church of Santa Maria Maggiore. The Pope immediately sent a groom to Giuliano da Sangallo to tell him to go right away
and see what it was. Michelangelo Buonarroti was often at our house,
and at the moment chanced to be there; accordingly, my father invited
him to go with us. I rode behind my father on his horse. We had scarcely
dismounted and glanced at the figures when my father cried out, 'It is the
Laocoön of which Pliny speaks!' The laborers immediately began dig-
ging to get the statues out. After having looked at them very carefully,
we went home to supper, talking all the way of antiquity."

Pope Julius was elated, for he was a collector of antiquities. Until then
his great prize had been a magnificent Apollo found in 1490 in the ruins
of a Roman villa which, on becoming Pope, he had installed in the place
of honor in the courtyard of the Belvedere, the papal summer palace.
The *Laocoön,* a legendary work of Greek art once owned by the Emper-
or Titus, was fit company even for the *Apollo Belvedere* and Julius immediately claimed it. To the man and his son who had found it he granted
a reward of 600 ducats, a generosity that so inflamed the already hot
search for buried masterpieces that Rome became pockmarked with dig-
gings. Julius, brandishing his papal prerogative like a club, bought most
of the best finds and added them to the Belvedere. And thus with his vigor
and taste and gold ducats he founded the Vatican collection of classical
sculpture, which grew to be one of the finest in the world.

Julius loved his reborn pagan deities and nymphs and creatures of old
mythology, but even more he loved the excitements of battle and the
rough pleasures of life in the field. So he was often away storming cities,
leading his troops with furious voice and flashing armor. The victory

won and his and God's enemies slaughtered like the Philistines or dispersed like the Sons of Edom, he would return in contentment to the Vatican to nourish the arts, to consult with his architects and painters and sculptors and spur them on to fulfill his vast plans for rebuilding and beautifying Rome. The project that above all others filled him with enthusiasm was to tear down the old St. Peter's and replace it with a glorious new basilica, a symbol of papal power commensurate with the grandeur and authority he was determined to win for the Vicar of Christ.

Such was Pope Julius, the holy terror who for eight years was to be the blessing and bane of Michelangelo's life—a greatly gifted and overpowering man who, among his other accomplishments, almost singlehandedly transferred the center of the Renaissance from Florence to Rome and there forced Renaissance art to its supreme flowering. And such was Julian Rome, a city as full of violence and clashing motifs and splendid purposes as the rambunctious man who ran it. And such was Italy in the early Cinquecento, when a great architect, the greatest of artists and a little boy could go and watch a Greek masterpiece emerge from its overburden of centuries of dust and discover, "It is the *Laocoön* . . .!"—and go "home to supper, talking all the way of antiquity."

Nowhere but in Julian Rome could Michelangelo have encountered a combination of time, place and circumstances so well designed to challenge and reward his protean genius. True, his relationship with Julius was frequently to be the source of exasperation and despair, for although they were so much alike that they were attracted to each other, they were too much alike to get along peaceably. As John Addington Symonds said, "Both aimed at colossal achievements in their respective fields. . . . Both were *uomini terribili,* to use a phrase denoting vigor of character and energy of genius, made formidable by an abrupt, uncompromising spirit." Sir Kenneth Clark has commented: "Gorki once said of Tolstoy, 'His relations with God are very uneasy: like two old bears in a den'; and such were Michelangelo's relations with God's vicar on earth. And yet it was one of those momentous conjunctions for which posterity must be grateful, for without Julius II, Michelangelo might never have had the opportunity of developing the full power of his imagination."

This being so, an understanding of Michelangelo's triumphs and trials during this period of his life requires some understanding of the Renaissance papacy. For Julius, far from being unique, was in many ways an archetypical Renaissance Pope, differing from the norm only in his extra intensity, determination and impetuosity. Because he led his armies in person he became known as the "warrior-pope," but actually for long years past popes had been waging wars with armies led by hired *condottieri* or by warrior-cardinals and warrior-bishops. Between their military campaigns and incessant diplomatic maneuverings, their intrigues and political machinations within the various city-states, and their eager pursuit of art and learning and other pleasures, sacred and profane, Julius' predecessors had been making their presence felt in all aspects of life in Renaissance Italy. It was Julius' uncle, Pope Sixtus IV, for example, who had abetted the Pazzi conspiracy to assassinate the Medici, which Lorenzo survived by the barest margin to become later the discoverer and

The famous Greek statue, the *Laocoön,* depicts Apollo's disobedient priest struggling with his two sons against sea serpents sent by an angry god as punishment. It is shown here almost exactly as Michelangelo saw it when it was wrested from its centuries-long sleep in the Roman earth. Though Renaissance and later sculptors added missing pieces, these have now been removed, but the right arm of Laocoön, which turned up only in this century, has been put back on. The effect on Michelangelo of these writhing, emotionally expressive figures was enormous: their influence can be detected in his frescoes for the Sistine Chapel, and in sculptures such as the two *Slaves,* shown on page 150.

mentor of the young Michelangelo. On the other hand, it was also Sixtus who built the great Sistine Chapel where in due course Michelangelo, commissioned by Julius, was destined to create his greatest work of art.

What purpose was the Church pursuing that caused the emergence at this time of such an exotic breed of popes—patrons simultaneously, and with equal certainty of God's grace, of the harshest arts of war and the most sublime arts of peace?

The roots of the matter wind deep through sedimentary layers of history laid down in the course of the perennial conflict between church and state, but the essential fact was that the papacy had acquired temporal sovereignty over much of central Italy including, besides Rome itself, such consequential cities as Bologna, Ravenna, Rimini, Ferrara, Urbino, Perugia—in all, several dozen political units of various sizes and degrees of autonomy. Some were ruled by hereditary nobility, some by bishops, some by relatives of the pope and powerful cardinals—all of whom, however, at least in theory ruled on behalf of the pope and were subject to his discipline; hence the term, the "papal states." They had been acquired by bequest, purchase, conquest, diplomatic deals and double-deals: in short, by most of the secular devices of empire building.

Consequently, when in 1309 the papacy was transferred from Rome to distant Avignon in southeastern France they soon were in disarray. The local rulers began running them as their own properties and remitting to the popes only a token revenue, if that. Some states were absorbed or brought under domination by powerful neighboring city-states such as Florence; many were seized by marauding *condottieri*. When finally the papacy returned to Rome the confusion was compounded, for some of the cardinals revolted, elected a rival pope and installed him at the old seat in Avignon. During this "Great Schism" there was a pope in Rome and another in Avignon, each commanding the loyalty of about half of Europe, each side hurling anathemas and edicts of excommunication at the other. The fantasy of popes, false popes and antipopes continued (for a while there were not merely two but *three* competing popes) until a Church council deposed all the claimants and elected Pope Martin V.

Bᵤₜ meantime more than a century had passed and the papacy's assets were in ruinous condition. Without the revenues of the papal states to support it and their physical territories to buffer it against the military power of the big secular states, the popes decided, the Holy See could not function effectively or remain independent. And without civil order in Rome and the countryside the popes and cardinals could not even be sure of their own safety. These hard facts produced men to match: popes and cardinals who, with few exceptions, were pragmatic and ruthless.

Martin V managed to pacify Rome during his reign. But his successor, Eugenius IV, had to save himself from rebel mobs by escaping down the Tiber; and he spent the next nine years in Florence as the guest of Cosimo de' Medici—until his military deputy, the bloodthirsty Bishop Vitelleschi, had slaughtered enough of the contentious local nobility to make it safe for him to return. Sixtus, though one of the leading scholars and theologians of his time, spent most of his 13-year reign at war against recalcitrant papal states and one or another of the big secular states. That

paragon of efficiency and iniquity, Alexander VI, made his son, Caesar Borgia, Captain-General of the papal armies. Caesar was not a good general but he was a brilliantly adroit and conscienceless scoundrel, his father's pride and joy. Mainly by Machiavellian guile (he was Machiavelli's principal model for *The Prince*), he not only subdued a number of truant states but was preparing to convert them into a Borgia kingdom when Alexander died and Julius II became Pope. After removing Caesar from command and exiling him to Spain, Julius took over his gains on behalf of the Church and prepared to finish the job. And after stupendous efforts, and occasionally stupendous defeats, he ended with such a general victory that the papal states remained subservient until the Italian national revolution of the 1860s made them part of the new Italy.

Just as Julius was the culminating figure in the long endeavor of the popes to rebuild their secular power, he was the culminating figure in their other major and corollary endeavor: to rebuild the city of Rome. Rome had lived on the papacy: the gold that flowed in from all over Europe, the pilgrims, the functionaries. Consequently, Rome without the papacy was in much the same position as a mining town when the mine shuts down, and it underwent the same swift decay. Its muddy, unpaved streets were littered with rubble and rubbish, its palaces and churches half-ruined. Even the basilica of St. Peter's, the Mother Church of Christendom, was crumbling. Martin V, on becoming Pope at the end of the Great Schism, confronted the ruined capital of a ruined domain.

Martin was the prototype of what was to become the common design: a tough man who nevertheless understood the uses of art both for itself and for its power to confer an aura of majesty on the city and papacy. As pope followed pope, each added something according to his tastes and resources; so did generations of wealthy churchmen. As a result most of the great artists of the Quattrocento—Fra Angelico, Filippino Lippi, Signorelli, Perugino, Ghirlandaio, Botticelli and others—came to Rome at one time or another, and they left an accretion of great works. But the size of the accomplishment had to be measured against the size of the need. By mid-century, Rome had a population of only 40,000 and the living city occupied only one fourth of the old Imperial city enclosed by the Aurelian Wall—the other three fourths still was rubble, ruins, and vineyards and pasture land. When Julius began his reign, the population still was only 40,000 and most of the city still was disfigured by the ravagement of the centuries and was offensive to sight and smell.

A great deal was needed to give Rome a grandeur commensurate with Julius' ambitions, which stretched far beyond the papal states. He hoped eventually to unify all Italy, perhaps even much of Europe, under papal authority. Short of that, he meant to make the Church so influential in the world that Rome, as its seat, would be in effect if not in fact the "capital of the world," the place where all roads led. And so Rome must become the most splendid city in the world. That is why he rallied his troops of artists and architects—and why he needed Michelangelo.

It was characteristic of Julius—so absorbed in his vast schemes that he seldom noticed, let alone comprehended or cared, that individuals had needs and obligations of their own—that having wrenched Michelange-

lo away from Florence he turned out to have no specific project in mind for him. He simply wanted him on hand and ready for use, like money in the bank or a weapon in reserve. Condivi relates, "At last it occurred to him to use his genius in the construction of his own tomb. The design furnished by Michelangelo pleased the Pope so much that he sent him off immediately to Carrara, with a commission to quarry as much marble as was needful. . . . After about eight months, back in Rome, he had . . . the stone blocks disembarked and carried to the Piazza of St. Peter's behind S. Caterina, where he kept his lodging, close to the corridor connecting the [Vatican] Palace with the Castel Sant' Angelo. The quantity of stone was enormous, so that, when it was all spread out upon the square, it stirred amazement in the minds of most folk, but joy in the Pope's. Julius indeed began to heap favors upon Michelangelo; for when he had begun to work, the Pope used frequently to betake himself to his house, conversing there with him about the tomb and about other works which he proposed to carry out. . . . In order to arrive more conveniently at Michelangelo's lodgings, he had a drawbridge thrown across the corridor, by which he might gain privy access."

This monument, the grandiose product of the perfect meeting of two minds that routinely functioned in terms of the ultimate and the colossal, deserves special attention. Not only was it in itself an astonishment, but for the next 40 years it was to become the bane of Michelangelo's life, attending him in everything he did, as if it were a chastisement Destiny had laid on him (as, in classical Greek drama, Destiny was bound to do) for the sin of *hubris,* or Overweening Pride—that destructive pride that made him attempt to do more than any mortal could possibly do.

For the "tragedy of the tomb," as Condivi called it, was implicit in its very design. It was to be some 36 feet long by 24 feet wide, rising like a step-pyramid in layers to a pinnacle over 36 feet high, adorned with more than 40 statues all bigger than life-size. "At the summit," as Condivi describes it, "two angels supported a sarcophagus. One . . . appeared to smile, rejoicing that the soul of the Pope had been received among the blessed spirits; the other seemed to weep, as sorrowing that the world had been robbed of such a man." This sarcophagus was only symbolic, however: the mausoleum contained a chapel, "in the midst of which was a marble chest, wherein the corpse of the Pope was . . . to be deposited."

For sheer splendor there had been nothing like this tomb since the mortuary triumphs of such Roman Emperors as Hadrian and Augustus. To Michelangelo, it offered a rationale within which he could use all his skills and artistic inventiveness to their fullest and from which he expected would emerge the supreme sculptural masterpiece of the ages. Apparently he believed that he could accomplish all this in five years. The tomb was to be "free-standing"—a structure independent in itself, not attached to the wall of a church. Where should it stand? Preferably not outside in the open, subject to the vagaries of wind and weather and human nature. But no church in Rome was big enough or architecturally suited to give it proper display. Pope Julius solved the problem by deciding to build a vast new basilica of St. Peter's.

The old basilica, as mentioned, was in decrepit condition, and plans

for a new one had been begun a half century earlier, but had been, in effect, long since abandoned. Now Julius called on both his official architect, Sangallo, and the other architect he most admired, Donato Bramante, to submit plans for it, starting fresh and thinking big. From that moment there was no question where the great tomb would stand: in the new basilica in the large central space under the dome. For purposes of display—and display was what Julius and Michelangelo wanted, each for his own genius—it would be impossible to imagine a better location.

However, this decision by Julius was the second of the circumstances that led to the "tragedy of the tomb." For the new St. Peter's distracted the Pope's enthusiasm, energy and money from the tomb. Further, it shortly brought Bramante into Michelangelo's life as an enemy. Even years later, looking back with the calmer emotions of old age, he was still convinced that Bramante had been the main cause of the troubles that now began to afflict him. How much truth there was in this has never been established, but since Michelangelo's belief in it decisively influenced his actions, it is necessary to know something about the characters and situation in order to follow the "plot" as it thickened.

Sangallo had good reasons for thinking he should be the architect of the new St. Peter's. Beginning in Florence under Lorenzo, his career had been distinguished and long. Among his notable feats in Rome was the beautiful ceiling of the great church of Santa Maria Maggiore, which he gilded with the first gold from the New World—the gift of Ferdinand and Isabella of Spain. He had been a personal friend of Julius since his days as Cardinal della Rovere, and had even followed him into exile when, the better to avoid Borgia poisons and to organize a cabal against Alexander VI, the Cardinal left Rome to live in France.

Bramante had come into Julius' ken by a very different route. Born near Urbino, he had worked here and there in northern Italy until settling in Milan under the patronage of the ruling Sforzas. There, with his powerful ambition and conspicuous talents, he considerably outshone the less obtrusive Leonardo da Vinci, and it was he rather than Leonardo who was considered the artistic star of the realm. When the fall of Duke Lodovico Sforza forced Bramante to find a new patron, he came to Rome. Inspired by the Roman ruins, he became a fervid antiquarian, adapting the classical style in his work with marvelous effectiveness. Thus his fame, lively originality and aggressive temperament combined to make Julius admire him, load him with projects, listen with interest to his ideas—and hence invite his ideas about the greatest project of all.

When Julius had the two plans in hand, he decided, friendship and loyalty or no, that he liked Bramante's better than Sangallo's, and that was that. And in point of fact Bramante's plan was better. But Sangallo was humiliated and bitter, and on his behalf so were his friends. For he —and they with him—had suffered what in the Renaissance was the least endurable blow: loss of status, of pride based on influence and power.

Bramante, armed with formidable new status, in the spirit of the times moved to attack the weakened Sangallist position with the aim of winning all, for he could not feel safe until he had driven Sangallo away from Rome. And he must attempt the same with Michelangelo, who,

The difficult and dangerous job of quarrying and transporting marble to a shipping site —a job Michelangelo once likened to taming the mountains—is re-created here in a drawing based upon methods in use at Carrara during his day. Blocks like the one shown above were first cut from a vein by chiseling a groove into a fault in the marble, inserting olive wood wedges and pouring water on them. The expansion of the wedges would split the stone along the line of the fault. Single blocks were then hauled on wooden rollers or iron balls to chutes carved from the living stone and greased with soap. Restrained by ropes or slings and resting on beams, a block would be eased down the chute to waiting carts. Michelangelo tells in a letter of 1518 what happened when a mistake in slinging caused a block to break loose— "one man had his neck broken and died instantly, and it nearly cost me my life."

as everyone knew, was Sangallo's friend and had been holding Julius spellbound with the great tomb project. Further, according to this line of reasoning—which might be termed "the devil theory" about Bramante, whose defenders offer a countertheory that Michelangelo was suffering from delusions of persecution—Bramante had become both inordinately jealous of Michelangelo and fearful of him. "For Bramante, as everyone knows," declared Condivi, "was much given to pleasure and very dissipated. The salary he received from the Pope, though it was great, was not nearly enough for him, so that he tried to make more by constructing walls of inferior material. . . . Bramante realized that Michelangelo would have discovered his mistakes, and so he tried to deprive him of . . . the influence which he had gained over the Pope."

If so, then Bramante's tactical objective was obvious: he must halt the plans for the tomb. Condivi relates that the wily Bramante plied the Pope with suggestions "that it was a bad augury to build your tomb while you were still alive." He also began to work on Michelangelo's nerves. There is no mention of what means were used, but Michelangelo himself wrote later that they "made me think that, if I were to remain in Rome, my own tomb would be prepared before that of the Pope."

In any event Julius began to see less and less of Michelangelo, seemed strangely uninterested in the tomb, advanced no money for expenses and one day soon, when Michelangelo came to call on him, refused to see him at all. As Michelangelo described it: "He had me turned away by a groom. A Lucchese bishop, seeing this, said: 'Do you not know who that man is?' The groom replied to me: 'Excuse me, sir, I have orders to do this.'" Michelangelo stormed out of the Vatican Palace and went home and wrote to the Pope: "Most blessed Father, I have been turned out of your Palace today by your orders; wherefore I give you notice that from this time forward, if you want me, you must look for me elsewhere than at Rome." He promptly left for Florence.

Julius received Michelangelo's letter within a few hours and sent his horsemen after him with an ultimatum: "Come back at once to Rome, under penalty of our displeasure." By the time they caught up with him, however, Michelangelo had reached the town of Poggibonsi, safe in Florentine territory, and he sent back the counterultimatum to Julius "that if he would fulfill the obligations he had toward me, I would return; but otherwise he must not expect to have me again." Next morning he continued to Florence, and there he took up his life where he had left off, working on the Cascina cartoon (and now finishing it).

Meanwhile, Julius fumed. Condivi relates: "During the months Michelangelo stayed in Florence three papal briefs were sent to the Signory, full of threats, commanding that he should be sent back by fair means or by force. When the second and the third were sent, [Piero Soderini] called Michelangelo and said: 'You have tried a bout with the Pope on which the King of France would not have ventured. . . . We do not wish to go to war on your account. . . . Make up your mind to return.' Michelangelo . . . thought of taking refuge in the East. The Sultan indeed besought him . . . to come and construct a bridge from Constantinople [across the Golden Horn] to Pera, and other great works." Sode-

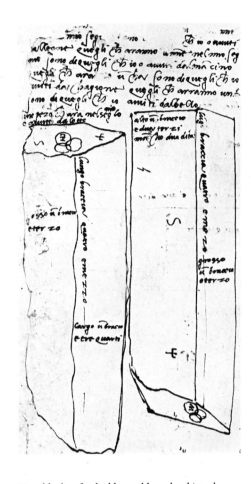

Two blocks of valuable marble to be shipped to Michelangelo from Carrara are firmly identified in this pen sketch which records his ownership. Not only has he noted the shape and measurements of each block, but he also shows the position of his mark, three interlocking circles, in which have been added the initials of the stonecutters themselves. A note at top, in his handwriting, identifies the men by name. And as a further guarantee that these blocks were indeed his, Michelangelo had this sketch and several others like it notarized by a solicitor at Carrara.

rini urged Michelangelo: "'It were better to choose death with the Pope than to keep life by going to the Turk. Nevertheless there is no fear of such an ending; for the Pope . . . sends for you because he loves you.'"

Knowing Julius, and having had time to reflect on his own *lèse majesté,* Michelangelo had reason to suspect that this was true only in the sense that the arena lions loved the Christian martyrs. However, for Florence's sake, for Soderini's and for his own—since Julian Rome was becoming the vital center of the arts—it seemed necessary to make some gesture of obeisance to Julius. After months of negotiations through intermediaries, rather like two warring states probing for mutually acceptable peace terms, the time for this clearly was at hand late in 1506.

That August, attended by a gorgeous wake of 12 cardinals and their retinues, leading a force of 500 knights in armor and 300 members of a new, special shock troop unit he had created—since famous as the Swiss Guards—Julius had launched his first military campaign against the truant papal fiefs of Perugia and Bologna. At Perugia the disobedient vassal was Giampaolo Baglioni, a bloody tyrant and all-round ogre whose wickedness was famous throughout Italy. But confronted by Julius' iron nerve and his absolute expectation of being obeyed absolutely, even the evil Baglioni lost his courage. He not only submitted without a fight but volunteered to contribute troops to the papal army. Bologna fell into a panic. Its disobedient rulers, the Bentivogli family, fled; the city gave up without resistance and Julius entered in triumph on November 11. Ten days later he sent a letter to the Florentine Signory asking that it arrange for Michelangelo to come there at once.

Michelangelo complied—sheltering, however, under credentials as an Ambassador of Florence, so that if the Pope had a mind to assault him he would be assaulting the Florentine republic. On arriving in the city his first act was to go to Mass at the cathedral. There papal attendants recognized him and brought him to the government palace and directly into the room where Julius was having lunch. Condivi relates:

"When the Pope beheld him, his face clouded with anger, and he cried: 'It was your duty to come to seek us, and you have waited till we came to seek you. . . .' Michelangelo knelt and prayed for pardon in a loud voice, pleading in his excuse that he had not erred through forwardness but through great distress of mind. . . . The Pope remained holding his head low and answering nothing, evidently much agitated, when a certain prelate, sent by Cardinal Soderini [brother of Piero Soderini] to put in a good word for Michelangelo, came forward and said: 'Your Holiness might overlook his fault; he did wrong through ignorance; these painters, outside their art, are all like this.' "

Julius himself had made a similar remark in one of his letters to the Signory about Michelangelo: "We for our part are not angry with him, knowing the humors of such men of genius." But, Condivi continues: "The Pope answered in a fury: 'It is you, not I, who are insulting him. It is you, not he, who are the ignoramus and the rascal. Get hence out of my sight, and bad luck to you!' When the fellow did not move, he was cast forth by the servants, as Michelangelo used to relate, with good round kicks and thumpings. So the Pope, having spent the surplus

of his bile upon the bishop, took Michelangelo aside and pardoned him.

"Not long afterwards he sent for him and said: 'I wish you to make my statue on a large scale in bronze. I intend to place it on the façade of San Petronio [the cathedral].'" The scale Julius had in mind turned out to be almost three times life-size—a seated figure 10 feet high. The great tomb was still in abeyance but here, encouragingly, was its spirit. Not wanting to renew their recent war, Michelangelo assented.

Julius put 1,000 ducats on deposit for him and prepared to go back to Rome. Condivi relates: "But before he did so Michelangelo had made the clay model. Being in some doubt how to manage the left hand, after making the Pope give the benediction with the right, he asked Julius, who had come to see the statue, if he would like it to hold a book. 'What book?' replied he. 'A sword! I know nothing about letters, not I.' Jesting then about the right hand, which was vehement in action, he said with a smile to Michelangelo: 'That statue of yours, is it blessing or cursing?' To which the sculptor replied: 'Holy Father, it is threatening the people of Bologna if they are not prudent.'" The friendly camaraderie of the past had been re-established.

Julius returned to Rome to a triumph seldom seen since the great days of the Roman Emperors. In Bologna, Michelangelo plunged into his work with his usual intensity. (He solved the problem of Julius' left hand by having it hold the keys of St. Peter.) But he was vexed in innumerable ways. Because he had worked very little in bronze casting, the cost estimate of 1,000 ducats he had given Julius had been only a rough guess. Hence his usual penurious way of living descended to the level of squalor. He hired three assistants for the cumbersome processes involved in casting, but rented only one room for living quarters and bought only one bed—which all four shared. To make this arrangement even less congenial, the weather turned miserably hot and an epidemic of plague broke out. He quarreled with his assistants and fired one; another quit. Everything merged into a nightmare. "If I were to make another statue," he wrote home, "I do not think I would be able to survive it."

But finally, on February 21, 1508, Julius the Colossus, in the polished bronze magnificence of full pontifical vestments and triple tiara, was set in place above the main doors of the cathedral. Little more than three years later the Bentivogli forces, temporarily regaining the city, toppled the statue and sent it crashing to the pavement below. From there it was dragged away and sold as bronze scrap to Alfonso d'Este, Duke of Ferrara, another strayed papal fief that Julius was attempting to discipline. An expert military engineer and gunsmith, Alfonso removed the head as a souvenir; then he melted the body and cast it as a great bronze cannon, which, in sardonic honor of Julius, he christened *La Giulia*. And so this product of Julius' pride and Michelangelo's toil came to nothing.

Arriving back again in Florence in the spring of 1508, Michelangelo prepared to resume his own life. He no longer had free occupancy of the house that had been built for him, but the Board of Works was willing to rent it to him; he signed the lease on March 18. Nevertheless, only a few weeks later he was in Rome again. And on June 15 the lease was canceled and the house relet—a date that might properly serve as the

Memorial Day for the Cascina fresco, the Twelve Apostles and the rest of the projects left undone in Florence, which were now doomed never to be done. Instead, and at first protesting every foot of the way, Michelangelo had been set to a new challenge that was to result in his greatest masterpiece, and in his own transmutation into a living divinity. The official date—a date that could properly serve as a celebrant Feast Day—is contained in his *Ricordi,* his journal of official transactions:

"I record how on this day, the 10th of May, 1508, I, Michelangelo, sculptor, have received from the Holiness of our Lord Pope Julius II, 500 ducats of the Camera . . . on account of the painting of the vault of the Sistine Chapel, on which I begin to work."

Just how this abrupt and total overturning of his plans had come about has eluded full explanation for some 500 years. As nearly as events can be pieced together, however, it appears that Pope Julius sent word that he should come to Rome for discussions, and Michelangelo obeyed not only to keep peace but because it might mean that the great tomb project was stirring again. After all, this never had been canceled: Julius' attitude throughout had been that it would be done, but not just now. Perhaps he implied that the time had come; perhaps he wanted Michelangelo to begin the work on some partial basis. These points are conjectural, but they fit into the hypothesis—which Condivi asserts as a fact and which Michelangelo himself must have believed—that the villain (or inadvertent hero) who engineered the Sistine commission was Bramante.

There is no doubt that Bramante now had even more compelling reasons for wishing to forestall the tomb project and discredit Michelangelo. Lack of money was already delaying the new St. Peter's. Julius' military campaigns were an increasingly heavy drain on his own energy and the papal treasury, and any part of these vital resources that was diverted to the tomb would be lost to the basilica. Bramante's problem then (according to Condivi's interpretation) was to think of a project that the Pope wanted done, that Michelangelo would dislike doing and in all likelihood fail at if he tried, and then to convince the Pope that Michelangelo was the essential man for the job.

Given these terms, the Sistine ceiling would be the perfect answer. The Pope did very much want it done; moreover, in his ponderings about a proper artist for it, he had thought of Michelangelo (or been given the thought) even in 1506. Michelangelo had excused himself on the grounds that he was a sculptor, not a painter. And, of course, this was almost literally true: his only experience in fresco had been during the brief apprenticeship with Ghirlandaio. His lack of experience and lack of interest, the sheer magnitude of the Sistine ceiling and the special technical problems of perspective and foreshortening imposed by its vault shape, all made it seem probable that if he attempted it he would have a miserable failure. The final element of this brew, according to Condivi's (that is, Michelangelo's) calculation, was that Bramante's young kinsman Raphael had been commissioned to do a set of large frescoes in the library of Julius' private apartments in the Vatican, and with his talent and perfect technique as a painter he was likely to have a success that would make Michelangelo's failure all the more conspicuous.

Michelangelo "tried in every way to extricate himself," Condivi relates. "He proposed Raphael in his place and gave as an excuse that this was not his art . . . and went so far in his attempts at refusal that the Pope began to grow angry and showed such obstinate determination that Michelangelo decided to undertake the job."

He had hardly begun painting, Condivi continues, "when the work began to throw out mold to such an extent that the figures could hardly be seen through it. Michelangelo thought that this excuse might be sufficient to get him relieved of the whole job. So he went to the Pope and said: 'I already told Your Holiness that painting is not my trade; what I have done is spoiled; if you do not believe it, send to see.' The Pope sent Sangallo, who, after inspecting the fresco, pronounced that the lime base had been put on too wet, and that water oozing out produced this moldy surface. He told Michelangelo what the cause was, and bade him proceed with the work. So the excuse helped him nothing."

Knowing that he would need skilled assistants to make up his own deficit of experience, he provided in the contract for five "painter-assistants who are to come from Florence." One was his old schoolmate Francesco Granacci, and the others were also friends or acquaintances. But in very little time relations began deteriorating because, as usual, Michelangelo imposed his own standards and viewpoint and proved as severe a critic of their work as of his own. He ended by dismissing them all. Then he destroyed the parts they had painted, barred the Chapel to visitors except the Pope and others by special permission, and determined to do the whole thing by himself.

Condivi relates: "While he was painting, Pope Julius used oftentimes to go and see the work, climbing by a ladder, while Michelangelo gave him a hand to help him on to the platform. One day the Pope asked him, as he had often done, when he would finish and Michelangelo answered, according to his custom, 'When I can.' The Pope, who was irritable, struck him with his staff, saying, 'When I can, when I can!' Michelangelo rushed home and began to make his preparations to leave Rome. The Pope sent hurriedly after him an amiable young man named Accursio, who gave Michelangelo 500 ducats, soothed him as well as he could and apologized for Julius II. Michelangelo accepted the excuses. The next day, however, the argument began again, and when the Pope threatened to have him thrown from his scaffolding Michelangelo had to give way. He had the scaffolding removed and uncovered the ceiling sooner than he had intended. 'That is why,' he said, 'that work was not carried on as far as I would have wished. The Pope's impatience prevented.'"

On October 31, 1512, the Chapel was opened for public viewing. All the artists and dignitaries of Rome came to see what Michelangelo had done—and what they saw, as Vasari said, was "a lamp for our art which casts abroad luster enough to illuminate the world." Michelangelo, the supreme master of sculpture, had proved himself also to be the supreme master of painting, and had put himself, as Condivi says, "above the reach of envy." He was, at the age of 37, The Divine Michelangelo—by the grace of God and His terrible Vicar, Julius II, who, at the age of nearly 70, died four months later.

Perhaps the most famous of Michelangelo's sonnets is the one he wrote about painting the Sistine Chapel ceiling. It is shown, in his own handwriting, together with a caricature of himself at work—standing rather than lying on his back as legend would have it. The sonnet is translated below.

In this hard toil I've such a goiter grown,
Like cats that water drink in Lombardy,
(Or wheresoever else the place may be)
That chin and belly meet perforce in one.
My beard doth point to heaven, my scalp its place
Upon my shoulder finds; my chest, you'll say,
A harpy's is, my paintbrush all the day
Doth drop a rich mosaic on my face.
My loins have entered my paunch within,
My nether end my balance doth supply,
My feet unseen move to and fro in vain.
In front to utmost length is stretched my skin
And wrinkled up in folds behind, while I
Am bent as bowmen bend a bow in Spain.
No longer true or sane,
The judgment now doth from the mind proceed,
For 'tis ill shooting through a twisted reed.
Then thou, my picture dead,
Defend it, Giovan, and my honor—why?
The place is wrong, and no painter I.

The Sistine Chapel

Only Michelangelo could have taken on two such awesome commissions as the Sistine Chapel ceiling and the *Last Judgment* and turned them into transcendent masterpieces. He was just 33 when he began the ceiling, and he poured all his youthful energy into it. Working on a scaffold high above the floor, his beard pointing to heaven and his face splattered with "a rich mosaic" of paint, so affected his eyes, says Vasari, that for months afterward he could read mail from his father and brothers only by holding the letters above his head. Increasingly he realized the Herculean nature of his labors: "I strain more than any man who ever lived . . . and with great exhaustion; and yet I have the patience to arrive at the desired goal." After four years of lacerating toil, during which time he worked almost unaided, the ceiling was done, its 5,800 square feet of surface peopled by a race of giants—more than 300 figures, although the original plan had called for only 12.

A quarter of a century later Michelangelo returned to the Sistine Chapel to execute the *Last Judgment* for Pope Paul III. In the intervening period Rome had been sacked and the papacy humiliated. Gone was Michelangelo's faith in man's power and yet, even with his painful awareness of the realities that restrain and ultimately bind men, Michelangelo again, as the subject of the *Last Judgment* unfolded to him, surpassed himself.

Of the many preliminary sketches Michelangelo made for the Sistine Chapel ceiling, only a few, like this study of a male model, survive. Transformed into a woman, the figure appears on the ceiling as the mighty Libyan sibyl, the seeress of Greek mythology.

Sketches for the Libyan Sibyl, c. 1510

The place is wrong," Michelangelo complained, "and no painter I."
The place, the Sistine Chapel, was a barn of a room measuring 132 feet by 44
feet, with its star-splattered ceiling arching a dizzying 68 feet over the marble
mosaic floor. Built in 1473 for Julius' uncle, Sixtus IV, whose name it bears,
the chapel had been designed with two contradictory functions in mind
—worship and defense. The three-foot-thick brick walls, high windows and
narrow entrance, the battlements on the roof and the quarters for soldiers above
the vault made it a fortress-refuge. Before Michelangelo set to work on the
ceiling, the walls were a showcase for art: they had been frescoed with
scenes from the lives of Christ and Moses by leading painters of the 15th
Century, including Ghirlandaio, Perugino, Signorelli and Botticelli. But
so unsure of himself did Michelangelo feel that he suspected a plot on the part
of the papal architect Bramante to embarrass him with failure. Complaining
to Julius, he pointed out that the scaffold Bramante had built for him hung
from holes in the ceiling. How, he asked, were the holes to be filled when
the scaffold came down? Julius ordered him to have Bramante's scaffold
destroyed and to put up one of his own. This Michelangelo did—happily
taking the ropes Bramante had used and giving them to a poor carpenter
who sold them to pay his daughter's dowry. Then, sometime in January 1509,
still assaulted by doubt, Michelangelo Buonarroti, sculptor, climbed
the scaffold to begin the painting that was to change the course of art.

In the late 15th Century, the Chapel ceiling was a pale blue, decorated with gold stars.

In the Chapel today, the *Last Judgment* is seen on the far wall.

The Sistine Chapel ceiling demonstrates the scope and power of Michelangelo's genius. To give coherence to his many-faceted subject, the world in the morning of time, he divided the ceiling into three zones. In the lowest zone, set off by zigzagging bands, he placed the Biblical ancestors of Christ, crushed by their burden of mortality, with heroic episodes out of the Bible filling the corners. In the second zone, he included enthroned sibyls and Old Testament prophets, still human, but elevated spiritually by their gift of clairvoyance. And in the third zone, running down the middle of the ceiling in nine separate panels, he painted episodes from Genesis.

By beginning in reverse order with the *Drunkenness of Noah* and ending over the altar with the *Separation*

of Light from Darkness, Michelangelo gave visual expression to a Neoplatonic notion popular in the Renaissance—that life should be a journey from the slavery of the body to the liberation of the soul in God. Working out this theme in paint, he became increasingly inspired, increasingly sure of himself, and the size of his figures began to increase dramatically. He allowed the sibyls and prophets to grow so big that he was forced to lower their pedestals to make room for them, and he gave such energy to the nude medallion-bearers that they had soon twisted out of their corners and were overlapping the Genesis scenes. In the final phase, it is thought that he required only about 100 working days to complete a section of the ceiling almost as big as the part he had already taken three years to do.

FOLD OUT: DO NOT TEAR ▶

Ceiling of the Sistine Chapel, 1508-1512

JUDITH AND HOLOFERNES		DELPHICA		JOSIAH		ISAIAH		EZEKIAS		CUMAEA		ASA		DANIEL		JESSE		LIBYCA		THE BRAZEN SERPENT
ZECHARIAH		DRUNKEN-NESS OF NOAH		THE DELUGE		SACRIFICE OF NOAH		TEMPTATION AND EXPULSION		CREATION OF EVE		CREATION OF ADAM		GATHERING OF THE WATERS		CREATION OF SUN MOON PLANTS		SEPARATING LIGHT FROM DARKNESS		JONAH
DAVID AND GOLIATH		JOEL		ZOROBABEL		ERYTHRAEA		OZIAS		EZEKIEL		ROBOAM		PERSICA		SALMON		JEREMIAH		THE HANGING OF HAMAN

OVERLEAF: God creates Adam as Eve watches from the shelter of His arm.

The *Deluge*, a detail of which is shown
here, was among the first of the nine Genesis
scenes to be completed by Michelangelo,
and it may well have had the most personal
meaning for him. Like the people who
flee the rising waters, he had fled the calamity
that Savonarola, in a terrifying sermon 15
years before, had predicted would visit
Florence for its sins. The father holding the
slack body of his dead son, the woman
balancing a table laden with her belongings
on her head, the young man staggering
under the weight of the girl clinging to his
back—all are ridden with anxiety of a kind
that Michelangelo must have known as
the invading French armies, fulfilling
Savonarola's prophecy, swept down on
Florence.

Done at a time when Michelangelo was
worried that painting "still just isn't my
profession," the *Deluge* looks like a
sculptured relief. The figures are small and
tightly drawn, in contrast to the large, freely
rendered subjects that fill later scenes. The
colors, however, are subdued, which was to
be true of the rest of the ceiling. "How
wrong," Michelangelo once said, "are those
simpletons of whom the world is full, who
look more at . . . color than at the
figures which show spirit and movement."

His doubts about himself were
compounded when the *Deluge* refused to
dry. He had no alternative but to scrape off
the fresco and start over again. This was
not the last disaster to befall the painting—in
1797 an explosion in a nearby gunpowder
magazine damaged much of the upper
right-hand portion.

Deluge, detail, 1509   125

Last Judgment, 1536-1541

Whereas the beneficent spirit of God the Creator pervades much of the ceiling, it is the terrible wrath of Christ the Judge that sweeps down through the *Last Judgment*, Michelangelo's later work for the Sistine Chapel. Heroic in size, arm raised in a gesture of damnation, the beardless Christ is the pivot of the composition, a great sun around which the action whirls. The Virgin sits at His side, and saints and martyrs, many with the symbols of their martyrdoms, crowd about Him (Michelangelo caricatured his own likeness among them, on a flayed skin held by St. Bartholomew, seated to the lower left of Christ). Below them, souls drawn to a smaller scale ascend and descend, abetted by wingless angels and clawed demons; while at the very bottom, the dead emerge from their graves, the damned are ferried by Charon across the Styx and the mouth of hell gapes open—right over the altar. In this somber spiritual message, the *Last Judgment* reflects the pessimism

that overtook the Renaissance. The Sack of Rome had occurred only nine years before, and now northern and southern Europe were teetering anxiously on the seesaw of reformation and counterreformation. Michelangelo himself was convinced that "I live in sin, I live dying within myself," and cried out to God, "Oh, send the light, so long foretold for all."

From beginning to end, the *Last Judgment* was as demanding as the ceiling. It required the destruction of frescoes by Perugino and others, as well as two of Michelangelo's own lunettes for the ceiling; the blocking up of two windows; the rebuilding of the entire wall; the erection of a scaffold, from which Michelangelo fell, seriously injuring himself, and six years of labor —two more than the ceiling took. When unveiled, this enormous fresco, measuring 48 by 44 feet, struck its viewers with the impact of a storm—even Pope Paul III fell to his knees in prayer, and all Europe felt its reverberations.

A man dragged down to hell by demons, Charon beating at his passengers with an oar—these are the kinds of tormented and tormenting figures that fill large stretches of the *Last Judgment*. Broader and fuller than even the muscular nudes on the ceiling, they embody Michelangelo's much later style, in which the stress was no longer placed on physical beauty alone. In their very massiveness, they seem to exert a gravitational pull on one another, and yet they remain soft and fluid, a new development in the treatment of the nude. They are depicted moving through space with miraculous ease. Michelangelo's angels do not need wings—they drive through the air under their own power. Nor do they—along with so many of the other figures—need the fluttering draperies they now wear. These were added after Michelangelo's death to placate counterreformation prudes who found their nudity offensive.

Last Judgment, detail, 1536-1541

Last Judgment, detail, 1536-1541

VI

An Age
of Lions

As dynamic an architect as he was a sculptor and painter, Michelangelo designed this dome for the Medici Chapel. In its lightness it seems to be hovering above windows deliberately narrowed to accentuate their upward thrust. From these and the cupola sifts down almost all the light needed to model the sculptured sarcophagi of the Medici Dukes below.

Michelangelo's feelings when Julius died are unrecorded, but among them, it can be assumed, were grief and a sense of loss. For despite their frictions Michelangelo admired the Pope and had a bristly, wary affection for him. He had readily forgiven all the abuse and even the caning, because, as Vasari said, "Michelangelo knew the Pope and was, after all, much attached to him." But mixed with his sorrow, it can also be assumed, was a sense of anticipation, for now the great sepulcher truly was needed and Michelangelo not only could but must work on it. Soon afterward he met with Cardinal Aginensis, Julius' nephew and chief executor, and signed a contract for a structure even grander than the one that had originally filled Julius with such enthusiasm. The number of statues was increased, the time for completion was lengthened from five years to seven, and instead of the 10,000 ducats that Michelangelo had agreed on with Julius, he was to receive 16,500.

From 1513 to 1516 Michelangelo worked on the tomb largely without interruption. During that rare interval of comparative peace he executed three of his most memorable statues. One was the *Moses,* a figure of such elemental force and grandeur that it often has been judged his greatest single sculpture. The others were those since known as the *Dying Slave* and the *Rebellious Slave.* In addition he did much of the architecture and sculptural decoration of the base of the tomb. He was at the height of his powers, and conceivably he might have finished all the major elements of the tomb in the time remaining. But then, in mid-1516, things began to be muddled again, and once more the masterpiece-that-might-have-been was submerged in the "tragedy of the tomb."

Yet once again circumstances were to lead him in circuitous ways to the creation of another grand masterpiece. And, in a reprise of still another theme from the past, the agents of Destiny were the two surviving sons and adopted son of Lorenzo the Magnificent, the same lads, now grown to manhood, who had been Michelangelo's boyhood familiars at the Medici Palace: Giovanni, the one his father had decided was the "clever" boy of the family and for whom he had secured a cardinalate; Giuliano, the "good" boy; and their cousin Giulio, son of Lorenzo's

murdered brother, and also "clever" enough, Lorenzo had decided, to make his career in the Church.

In September 1512, 18 years after the misrule of Lorenzo's firstborn son Piero had driven them all from Florence into exile, the three men had returned to the city—at Julius' wish and supported by Spanish troops allied to the papal armies—and re-established dominion over its government. When Julius died six months afterward, Cardinal Giovanni became Pope Leo X and forthwith made his cousin Giulio a cardinal. Thus the Medici now controlled both Florence and Rome, the two locales of Michelangelo's life and art. For the next two decades his career was to be inextricably bound to theirs. Accordingly, it will be useful to summarize the events that had brought their stars into this strange conjunction so many years later.

After the fall of the House of Medici on November 9, 1494, the four young Medici males had assembled in Bologna. Reports from Florence in the next weeks convinced them that there was no chance for a countercoup by their friends. Moreover, the Signory was offering a rich bounty for the two older sons—4,000 florins for Piero, 2,000 for Giovanni. The outcome of the family council was to send the Medici off on three separate tangents.

Piero set out on his reckless and futile series of attempts to regain Florence by conquest. His youngest brother, the good Giuliano, who was only 15 when the exile began, went to the little mountain duchy of Urbino, a sort of miniature Florence as a center of culture, where his natural gentility made him a welcome guest at the ducal court.

As for Giovanni, "the boy Cardinal," his logical destination would have been Rome. But he had already aligned himself with the faction of cardinals led by Giuliano della Rovere (the future Julius II) against the incumbent Pope, Alexander VI, and he now followed della Rovere's example by boycotting Rome. Accompanied by cousin Giulio and a small entourage of friends and retainers, he embarked on a wandering course through France, Flanders and Germany, where as a Cardinal and a Medici he found ready hospitality at the great abbeys and noble courts. With his horizons much broadened, he returned to Rome in 1500 and established a peace-of-convenience with Alexander. Hence he was on the scene to help secure the election of Cardinal della Rovere to the papacy in 1503. He was then 28, and Julius nearly 60. What began as gratitude and affection on Julius' part for his young supporter developed into a full measure of respect as Giovanni handled a variety of assignments with finesse and intelligence. Finally he came very near to being, in effect, Julius' first deputy, the strong staff of his old age.

Florence had defied Julius during the later military campaigns of his reign by siding with its traditional ally, France, at a time when Julius' policy had turned against the French. When Julius at last won the general victory noted earlier, Florence was at the Pope's mercy: he could impose a new government of his choosing. The choice was obvious. The republic fashioned by Savonarola and Piero Soderini was overturned and the Medici-style republic reinstated—under the control of Cardinal Giovanni, who Lorenzo had long ago foretold would be "clever."

It was another measure of Giovanni's cleverness that he arranged for his "good" brother, Giuliano, to be the first Medici to re-enter the city. When Giuliano had fled as a stripling the Florentines felt only sorrow and sympathy for him; when he returned at the age of 33 he was received, if not with enthusiasm, at least with smiles. Two weeks later Cardinal Giovanni arrived, prudently accompanied by Spanish mercenaries and with all the pomp appropriate to his station as a Prince of the Church. With him, as always, was his cousin and intimate Giulio, efficient, intelligent, and pleasant of manner. And with him, too, was his 20-year-old nephew Lorenzo. As the only son of Piero the Unfortunate, and with a double heritage of Orsini blood (from both his mother and grandmother), he had a background, in the Florentine view, sufficient to produce a congenital monster. But actually he seemed to be a rather glorious youth, handsome and charming and courteous to all. In tandem, the new Medici generation was too much to resist. Giuliano served awhile as "first citizen," then retired to the quiet life he preferred, and young Lorenzo took his place. It seemed very natural, and Florence subsided into a somewhat stunned acceptance of its fate.

After only half a year Cardinal Giovanni had to go to Rome to vote for a successor to Julius II. Against general expectations and somewhat to his own surprise it was he who was elected. He was only 37, a good 22 years younger than the average age of his four predecessors at accession. The frame of mind in which he accepted the honor was reflected in a well-circulated remark he is supposed to have made to his brother Giuliano: "Since God has given us the papacy, let us enjoy it."

And enjoy it he did. As his father had so stamped the Golden Age of Renaissance Florence with his own personality that it became known as the Laurentian Age, so the Golden Age of Renaissance Rome took its name from Pope Leo and passed into history as the Leonine Age.

The spirit of Lorenzo was everywhere evident in Leo's Rome. He subsidized scholars, writers, poets, composers and musicians; imported singers for the Sistine Choir (founded by Sixtus IV) and made it unrivaled in the world; recruited teachers for the University of Rome and founded a college, known as the Medicean Academy, to foster Greek studies. He assigned traveling prelates to seek out classic and Christian manuscripts and buy them or borrow them for reproduction, and he had all the ancient inscriptions in the city copied and catalogued in a great work of archeological scholarship. He continued Julius' program of beautifying Rome, commissioned numerous works of art and, following Bramante's death in 1514, made his special favorite, Raphael, chief architect of the new St. Peter's.

Like his father, Leo did not neglect the pleasures of the people or stay aloof from them. There were pageants and entertainments—even a bullfight in St. Peter's Square—and not even the Florentine *carnevali* surpassed the gaiety of those he staged in Rome. The transfusions of gold and talent filled the city with vital energy. With the waning of the Florentine Renaissance and its new blooming in Rome, there was such a migration from Florence and other northern cities that more than 500 new houses a year were needed. Rome was "the rendezvous of the world."

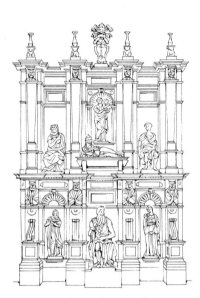

Tomb of Julius II Today

The tomb of Pope Julius II as it exists today
(*above*) is a far cry from what Michelangelo
once had in mind for it. His original
concept, the 1505 version, is shown opposite in
the first of four reconstructions based on
the researches of Charles de Tolnay. This called
for a freestanding tomb, decorated on
all four sides with some 40 figures, including
a *Moses* to be positioned on the right
corner of the second level. The 1513 version
made the tomb over into a wall monument, and
it was for this version that the *Moses* and
the two Louvre *Slaves* were carved; these have
been shaded to indicate their intended
positions. For the 1516 version, Michelangelo
retained the *Moses* and the *Slaves,* but modified
his concept still further—the wall monument
became a mere façade. In the 1532 scheme,
he dropped the *Moses* but included the four
Captives and started the *Victory (shaded).*

Of the seven freestanding statues that
adorn the monument today, only three—the
Moses, the *Leah* and the *Rachel* on the
lower level—are actually by Michelangelo. His
four *Captives* are on display in the Accademia
in Florence; the *Victory* is in the Palazzo
della Signoria. And as a final irony, the
reclining figure of the Pope rests on top of an
empty sarcophagus: Julius' bones were
never moved to his much altered tomb.

The Medicean spirit was equally evident in Leo's tireless attentions to
the welfare of his family. During a peaceful phase in the cyclical friend-
foe, foe-friend relationship of the papacy and France, Leo proposed to
King Francis I that they bind their interests by a marriage between his
brother Giuliano and a French princess of suitable charms, fortune and
royal blood, adding that for the sake of domestic and international har-
mony Giuliano would need a title at least as imposing as his wife's. Francis produced an attractive 17-year-old aunt, Philiberte of Savoy, and a
properly resonant title: in 1515 Giuliano emerged as the Duke of
Nemours.

The next year Leo expelled Francesco Maria della Rovere, who was
Duke of the papal fief of Urbino—and also nephew of Leo's mentor and
predecessor, Julius II—for treasonable activities. He then installed his
own nephew, Lorenzo, as Duke. Two years after that, in another period
of rapport with King Francis, Leo arranged the marriage of the newly
minted young Duke with a French princess, the lovely and rich Madeleine de la Tour d'Auvergne.

These were landmarks: henceforth few Medici would marry on a level
beneath that of high nobility. And the baby daughter born the year following to Duke Lorenzo and his princess was to become the famous
Catherine de' Medici, who would one day marry a King of France and
become the mother of three successive French rulers.

It was, of course, inevitable that Leo should want to enlist Michelangelo to work for the glory of his papacy and the glory of his House. He
had reason to know that Michelangelo was difficult to manage, and was
more attracted personally to the gentle, amenable Raphael. But the fact
remained that Michelangelo was the greatest artist of the age. As a youth,
Leo had spent part of his time away from the Medici Palace studying at
the University of Pisa, but as Pope he found it useful to stretch a point by
saying to friends, "Buonarroti and I were educated together under my
father's roof." If Michelangelo had been engaged on almost any other
project than the tomb of Julius, Leo could have used his papal prerogative to detach him from it. However, in view of his own close association
with Julius and Michelangelo's consuming devotion to the tomb, he had
no decent alternative but to wait. And thus it was that Michelangelo enjoyed the near-miracle of three years of undisturbed work.

It took a whole concatenation of circumstances to end this interlude,
but they can be dealt with in brief. Francesco Maria della Rovere, whom
Leo had removed as Duke of Urbino, was, if anything, even more hot-
blooded than his late uncle Julius. To subdue him Leo had to raise a papal
army which, under Duke Lorenzo's generalship, fought for eight
months before enforcing the papal verdict. Since Francesco Maria's relatives naturally sided with him, the previous friendship between the Medici and della Rovere was embittered. The result was that Leo, however
grateful his memories of Julius, began to take a cold view of the project
that beyond glorifying Julius was bound also to shed a great deal of reflected glory on the House of della Rovere.

In June 1515, a few months after Leo's troubles with Francesco Maria
began, Michelangelo mentioned in a letter to his father that "This sum-

mer I must make a great effort to finish this work [on the tomb] . . . because I think that I shall soon have to enter the service of the Pope." A year later, when the troubles were heading toward their climax, on the initiative of Julius' executors Michelangelo signed a new contract for a much shrunken version of the tomb. The overall size was cut by nearly half and so was the number of statues. Yet the price remained the same, Michelangelo was given an extra two years to finish, and was allowed to do the work anywhere he chose. In return the executors secured his promise not to accept any work that would interfere with the completion of the tomb—a clause hopefully designed to keep him from becoming involved in a new project Leo was then considering.

Project of 1505

As noted earlier, the Medici family church in Florence, San Lorenzo, had been redesigned for Cosimo *pater patriae* by the great architect Brunelleschi. The twin pulpits had been modeled by Donatello and completed after his death by his pupil and Michelangelo's teacher, Bertoldo. The sacristy, which contained the family tombs, was also designed by Brunelleschi. For it Donatello had designed the splendid pair of bronze doors, as well as the tomb of the family patriarch, Giovanni. Verrocchio had executed the tomb of Piero *Il Gottoso*. Lorenzo himself and his brother Giuliano also were buried in the sacristy. Here, in short, in the small compass of church and sacristy, was a shrine to Michelangelo's greatest predecessors among Florentine sculptors, to his old teacher, and to the great patron to whom he owed his start on his own career.

Project of 1513

However, San Lorenzo lacked a façade: as was customary, this had been left to the last, and due to the long exile of the Medici it had remained undone. Thus, although the church was a model of classic perfection in its interior, it still presented to the world a front of drab brick and mortar. Pope Leo had spent part of the Christmas season of 1515 in Florence, prayed in the sacristy and, it is related, wept on his father's tomb. Very soon afterward he decided to build the façade and asked several notable artists and architects to submit plans to him.

Michelangelo heard of the project and sent his own suggestion in the form of a sketch. Leo was delighted with it. He pressed Michelangelo to undertake the work with the help of the architect Baccio d'Agnolo. And Michelangelo accepted, having somehow persuaded himself that he could do the most important pieces of sculpture and superintend the rest of the job without letting this interfere with his work on the tomb of Julius.

Project of 1516

But no sooner had he received notice from Leo that he was to proceed than he had an attack of conscience, and, as Condivi relates, "made all the resistance he could, saying that he was bound to Julius' executors and could not fail them. But the Pope, who was determined in this matter, replied, 'Leave me to deal with them; I will content them' . . . and he sent for them and made them release Michelangelo." According to Vasari, Michelangelo "left Rome with tears in his eyes."

Yet once he was engaged on the San Lorenzo project the inevitable happened. His imagination caught fire, and soon the façade was no longer Leo's—any more than the Sistine vault had been Julius'—but his own. Soon, too, he became dissatisfied with d'Agnolo's contributions and de-

Project of 1532

135

cided—just as he had done in the case of the Sistine ceiling—that if the job was to be done properly he must do it all himself. By July 1517, he had worked himself into such a passion of creation that he wrote to Leo's representative: "I feel it in me to make of this façade of San Lorenzo [a work] such that it shall be a mirror of architecture and of sculpture to all Italy."

Michelangelo spent the next three years on this project—and achieved a total disaster. He insisted on going personally to Carrara to supervise the quarrying of the needed marble. Then the Medici family decided that the stone must come instead from the quarries of Pietrasanta, which had recently been acquired by Florence. The irate people of Carrara promptly conspired to prevent Michelangelo from obtaining barge transport for his marble. He managed to find some boatmen, but had to arrange to have a road built across the mountains to get the stone to port. During this time he fell ill from strain and worry. Added to this calamity, the Arno went dry and the shipment was further delayed. When at last the marble arrived in Florence, Michelangelo returned to the quarries to get more; he was obsessed with the notion that he could not begin work at San Lorenzo until all the materials had been brought to Florence. Of the second shipment from the quarries, four of six huge blocks were damaged either en route or in Florence. Finally, in March 1520, Leo lost patience and canceled the agreement.

Michelangelo was crushed and outraged. Yet the fact was that he had done nothing whatever toward the actual building of the façade. The brick-and-mortar front of San Lorenzo remained exactly as it had been; and so it remains to this day, a blank memorial to the irrational and self-destructive components of Michelangelo's genius.

Despite the fiasco, Leo was not angry; rather, he was saddened and perplexed. Not long afterward Michelangelo's friend and protégé, the painter Sebastiano del Piombo, who had been to Rome to see Leo about a possible commission for himself, wrote that "if you were to come to Rome you could obtain anything you wanted, not castles, but a city, because I know in what esteem the Pope holds you. When he speaks of you, it is, as it were, of a brother and almost with tears in his eyes. He told me that you were brought up together and he made it clear that he knows and likes you, but you frighten everyone, even popes."

The question that presented itself to Leo was not whether to continue to engage Michelangelo, but how to confine his erratic, discursive tendencies and direct his genius toward a feasible goal. Events had already furnished a melancholy answer as to what this should be. The good Giuliano, Duke of Nemours, had died of tuberculosis in 1516, hardly more than a year after his marriage. Madeleine, wife of Duke Lorenzo of Urbino, had died in 1519—a fortnight after giving birth to their daughter Catherine. Lorenzo's robust health had been damaged earlier: some said by profligate adventures during visits to France, others by the winter campaign in the Apennines that had secured his dukedom. In any case it now gave way and in less than a month he too died, at the age of 27.

Leo and Cardinal Giulio decided to build a New Sacristy at San Lorenzo. It would be a mausoleum and memorial chapel to these two

young men and, as well, to the two men for whom they had been named, Lorenzo the Magnificent and his murdered brother, Giuliano: that is, the Pope's and the Cardinal's own respective fathers, whose bodies would be moved from the old Brunelleschi sacristy.

They asked Michelangelo to design the New Sacristy and to carve the funerary monuments. He accepted the commission—which was not, of course, a commission but a labor of the mind and heart.

He worked at it over a period that stretched all the way to 1534—until he was nearly 60—and then left it so incomplete that it is difficult even to guess his final intentions. Apparently he revised continually as he went along, refusing to be bound by his own earlier ideas just as he refused to be bound by the ideas of his patrons. As the critic John Pope-Hennessy has observed, "With Michelangelo nothing was settled until it was finally carved." As to why he did not finish, the reasons are woven into the fabric of his life and are related in the next chapters. What matters, after all—and matters enormously—is what he actually did manage to do.

The New Sacristy itself was meant to balance Brunelleschi's Old Sacristy, and Michelangelo therefore made it nearly a twin in its outer structure. The interior, however, with its solemn harmonies and soaring lines, is a spiritually moving work of sculpture in itself, as well as a perfect setting for the sculptures it contains. There are seven of these figures by Michelangelo's hand: a *Madonna and Child,* the four allegories called *Dawn* and *Dusk* and *Night* and *Day,* and the statues of Lorenzo and Giuliano de' Medici. The latter are not—as many visitors to the sacristy assume—Lorenzo the Magnificent and his brother Giuliano but Dukes Lorenzo and Giuliano. In fact, the elder Lorenzo and Giuliano are memorialized only by modest inscriptions on the marble slabs above their grave crypts. It is one of the strangest and most perverse ironies of Michelangelo's life that he should thus have immortalized the lesser Medici and done nothing for the memory of his great patron, Lorenzo the Magnificent. The reason was simple: because the younger men had died recently and the grief felt for them was still fresh, the Medici had decided that their tombs should be done first; and before he could even begin the others Michelangelo, as will be detailed later, had to leave Florence.

Yet, incongruous though the priority given the young Dukes may seem, it is saved from absurdity by the fact that their statues are really not effigies of them at all. We have the explanation from the Florentine poet Niccolò Martelli, who had it from Michelangelo, that he felt no need to show them as they were because a thousand years later the question of what they had looked like would be of no importance to anyone. Instead he used them as an artistic device for the creation of allegories which, for the sake of convenience, have come to be known as the Contemplative Life and the Active Life, but which are so profoundly rich in meanings, so evocative and yet so mysterious, that no titles suffice. Every beholder brings to them the thoughts that lie deep within himself. The titles are not important because the statues are not those of any two men who ever lived but representations of all mankind, and deal with the ultimate theme: the nature and destiny of the human soul.

San Lorenzo, Wooden Model

San Lorenzo Today

The façade of the Medici church of San Lorenzo, which Michelangelo planned to make "a mirror of architecture and of sculpture to all Italy," remains to this day a rough wall of jagged brick and eroding mortar *(bottom).* How it might have looked had Michelangelo been able to follow through on his project is suggested in part by the wooden model *(top),* which puts classical motifs in serene counterbalance to each other. More than a screen to conceal the unequal heights of the nave and aisles, the façade was to have been a three-dimensional structure, almost a building in its own right, with its surface brought brilliantly alive by reliefs and statuary.

The House of the Dead

Although far from finished, the Medici Chapel in Florence's church of San Lorenzo is in its own way as important a monument as the Sistine Chapel in Rome, expressing through its sculpture and architecture some of Michelangelo's deepest insights into death and immortality. Even as he was working on it his father and his favorite brother died. Their deaths appeared to him the final blows in a long succession of troubles, born of the alarms, anxieties and intrigues of the period, which had left him, still only in his fifties, convinced that he was in the autumn of his life. "My powers are small, I am old," he said once. Yet out of the struggles of this period emerged "firm faith." "By thine own death . . ." he wrote of his father in a poem, "I learn to die."

The Chapel, or New Sacristy as it is sometimes called, as first conceived was to have contained a single, free-standing tomb in the center. But what Michelangelo eventually did was to make the Chapel the tomb. Thus it is a place of blank windows and blank doors, a palace façade behind which no one lives, a house of the dead aspiring heavenward, in which marble figures like that of Duke Lorenzo (opposite), rather than the people who come to see them, seem like the real inhabitants. For here, as Michelangelo intended, is time at work—"time which consumes all things."

Chin resting on hand, Lorenzo, Duke of Urbino, in an idealized portrait represents the thoughtful life. Michelangelo ignored the Duke's beard, long nose and bulging eyes, to give him, as one critic has said, "the image of his immortal soul in the existence beyond the grave."

Tomb of Lorenzo de' Medici, Duke of Urbino, detail, 1520-1534

Raphael: *Pope Leo X with Cardinal Giulio de' Medici (left) and Luigi de' Rossi,* c. 1518

Raphael: *Giuliano, Duke of Nemours*, c. 1515

Bronzino: *Lorenzo, Duke of Urbino*, c. 1540

The Crowded Medici Tombs

The Medici Chapel, shown in the drawing above, was the first of Michelangelo's architectural projects actually to be built. Although modest in size compared to St. Peter's, it gives full expression to his dynamic concept of a building as a living organism with muscles and bones of its own which continuously act and react on one another. Here the forces in opposition are the plain stucco walls, edged in dark stone, and the elaborate architecture of the wall tombs, carried out in a style entirely Michelangelo's invention. Vasari found the Chapel so original that he credited it with having freed architects from their bondage to the past.

The portraits reproduced on these pages show the men most intimately connected with the Chapel. Michelangelo's patrons, Pope Leo and Cardinal Giulio, can be seen in the Raphael opposite. It was their intention that Michelangelo design tombs for their fathers, Lorenzo the Magnificent and his brother Giuliano, and for their young relatives, Duke Giuliano *(above, left)* and Duke Lorenzo *(above, right)*. But when Michelangelo left Florence for good in 1534, only the ducal tombs had been designed —with the result that the older men today lie all but ignored in a *cassone,* or chest, opposite the altar. In the tomb on the left is Duke Giuliano; Duke Lorenzo is in the one on the right, sharing it—a fact not generally known—with Duke Alessandro, the Moor *(right)*. Ironically, it was this tyrannical despot's rise to power that forced Michelangelo to flee the city, leaving the Chapel unfinished, and it was Alessandro's murder in 1537 that provided a reason for finally assembling the tombs. After the young Dukes were transferred to the Chapel, the body of the despised Moor was unceremoniously placed on top of Lorenzo's remains.

Bronzino: *Alessandro, First Duke of Florence*, c. 1540

Tomb of Giuliano de' Medici, Duke of Nemours, 1520–1534

F acing each other, the ducal tombs are flanked by empty niches in which
Michelangelo planned to put standing nudes; river gods were to have reclined
at the bases. And yet so powerful an effect did he achieve that nothing
seems to be missing: in their serene setting, the tombs speak movingly of death.
On the sarcophagus of Duke Giuliano *(above)*, the allegorical figures of *Night*
and *Day* rest uneasily, grieving over the Duke, whose death "has stolen

Tomb of Lorenzo de' Medici, Duke of Urbino, 1520–1534

the light from us." Almost mirror images of *Night* and *Day, Dusk* and *Dawn*
on Duke Lorenzo's sarcophagus also seem overwhelmed by sorrow.
The anguish of these figures, expressing awareness of life's transiency, contrasts
with the calm acceptance of the Dukes seated in the niches. Michelangelo
turned their heads away from the site of their mortal remains and toward
a reminder of eternity—the statue of the *Madonna and Child* on the far wall.

Perhaps no two of the many works to have come from Michelangelo's hand have stirred more controversy than *Night* and *Dawn,* which seem to have as many detractors as they do admirers. In their massiveness and muscularity, these oversized allegorical nudes hardly look like women at all, and it is true that Michelangelo used male models for them. His concern here, however, was not with beauty or delicacy of form but with power. Both figures had to stand for concepts larger than reality—just as the mighty figure of Duke Giuliano, dressed as a Roman emperor and seated in the niche above *Night,* was intended not to represent his likeness in life but his soul in death. Yet, for all their masculinity, even *Night* and *Dawn* are undeniably voluptuous in their languid contours. Rubens, painter of some of the world's most voluptuous women, was quick to recognize this—he made a detailed, appreciative sketch of *Night.*

Dawn, 1526-1531

The fitful sleep of *Night* is accentuated by the emblems of darkness all around her: a crescent moon and star in her diadem; a flint in her hand, source of her own destruction at the first spark of dawn; and the owl and leering satyr's mask shown here. The owl, sheltered in the crook of *Night's* bent leg, is an obvious creature of darkness, and here it seems to be raking with its talons a garland of poppies, suggestive of opium and drugged sleep. The mask, with its sockets—"horrid and black" in Michelangelo's line, "the portent of time"—is perhaps a less obvious symbol. But its full sensuous lips and nightmare grin may indicate that Michelangelo intended it to suggest an incubus, an evil spirit that people believed swept down upon women in their sleep. What meaning, if any, the gap-toothed, grimacing grotesques *(below)* may hold is not clear. Running in a narrow band behind the sarcophagi of both Dukes, they may well stand for the horrors of death.

The Laurentian Library

Just as he never finished the Medici Chapel, Michelangelo left undone his other architectural project in San Lorenzo: the library for the Medici collections of books and manuscripts. When he left Florence for good, the library lacked, among other things, its extraordinary staircase. Years later Vasari asked Michelangelo what he had had in mind for the stairs so the library might be completed. Michelangelo replied, "I recall a certain staircase, as it were in a dream, but I do not think it is exactly what I thought of then, because it is a clumsy affair." Pressed for details, he came up with a description; in time, he prepared a clay model for the builder to work from and sent it off in a box to Florence.

Never was there a staircase like this one, so entirely the product of a sculptor's imagination that it suggests, in its extreme plasticity, a lava flow. To climb it is to feel somehow impeded, as though advancing against a current—upward through the towering vestibule that exerts a peculiar pressure of its own, with walls that seem almost to be swelling out beyond the paired columns set back in recesses. But relief comes in the more than 160-foot-long reading room behind the double door *(above)*, a scholar's retreat with its light, subdued architecture, rows of carved desks and rich parquet floor.

VII

A Tyranny
of Tombs

Begun when Michelangelo still had
high hopes for the Julius tomb, the
Dying Slave (left) and the *Rebellious
Slave* express, in their tortured poses,
a vain struggle for freedom. As
the project dragged on, however,
even these figures, so close to
completion, were abandoned and
Michelangelo came to regard himself
as the slave of the tomb.

Dying Slave, 1513–1516
Rebellious Slave, 1513–1516

In the year 1520 Michelangelo became forty-five years old. In his own
mind, his letters show, he was already an "old man"—weary, prone to
illness, abused by life, haunted by the premonitory shadow of death. The
fact was, of course, that he would live on robustly into his 90th year:
at 45 he had literally just reached middle age. And in several ways this
time, which saw the end of the futile period of the San Lorenzo façade
and the beginning of the fertile period of the Medici tombs, acted as a
kind of hinge not only of Michelangelo's life-span but of the circumstances of his life.

Leonardo da Vinci, his old rival, died at the age of 67 in May 1519.
Raphael, his young rival, died at the age of only 37 in April 1520. Thus,
of the trio of towering geniuses whose names together define the High
Renaissance, Michelangelo alone remained: so literally alone, so far beyond comparison with any living artist that simply by continuing to exist and work he dominated the arts and molded them in his own image.

In 1521 Pope Leo died—probably of the "Roman fever," malaria,
though there were lurid stories of poison. Rome was stunned at his passing, and the historian Paolo Giovio said: "Knowledge, art, the common
well-being, the joy of living—in a word, all good things—have gone
down into the grave along with Leo." But while Leo had made Rome
the most cultivated city of Europe, he had spent at such a rate that he
not only drained the papal treasury but left it 400,000 ducats in debt.

Consequently, directly after his death, Cardinal Giulio, as the new
head of the House of Medici, put a halt to all of Leo's undertakings—
suspending but not canceling them—and kept the suspension in force
throughout the pontificate of the next Pope, a Netherlander who took
the name of Adrian VI. With the San Lorenzo project thus held in abeyance, Michelangelo resumed work on the tomb of Julius.

But then Adrian also died, after reigning only 20 months. He had been
a devout, plain-living man who "loved poverty," disapproved of classical statues as "idols of the pagans" and in general viewed the secularized
papacy of Leo, Julius, Alexander *et ante* with almost the pious horror of
Savonarola. As a result, he made himself thoroughly despised in Rome.

In his 89 years, Michelangelo lived to see the reigns of 13 Popes. They are listed here with their papal names and crests, and their family names and cities.

SIXTUS IV 1471–1484
Francesco della Rovere
Savona

INNOCENT VIII 1484–1492
Giovanni Battista Cibò
Genoa

ALEXANDER VI 1492–1503
Rodrigo Borgia
Valencia

PIUS III 1503 (10 days)
Francesco Todeschini-Piccolomini
Siena

JULIUS II 1503–1513
Giuliano della Rovere
Savona

LEO X 1513–1521
Giovanni de' Medici
Florence

ADRIAN VI 1522–1523
Adrian Florensz
Utrecht

CLEMENT VII 1523–1534
Giulio de' Medici
Florence

PAUL III 1534–1549
Alessandro Farnese
Rome

JULIUS III 1550–1555
Giovanni Maria Ciocchi del Monte
Rome

MARCELLUS II 1555 (3 weeks)
Marcello Cervini
Montepulciano

PAUL IV 1555–1559
Gian Pietro Carafa
Naples

PIUS IV 1559–1565
Giovan Angelo de' Medici
Milan

One of Leo's dispossessed artists tried to stab him; later he barely survived poisoning. When he died it was assumed he had been murdered—but, again, the real culprit probably was an infected mosquito.

This brief brush with austerity made the College of Cardinals treasure Leo's memory all the more. In the next papal election they sought his nearest equivalent in his cousin and virtual alter ego, Cardinal Giulio de' Medici, who, in November 1523, became Pope Clement VII. It was an immensely popular choice, especially among artists, writers and scholars; Michelangelo wrote that he thought the election "will rejoice everyone. I expect that as far as art is concerned many things will be executed here."

He had always been more at ease with Giulio-Clement than with Giovanni-Leo. He and Giovanni were temperamentally so unlike that they could never reach an empathic understanding. But Giulio, being somewhat sensitive himself, could penetrate Michelangelo's moodiness and accept his intense individualism. He forgave him his trespasses, sympathized with his difficulties, and tried to find productive release for the fierce energies of his genius. In turn, Michelangelo was devoted to him, though never awed by him. "Whenever Buonarroti comes to see me," Giulio once observed after he became Pope, "I always ask him to sit down, because he certainly will, without leave or license."

With a new Medici in the papacy work could be renewed at San Lorenzo. So once again Michelangelo put aside the tomb of Julius, but by this time apparently without really great regret. Further, he soon learned that Pope Clement wanted him to design the Laurentian Library in Florence—and this, for strong reasons of personal sentiment, was another offer that could not fail to appeal to him.

Needed to house the great Medici collection of classical and early Christian manuscripts, the library was another long-contemplated family enterprise. Clement resolved to have a structure ample enough for present needs and future growth, and the most appropriate site for this, he decided, would be the cloisters of San Lorenzo. These adjoined the church and comprised a large rectangular lawn and garden enclosed by a lovely loggia, with arches and columns in Brunelleschi's classical style. The library would be built over one side of the cloisters, and entrance to it would be up a grand staircase from the loggia.

Michelangelo's first official knowledge that he was to be the architect came from an old friend, Giovanni Fattucci, a chaplain of the cathedral of Florence, who was in Rome on church business and while there was acting also as his personal agent. Hence Michelangelo's letter to Fattucci in January 1524: "I learn from your last that His Holiness Our Lord wishes the design for the Library to be by my hand. I have no information about it nor do I know where he wants to build it . . . I will inform myself . . . and will do all that is in my power, although architecture is not my profession." That he accepted such an additional very large commission on such a vague basis reflects not only his feeling for Clement and for the library but his still apparently unreformable willingness to pile great project on great project. And before long this latest surrender to an old weakness produced a new harvest of trouble. For the past had arisen, ghostlike: the "tragedy of the tomb" was ready to resume.

The rambunctious Francesco Maria della Rovere, who, as noted earlier, had been ousted as Duke of Urbino by Pope Leo, had been reinstated by Pope Adrian in 1523. By then the time limit specified by the della Rovere family for completion of Julius' tomb had passed—and Michelangelo was still far from finishing. Consequently the Duke prepared to sue him to force him either to complete the tomb or return all the money that had been advanced to him, plus interest, plus damages. Adrian's death and the accession of a new Medici Pope inhibited but did not deter the intrepid Francesco Maria: by the following spring he was again brandishing the suit which, if successful, would have meant Michelangelo's financial ruin. Since Clement had meantime added the library to his other assignments and was pressing him to work full speed at San Lorenzo, Michelangelo found himself trapped between the rival demands of Pope and Duke. He decided he must go directly to Clement in Rome and plead to be extricated from the jaws of this conundrum.

Clement was sympathetic, but rather than overrule the Duke's claims arbitrarily arranged for the whole matter to be examined by the Duke's representatives and Michelangelo's friend Fattucci. After some months these negotiations reached a stalemate, the suit was revived, and Michelangelo sank to new depths of despair. He wrote: "I don't want to go to law. They can't go to law if I admit that I'm in the wrong. I'll assume that I've been to law and have lost and must pay up. This I'm prepared to do. . . . As an intermediary, [the Pope] might express his desire that I repay what I have received . . . so as to free me from this burden, and to enable the relatives of Pope Julius to have it made by any master of their choice. . . . As it is, worries hardly let me live, let alone work."

Thus the grand dream of his young manhood had become the "burden" of his middle age; the work he had passionately yearned to do he now desperately yearned not to do.

Eventually, agreement was reached in principle that he would finish the tomb but that it would be of a different style and on a still more reduced scale: a sort of sculptural façade including only half a dozen figures by Michelangelo. And even this arrangement depended on Duke Francesco's approval of the new design that he would prepare.

It took Michelangelo a year to deliver the design—and the Duke, seeing it, vehemently did *not* approve. Michelangelo, fearing "ruin and disgrace" unless the Pope rescued him, wrote: "I desire to free myself from this obligation more than to live . . . I am completely out of my mind." But by then it was too late for anything to be settled. For meanwhile a disaster had been brewing that would devastate both Rome and Florence, end the High Renaissance, and pit Michelangelo and Clement against each other as enemies. Finally, in the aftermath, it would drive Michelangelo from Florence forever. To see how this chain of disasters developed, it is necessary to refer again to the hinge-time around 1520.

Clement, and Leo before him, had long nursed a careful if covert plan for the future of the House of Medici. This plan was nothing less than to end the Republic of Florence and formally install the Medici as its hereditary rulers. Death, however, had intervened to shatter this dream by striking down young Lorenzo and Giuliano-the-good—the only

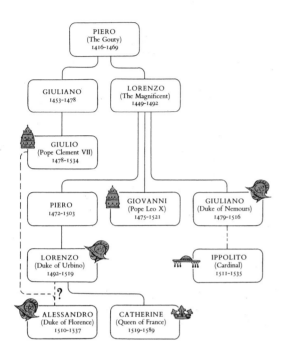

The phenomenal rise to power of the
descendants of Piero de' Medici is shown in
this abbreviated genealogy, with symbols
designating the lofty positions attained by
various members of the family. A tiara stands
for the papacy, a helmet for a dukedom,
a broad-brimmed hat for a cardinalate and
a crown for a throne—in this case, the throne of
France, achieved by Catherine de' Medici
through her marriage to the future Henry II.
The broken lines indicate illegitimacy, with
the question mark underscoring the confusion
that still persists over whose son the
bastard Duke Alessandro actually was
—Pope Clement VII's or Duke Lorenzo's.

male laymen of the senior Medici line and thus the only feasible founders
of a dynasty. Since the family had always followed the custom of male
primogeniture, with the chieftainship of the House passing from oldest
son to oldest son, it was Lorenzo who had been the pivot of the dynastic
plan. But he had left no male heir—only the infant Catherine de' Medici
—and the marriage of Giuliano had been childless.

Thus, at the very summit of its power, the House of Medici suddenly
faced an equivocal future. The two untimely deaths had occurred when
Leo was still Pope and the future Pope Clement was still a Cardinal and
Archbishop of Florence. Leo needed time to ponder the situation and accordingly sent Cardinal-Archbishop Giulio to Florence to take over the
city as interim "first citizen." Giulio proved himself to be extremely
good in the role, which he filled from 1519 to 1523. But when he in his
turn became Pope he confronted the difficult problem of who should
succeed him at Florence. His answer, after some hesitation, was to intro-
duce to the startled Florentines not one but two bastard Medici boys.

Their very existence had been almost unknown except within the im-
mediate family and a small circle of trusted aides. Clement, however,
confided so few of their vital statistics that then and for long afterward
there was uncertainty as to how old they were and which was the elder.
Their mothers were not identified—and have not been to this day. Ippolito, an exceptionally handsome and winning lad of about 13, was the son
of the good Giuliano, Duke of Nemours, by a woman of Pesaro or possibly of Urbino. Alessandro, who was about 14, was presented as the son of
Duke Lorenzo of Urbino. However, as Schevill has written: "If Ippolito's birth was enveloped in uncertainty, Alessandro's has remained an
impenetrable mystery. His villainous disposition coupled with his dusky
skin, Negroid lips and crisp hair caused people to regard him as a monster and to put faith in the unsubstantiated rumor that his mother was a
Moorish slave. Nor was that the worst of the whispers . . . Clement VII's
manifest preference of the 'monster' over . . . Ippolito lent credence to
the opinion . . . that, instead of his being the bastard son of Lorenzo, he
was in point of fact the bastard son of the Pope."

Neither bastardy nor racially mixed blood was necessarily a handicap.
In a famous example cited by the historian Jacob Burckhardt, when Pius II
passed through Ferrara he was met by "eight bastards of the [ruling]
House of Este . . . among them the reigning Duke Borso himself and
two illegitimate sons of his illegitimate brother and predecessor Lionello.
The latter had also a lawful wife, herself an illegitimate daughter of Alfonso I of Naples by an African woman. The bastards were often admitted
to the succession where the lawful children were minors and the dangers
of the situation were pressing; and a rule of seniority became recognized,
which took no account of pure or unpure birth. The fitness of the individual, his worth and capacity, were of more weight than all the laws
and usages which prevailed elsewhere in the West. It was the age, indeed,
in which the sons of Popes were founding dynasties."

Nevertheless, legitimate children had preference, and there was some
social disadvantage in being a bastard. A common slang term for them
was "mule"—a hybrid, in-between product, with the imputation that

such a child was the product of a mating between a gentleman and a woman of inferior station. The Florentines took it as a rude shock when these two young mules suddenly were produced from nowhere, manifestly to be groomed as their rulers. They did not at all like what they saw and heard of Alessandro. And they soon developed a fine loathing for Cardinal Passerini of Cortona, whom Clement appointed the boys' guardian and thus in effect the interim "first citizen" of Florence, and who suffered from the defects of boorishness and open avarice. Resentment grew and needed only the right opportunity to overflow into revolt.

The opportunity came in May 1527 when word reached the city that the army of Charles V, King of Spain and Emperor of the Holy Roman Empire, had captured Rome and was besieging Clement in the Castel Sant'Angelo, his fortress near the Vatican.

This calamitous event was the culmination of a pair of major and by now familiar themes of Italian life: one the chronic struggle between France and Spain for dominance in the affairs of the Italian peninsula, and the other the chronic efforts of the popes to protect and extend their own secular possessions, which had involved them in playing the contending powers against each other. Leo had allied himself with the Spaniards to fight the French, who had become too strong. But in the latest round, Spain had won so overwhelmingly that Clement feared it would dominate the papacy and engulf the papal territories. Therefore he had entered into a secret coalition with France and some of the Italian states to war on Spain; and Charles V, learning of this cabal and deciding the Pope was its ringleader, took advantage of a delay in the French invasion to send an army to deal with him before the French could arrive.

I t was a raggle-taggle army of Spaniards, Italians and German mercenaries who were interested primarily in loot. However, the Germans, who comprised over half of the force, included many followers of the fiery reformer Martin Luther; they had an extra interest in entering Rome for the pleasure of despoiling churches and abusing Catholic clergy. The so-called Imperial army arrived at the gates of Rome on May 4, 1527, and in only two days broke the defenses and came storming into the city. Clement and his aides fled to the Castel Sant'Angelo, leaving the Vatican and its treasures at the mercy of the rabble soldiery. The Vatican loggias designed by Bramante and decorated by Raphael became a barracks, the Sistine Chapel a stable. For the next eight months the Pope and his small band were first besieged, then held prisoner in their citadel, while—in Symonds' evocative words—they "watched smoke ascend from desolated palaces and desecrated temples, heard the wailing of women and the groans of tortured men, mingling with the ribald jests of German drunkards and the curses of Castilian bandits. Roaming those galleries and gazing from those windows, Clement is said to have exclaimed in the words of Job: 'Why died I not from the womb? Why did I not give up the ghost when I came out of the belly?'"

This was the Sack of Rome—done under the banner of the Holy Roman Emperor—an ordeal as steeped in destructiveness as Rome had ever suffered at the hands of the earlier so-called barbarian hordes.

The news of Rome's and Clement's catastrophe reached Florence on

May 11. When the first shock subsided, the Florentines knew what they must do. And Cardinal Passerini also knew what he must do. On May 17 he and his two young wards quietly vanished from the city. Immediately the Florentines revived the republican constitution they had created 33 years earlier at the time of the previous Medici exile. Then, as they watched events develop, their jubilation chilled and they began to see to their military defenses.

Technical advances during recent decades had outmoded the city's old fortifications. Clement himself had begun remodeling them in 1525, assisted by the advice of, among others, the one-time Florentine Secretary of War, Niccolò Machiavelli. Now these works needed to be improved and extended for defense against Clement—for it was virtually certain he would try to reassert Medici control in Florence as soon as he found a way out of his troubles with Emperor Charles V. At the moment he was still at Charles's mercy, but he was not powerless: most of the other rulers of Europe had been scandalized by the Sack of Rome and were bringing pressure to bear on Charles. Actually Charles himself had been nearly as shocked: he disavowed the deeds of his undisciplined hirelings, but his conscience was sore and he was looking for a way to make amends and to refurbish the papal dignity. Negotiations for a settlement had begun; consequently so had Florence's military preparations.

For Michelangelo the situation presented a painful choice of loyalties. His life and fortunes had been intimately bound up with the Medici. He owed them much, and Clement had enlarged the debt. He had settled a lifetime pension of 50 ducats a month on Michelangelo and given him a house rent-free near San Lorenzo; had interceded several times to keep the della Rovere heirs at bay; had borne with his foibles and delays on the Medici library and tombs and insisted on providing him with first-rate assistants to relieve him of details; had cautioned him to preserve his health and to refrain from worry ("Fear not that you will ever want for work or rewards while we live," he had written in 1525, signing the note not with his papal signature but simply "Giulio"); and in a hundred other ways had shown the great affection and esteem he felt for Michelangelo. And Michelangelo had responded gratefully to this warmth, writing in 1525 to Fattucci that "I will always go on working for Pope Clement with such powers as I have, which are slight, as I am an old man."

Nevertheless, he volunteered his advice and services to the Signory in the work of refortification. Since Michelangelo never explained himself afterward, romantics have interpreted this decision and his activities in defense of Florence to suit their own preconceptions. As de Tolnay has said: "His behavior is regarded by some as proof of his great Italian patriotism, of his republicanism, of his violent hostility toward the Medici —and he is cast in the mold of a national hero. . . . In fact Michelangelo, even though he was a Florentine republican, never repudiated the Medici . . . his notion of freedom did not apply to the *popolani,* the lower orders . . . he was an aristocrat, and proud of his noble birth, seeing in it a special virtue. All of which means that Michelangelo's political attitudes cannot be understood according to modern ideas. They were dictated not so much by reason and interest as by feeling and instinct."

As we have seen, it was entirely possible to be both pro-republican and pro-Medici, provided the incumbent Medici operated with skill and discretion within the republican forms and with a proper display of republican spirit. To Michelangelo, Lorenzo the Magnificent probably had represented very nearly the republican ideal. There is no reason to suppose that later on he disliked the regimes of either the younger Lorenzo or Cardinal Giulio as "first citizen," and in fact most Florentines apparently had been fairly content with them. Accordingly, the most reasonable explanation for the revolutionary discontent which erupted in 1527 was that it grew from Clement's incredible tactlessness—a well-nigh amnesic lapse in his understanding of the Florentine psyche—when he tried to solve the Medici dynastic problem: the arbitrary way in which he imposed the bastards Alessandro and Ippolito; the appointment as his personal representative in Florence of the Cardinal of Cortona, who was something of a scholar but no gentleman; and not least, the character of young Alessandro, who emerged ever more clearly as Clement's choice as future head of the House of Medici, and who seems to have exuded a baleful quality that only a father who was a Renaissance Pope could love. The Florentines rebelled against Clement because, in the foregoing circumstances, they had smelled—correctly—the intention of tyranny.

Michelangelo had always steered clear of political affairs; he felt he had better things to do with his time. Nevertheless, it seems obvious that *despite* his long-standing allegiance and gratitude toward the Medici in general and, recently, especially toward Clement, he had come to believe that the return of Clement's two "mules" truly would jeopardize the republic. If it were to be a choice between the Medici and the republic, he must as a man of conscience choose the republic.

In any case, once he had made his decision a familiar characteristic came to the fore: he became wholly absorbed in the defense of Florence, enveloping it in the giant embrace of his passions and intelligence and attempting to make it all his own. He progressed rapidly from the status of volunteer adviser to membership at the beginning of 1529 on "The Nine"—the board in charge of the city's military preparations. That April, the Signory appointed him "Governor and Procurator-General over the construction and fortification of the city walls, as well as every other sort of defensive operation and munition for the town of Florence," at the pay of a golden florin a day.

As to the design of fortifications, Michelangelo could have said in fullest truth what he had said consecutively about bronze sculpture, fresco painting and architecture: "It is not my profession." However, so great had his reputation grown as an invariable producer of masterpieces no matter what the medium that the Signory had no misgivings; and this time, apparently, neither did he. De Tolnay notes: "He drew a series of magnificent large plans for the fortifications of the walls and gates . . . [which] by their originality and ingenuity, marked a decisive turning point in the history of the architecture of fortification. . . . By means of diagonal and curved walls [he] devised a system which ensured that the artillery fire of a besieging army could only attack the walls obliquely. . . . These designs also have artistic beauty; conceived as they were by a

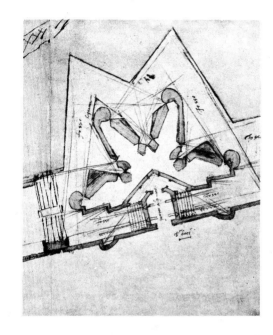

How Michelangelo rose to a new challenge as chief of Florence's fortifications is shown by this drawing made shortly before he assumed that office. In this bastion to be built at one of the city's gates, he gave the moated walls (shaded) bold curves, apparently to reduce the shattering impact of cannon balls. Even more important, he made them reach out toward the enemy—thus enabling the defenders to shoot at their besiegers from any angle, and to lay down a blanket of cross fire (faint bisecting lines). Ingenious though they were, not one of the dozen or so bastions Michelangelo proposed for the defense of Florence was ever built.

sculptor's imagination, they have the organic character of living creatures, and look rather like the silhouettes of crustaceans, with their long antennae."

The designs were so far ahead of their time that, in fact, they were not accepted by the city's leaders. In the same way their lack of understanding nearly prevented his major strategic contribution, the fortifying of the hill of San Miniato. This lies directly across the Arno, and from it, as Michelangelo soon realized, enemy artillery could devastate the city. Yet this key position never had been fortified and Michelangelo found, to his consternation, that his superiors in the government were lukewarm about his plans for doing so now. In the first weeks of June they sent him—to distract him from his work at San Miniato, he suspected—to inspect the fortifications at Pisa and Livorno and along the Arno.

On June 29, Pope Clement and Emperor Charles came to terms on a peace treaty that confirmed the worst apprehensions of the Florentines. Charles put an Imperial army at Clement's disposal. They agreed that when Florence was subdued, the republic would be abolished and Florence and Tuscany would become a Medici dukedom, with the bastard Alessandro as Duke. To seal the bargain, Charles pledged that Alessandro would have for his bride in proper course (she was still only seven) his own illegitimate daughter Margaret.

The Florentine government continued to delay the work at San Miniato and at the end of July sent Michelangelo to study the fortifications at Ferrara, whose Duke Alfonso was Italy's greatest expert both on artillery and fortifications. Thus Michelangelo finally met the man who two decades earlier had converted his statue of Pope Julius (*sans* head) into the famous bronze cannon *La Giulia*. In an aggravating oversight none of the chroniclers of the time, not even the gossipy Vasari, mentions whether Michelangelo saw *La Giulia* or Julius' head or whether he and the Duke had anything at all to say to each other about the peculiar fate of the statue. However, Condivi does report that "The Duke received him with great demonstrations of joy. . . . There was nothing appertaining to the business of his mission which the Duke did not bring to his notice. . . . Besides this, he opened his own private treasure-room, displaying all its contents, and particularly some pictures and portraits. . . . The Duke jestingly said to him, 'You are my prisoner now. If you want me to let you go free, I require that you shall promise to make me something with your own hand, according to your will and fancy, be it sculpture or painting.' Michelangelo agreed; and when he arrived at Florence, albeit he was overwhelmed with work for the defenses, he began a large piece . . . representing the congress of the swan with Leda."

Almost immediately, however, there came a new and unexpected turn of events. Rumors of treason reached Michelangelo; quiet inquiry brought him to the shocking suspicion that the chief traitor was none other than the man the Signory had hired as commander-in-chief of the defending forces, the *condottiere* Malatesta Baglioni, kinsman of the same Perugian ogre whom Pope Julius had brought to heel. Suspicion became near-certainty when he found that Baglioni had mounted his guns not within but below the bastions of San Miniato and that, moreover, he had

not even set men to guard them. Condivi relates that Michelangelo "approached the Signory and laid before them what he had heard and seen. . . . Instead of receiving thanks for this service, he was . . . rebuked as being timorous and too suspicious. . . . When Michelangelo perceived how little his words were worth, and in what certain peril the city stood, he caused one of the gates to be opened, by the authority which he possessed, and went forth with two of his comrades, and took the road to Venice."

The flight of the "Governor and Procurator-General"—*molto disordinatamente,* "in great confusion," as he later admitted—left Florence thunderstruck. He himself soon supplied the explanation in a letter from Venice to his friend Battista della Palla. After remarking that he had been "quite resolved, and without any sort of fear, to see the end of the war out," he went on: "But on Tuesday morning, September 21, a certain person came . . . where I was attending to the bastions and whispered in my ear that, if I meant to save my life, I must not stay in Florence. He accompanied me home, dined there, brought me horses, and never left my side till he got me outside the city, declaring that this was my salvation. Whether God or the devil was the man, I do not know."

The man, according to the Florentine historian Varchi, was Rinaldo Corsini, a respected city councillor, and what his true motive was is still unknown. Baglioni—who naturally had learned of Michelangelo's denunciation of him to the Signory—may well have planned to dispose of such a dangerous outspoken enemy. On the other hand it was well known that Michelangelo was prone to nervous suspicions, unreasoning alarms and sudden panic, and that more than once he had fled from what he believed were threats to his life; thus Corsini may have been a provocateur sent by Baglioni or someone else who wanted to discredit him.

In any case the episode ended not too unhappily. Della Palla pleaded with Michelangelo to return and sent along letters from 10 other friends urging the same. He did return late in November. The siege of the city by the Imperial-papal army had already begun, but the roads on the northern side were still open and he was able to enter through a northern gate. The Signory extracted a forced loan of 1,500 ducats from him and banned him from membership in the Grand Council for three years, but revoked the much more severe penalties it had imposed on him as a deserter. It even reinstated him as chief designer and builder of fortifications.

The siege brought dreadful hardships to Florence, but it held out for 10 months. Michelangelo's fortifications at San Miniato never were breached: the enemy commander decided instead to starve the city out. Even so, it was not this that finally brought surrender but the treachery of its chief defender—Baglioni, who fulfilled Michelangelo's warning on August 3, 1530. Nine days later Florence capitulated.

Clement, who had regarded the revolt and resistance as a supreme perfidy, had been storing up his anger for more than three years. Most leaders of the resistance were imprisoned, often with benefit of torture, and many were executed, among them Michelangelo's friend della Palla. Michelangelo, of course, had reason to fear Clement's wrath. Not only had he been a member of the Nine and chief of fortifications, but a story (a false one) was widely circulated that he had proposed demolishing the

Medici Palace and renaming the site on which it stood the "Place of Mules."

For weeks Michelangelo stayed in hiding. Then came the surprising denouement, described by Condivi: "When Clement's fury abated, he wrote to Florence ordering that search should be made for Michelangelo, and adding that when he was found, if he agreed to go on working at the Medicean monuments, he should be left at liberty and treated with due courtesy. On hearing news of this, Michelangelo came forth from his hiding place, and resumed the statues in the sacristy of San Lorenzo, moved thereto more by fear of the Pope than by love for the Medici."

Clement nevertheless gave every sign of being moved by love for Michelangelo. Within weeks he had seen to it that Michelangelo was again receiving his 50-ducat monthly pension. A few months later, responding to some apprehension of Michelangelo's, his friend Sebastiano del Piombo wrote from Rome: "One letter to your friend [the Pope] would be enough; you would soon see what fruit it bore. . . . A father could not say of a son what he does of you. It is true that he has been grieved at times by buzzings in his ear about you at the time of the siege of Florence. He shrugged his shoulders and cried: 'Michelangelo is in the wrong; I never did him any injury.'"

M oreover, when in its cyclical fashion, like some dread disease, the matter of the tomb of Julius was raised again in 1531 by Duke Francesco Maria, and Michelangelo in desperation offered to give back the studio-home mentioned earlier, refund 2,000 ducats besides, and have the Duke hire other sculptors to finish the tomb, Clement vetoed the offer as too generous. That autumn Michelangelo's health broke down from overwork and worry. Clement fired a papal brief at him ordering him to take care of himself and stop working so hard—under pain of excommunication. "The best remedy" for his nervous despondency, an intermediary suggested, "would be if His Holiness could accommodate matters with the Duke of Urbino." By the following spring Clement had done so. On April 29, 1532, with the Pope presiding, and in the presence of a glittering assemblage of high dignitaries, a new contract for the tomb of Julius was signed at the Vatican by Michelangelo and agents of the Duke.

In the massive, drawn-out history of the tomb this agreement is known as the Third Contract; actually, it was the fourth, counting the original oral arrangement between Julius and Michelangelo. Under this contract, Michelangelo was required to supply six statues by his own hand, and models or drawings for five other statues to be carved by other sculptors. Clement would allow him to come to Rome to work on the tomb two months a year for three years. Like the tomb itself, the grandiose idea of making it the centerpiece of the new St. Peter's had undergone attrition. Among the alternate sites that had been considered, the one now chosen definitely was the rather small church of San Pietro in Vincoli ("St. Peter in Chains") which had been the titular church of Julius' cardinalate.

"In this way the thing was settled for the time," Condivi goes on to relate, "but it did not end there; for when [Michelangelo] had worked . . . in Florence and came back to Rome, the Pope . . . ordered him to paint the wall above the altar in the Sistine Chapel. He was a man of excellent

judgment in such matters, and had meditated many different subjects for this fresco. At last he fixed upon the Last Judgment. . . ."

In a reign filled with errors and troubles innumerable, Clement's unwavering support of Michelangelo was one of the few redeeming satisfactions. He could scarcely have derived much gratification from an event which took place the same month as the signing of the Third Contract, though it was one he had no less zealously supervised. He formally established the bastard Alessandro as Duke of Florence, thereby bringing five centuries of Florentine republicanism to an end. Knowing the character of this strange being to whom he was handing over the city, Clement must have carried a heavy burden of conscience to his grave.

For Alessandro, a "monster" in youth, had become even more brutish in young manhood: tyrannical, flagrantly licentious, glorying in every violence and sordid vice, irrational and unpredictable in his sudden passions and particularly his hates. For reasons never well explained—Condivi simply refers to "old grudges"—his feeling toward Michelangelo was especially venomous. And Michelangelo in turn was frankly terrified of him. "He remained in continual alarm," says Condivi, "because the Duke, a young man, as is known to every one, of ferocious and revengeful temper, hated him exceedingly. There is no doubt that, but for the Pope's protection, he would have been removed from this world."

Nevertheless Michelangelo continued to work in Florence, so far as his involved circumstances would allow. The last time he saw Clement was in the fall of 1533, when the Pope was en route to Marseilles to perform his last public act: the marriage of his niece, Catherine de' Medici, to the future Dauphin of France, King Francis I's 14-year-old second son, Henry; Catherine, by now a lively girl of 14, was destined to become the most powerful Medici of them all, and perhaps the greatest single influence in instilling the arts and graces of the Italian Renaissance in the aristocratic society of France and hence the culture of Europe.

In the spring of 1534 Clement's health began failing. When the realization grew that his death was not far off, Michelangelo knew that Florence, his "nest," could become his trap. The two human relationships that had bound him to the city had already been broken. His favorite brother, Buonarroto, had died of plague in 1527; then in 1531 had come the death of his father Lodovico, that querulous, demanding, ungrateful old man whom Michelangelo had never stopped trying to please.

Unobtrusively, therefore, without farewells and even without instructions to his assistants about the work ahead at San Lorenzo—where the two Dukes, the brooding *Night, Day, Dawn* and *Dusk*, and the unbearably sad *Madonna* were strewn at random around the sacristy floor amidst debris and marble dust, waiting to be finished and placed on the Medici tombs—he made his arrangements to leave Florence.

At times in the past, his protective Destiny had seemed over-protective; but not now. Michelangelo arrived in Rome on September 23, 1534. Two days later Pope Clement died, ancient and defeated at the age of 56. Condivi, recording what Michelangelo himself had believed, wrote: "It was certainly by God's aid that he happened to be away from Florence when Clement died." He never saw Florence again.

The Magnificent Failure

The Julius tomb, on which Michelangelo labored intermittently for 40 years, is often called his greatest failure—and indeed, it would seem difficult to understand how a man so deeply conscious of his duty and his own artistic integrity could allow himself to fall so short of his original conception. Why had he not abandoned the project altogether and spared himself the misery it brought him? The contracts which bound him made this all but impossible, true; but certainly important too was his grandiosity—his own tendency to thrive "on precisely what kills others." In his bondage to the tomb, as in other things, Michelangelo was for a long while like the giant of one of his poems, who, yearning for sun, sought lofty towers on which to stand to reach for it.

But when at last the project came to its final stage, Michelangelo had become an old man for whom the only truth was God, and the elaborate tomb of his early imagination must have seemed vainglorious indeed. Yet, anticlimax that it is, it does not represent failure in a broader, spiritual sense. In the works which Michelangelo carved for it—many of them discarded —there is a stirring record of his pilgrimage. While the *Moses* speaks for the almost divine nature of the sculptor's power and his identification with the spirit, the four *Captives* still trapped within the marble tell of his awareness of the body as "the soul's dark prison."

Moses, described by one critic as "a cataclysm made man," sits at the foot of the Julius tomb, tablets under his muscled arm. Instead of having light beams radiating from his head, a the Old Testament describes him, he has horns—reflecting a mistranslation, in the Latin vulgate, of the Hebrew word for "light."

Moses, c. 1513-1515

Michelangelo made the *Moses* a penetrating character study, rather than portraying the prophet and lawgiver at some historic moment in time. The intelligent face with its intense gaze, furrowed brows and tightly set lips proclaim him to be a man of action, power and potential wrath; the strong and sensitive hand *(above)*, by contrast, bespeaks the more relaxed and contemplative side of his nature—here Moses seems almost to be stroking his beard. And although the figure is seated, it fairly explodes with movement: the torrent of beard flows from cheek to waist, the thick robes cut across legs and chest in broad folds and creases, the pulsing veins bulge through the skin as they wind down arms and hands. Yet despite the almost flamelike agitation these details give to the work, there is also a certain quiet to it, the same action-in-repose which marks the colossal *David.*

The *Moses* belongs to the period in Michelangelo's career as a sculptor when it was important for him to display his technical virtuosity. All the parts are absolutely perfect, exquisitely controlled, finished to the last detail—in marked contrast to the *Captives* shown on the following pages, whose unpolished surfaces and vague outlines point the way to the soft modeling of Michelangelo's late, far more personal, style.

Youthful Captive, 1530-1534   *Atlas*, 1530-1534

The constant struggle between physical and spiritual forces that was
so much a part of Michelangelo's driving genius is beautifully expressed by four
unfinished statues, the *Captives,* meant for an early version of the tomb
and then abandoned. They seem to be battling to free themselves from the
rough-hewn stone, pressing out from within, as the force that drives through
them flexes their muscles to the breaking point. And yet they are bound

Bearded Captive, 1530-1534   *Awakening Captive, 1530-1534*

by the dimensions of the block, and it is likely that even if Michelangelo had
finished them, he would have retained in their shapes a hint of their stone
prisons. They even offer a clear demonstration of how the sculptor worked: he
would advance through the marble in so many parallel planes, almost
as though he were peeling off layer upon layer of superfluity in search of the
figure he had already seen in his mind's eye lying locked inside.

VIII

Architect
to the Ages

"In the record of the Florentines," Ferdinand Schevill concludes in his great history of Florence, "there clearly is something akin to what, vaguely enough, we call genius when manifested by an individual. Genius falls where it chooses to fall; it is given and taken away. . . . With the heroic spasm culminating in the siege of 1530 . . . the spirit or genius or soul of Florence—call it what you will—took its departure."

In somewhat the same way, the Sack of Rome and the evil events leading to and stemming from it afflicted "the spirit or genius or soul" of the whole Italian Renaissance. For it undermined Renaissance man's strongest sustaining faith, his belief that humanity had at least the potentiality of being able to control its own destiny. Added to the Imperialist assault, the Sack, and the bloody months of the Occupation, Rome had had to contend with two virulent outbreaks of plague. The combination of malignant Nature and malignant human nature, equally senseless and uncontrollable, killed or dispersed some two thirds of the Roman population and made the Renaissance "discovery of the world and of man" a horror rather than an inspiration.

The decline of the era was not something that happened suddenly, of course. Rather it was a wasting process that took place over a number of decades, and during these years the splendid works produced in Florence, Rome and Italy suffered only by comparison with the past. When Michelangelo left Florence in 1534, the city's future still held, for instance, the marvelous bronze *Perseus* of that roustabout genius Benvenuto Cellini, the sculptures of Giambologna, the portraits of Bronzino and the phantasmic drawings of Pontormo. And Rome, during the pontificate of Clement's successor, Pope Paul III, enjoyed a brilliant—if transitory—burst of creative energy. As sometimes happens in fatal illnesses, the Italian Renaissance had a period of euphoria before the end finally came.

And again Michelangelo's life moved along in peculiarly apt concordance with the circumstances of time and place. When he settled in Rome he was nearing 60: his energies declining, self-doubting, half-sick of himself and the world. But like the era itself he was propelled by the force of his own momentum, and he had noble works yet to perform.

The Campidoglio, designed as a civic center by Michelangelo a year before he began his work on St. Peter's, crowns the Capitoline Hill, which Romans considered to be the axis of their world. As though to dramatize its symbolic meaning, Michelangelo gave the square a radiating, starlike pavement.

Again it was a Pope who was his patron, protector and to some degree his persecutor. Paul III was the former Cardinal Alessandro Farnese, member of an old Roman family. His sister, the golden-haired Giulia, had notably advanced the Farnese cause not only by marrying an Orsini but—so it was said, probably rightly—by becoming the mistress of Pope Alexander VI and having a child by him; the irreverent called her *la sposa di Cristo,* "the bride of Christ." Supposedly it was to Giulia's bedchamber diplomacy that her brother had owed his cardinalate, and for years he was known as *il cardinale della gonnella,* "the cardinal of the petticoat."

Nevertheless Paul III had remarkable qualities of his own. Learned, a brilliant conversationalist, a connoisseur, he was at the same time a tough-minded realist and man of action. He was 66 when elected, but he had one of the longest reigns in history, 15 years—a period which spanned fully half of the remaining years of Michelangelo's own life.

Michelangelo had known Paul as a Cardinal and liked and respected him, but he had no intention of working for him. Ever since 1505, when Julius had first summoned him to Rome, he had not been able to call his life his own; he had had enough of popes, and his one desire now was to discharge his obligation to the implacable Duke Francesco Maria by finishing the tomb of Julius. Through one of the contracts he had become owner of a substantial house, with grounds and outbuildings, in Rome. He had a large studio there containing the *Moses,* the two *Slaves* and other portions of the tomb in various stages of completion; here, too, apparently, he had done a good deal of preparation for the *Last Judgment* before Clement died. He was no longer so addicted to feverish habits of work, and he had grown away from his disordered mode of life. He still lived frugally (although by now he was comfortably wealthy) but on a dignified scale; he paid attention to his person, dressing neatly in good linens, fine Cordovan leather boots of his own design and well-fitted jacket and trousers, the jacket usually of black damask. He had acquired a sense of decorum; and although tranquillity was not in his nature, he did want peace and independence. But then, as Vasari wrote:

"Pope Paul III soon summoned him . . . and said he wished the master to enter his service. Michelangelo excused himself, saying he was under contract to the Duke of Urbino. . . . Paul was much displeased. 'For thirty years I have wished this! And now that I am Pope, will you disappoint me? That contract shall be torn up. I will have you work for me, come what may.'" Condivi adds that Paul "one day . . . visited Michelangelo at his house, attended by eight or ten Cardinals . . . and having gone through the whole workshop, renewed his request. . . . When Michelangelo still resisted, he clinched the matter by saying: 'I will provide that the Duke . . . shall be satisfied with three statues from your hand, and the remaining three shall be assigned to some other sculptor.'"

As things turned out not even Paul found it possible to cut that briskly through the incredible complexities of the tomb. It will suffice to note that Duke Francesco Maria died and that his son Guidobaldo, perhaps because he was courting the Pope's niece, proved easier to deal with and fulfilled Paul's promise; and that because of the still-more-shrunken scale specified by the new Fourth Contract Michelangelo decided to substitute

for the two *Slaves* two smaller Old Testament figures, *Leah* and *Rachel*. The tomb of Julius was unveiled at San Pietro in Vincoli in February, 1545—four decades after Michelangelo had begun it.

"And so the Tragedy of the Tomb came at last to an end . . . though, truth to tell, it is but a mutilated and botched-up remnant of Michelangelo's original design," Condivi wrote, adding in an excess of loyalty, "the monument is still the finest to be found in Rome"—wishful thinking that Michelangelo did not share. He was ashamed of it, yet, after so many years of bearing its curse, almost beyond caring. And so also, it would seem, were Julius' heirs, for Julius' body lies beside that of his uncle Sixtus IV in the chapel of the Blessed Sacrament in St. Peter's. The so-called tomb of Julius by Michelangelo is empty.

But the end of the tragedy of the tomb was unknowable in 1535, and Michelangelo found himself swept along by Paul's admiration and imperious insistence. That September the Pope issued a brief declaring Michelangelo to be the world's foremost sculptor, painter and architect and putting him in charge of those arts at the Vatican, at a lifetime income of 1,200 golden ducats a year. Paul addressed him as a peer, and Michelangelo once remarked to a friend, "Sometimes, I may tell you, my important duties have given me so much license that when I am talking to the Pope I put this old felt hat nonchalantly on my head and talk to him very frankly, but he does not eat me up on that account."

Within months of Paul's election to the papacy, Michelangelo was engaged once more on the *Last Judgment:* the fresco was unveiled on Christmas Day, 1541. A few months later he began work on a pair of frescoes, the *Conversion of St. Paul* and the *Crucifixion of St. Peter,* for the new Pauline Chapel at the Vatican. These took eight years, until 1550, to finish. In the interim, in 1547, the Pope had named him architect-in-chief of St. Peter's. Along with all this, at Paul's behest he drew plans for the redesign of Rome's ancient and blighted Capitoline Hill—the Campidoglio. Between times Paul also involved him in the reconstruction of the fortifications of Rome and in the completion of the vast new Farnese family palace.

In short, what might have been an embittered decline into old age turned out to be a glorious autumn of life for Michelangelo—on the whole the happiest span of years since his youth. The reason lay partly in Pope Paul's affection and unswerving confidence, but even more in the satisfactions of close friendships.

Michelangelo had never been the terrible-tempered troglodyte his enemies liked to portray. It is true that in his blackest moods he was, to put it plainly, impossible, and at such times he seemed almost to take a savage satisfaction in being unloved and unlovable. Yet he somehow stirred the protective instinct in people; they wanted to take care of him. They loved him; and it should be emphasized that this word, which in our times causes nervous embarrassment if used to describe the feelings of two men toward each other, was then a quite customary term for the affection that might exist between men.

For a great many years Michelangelo's commitments to friendship had been limited by his obsessive commitment to his art. Now, however, ad-

Michelangelo in his eighties is portrayed on the front of this medallion, made for him as a gift by the sculptor Leone Leoni. The relief on the back showing a blind beggar being led by a dog may have been executed from a drawing supplied by Michelangelo; the beggar's features bear a resemblance to the artist's. The significance of the motif may be simply this—that man is a helpless thing guided by faith alone.

Medallions enjoyed a vogue during the Renaissance since they could be given as keepsakes to friends. Michelangelo was so pleased with the medallion that he reputedly gave Leoni in return a wax model of one of his own works, *Hercules and Antaeus.*

vancing age, personal griefs, and the failure of so many of his hopes put him in such need of solace as he had never felt before. On settling in Rome, as Rolland remarks, "He was in a condition of great mental unrest, his heart hungry for love. This was the period of those strange, violent and mystical passions for beautiful young men like Gherardo Perini, Febo di Poggio and, most loved and most worthily so, Tommaso dei Cavalieri. These attachments . . . were an almost religious delirium of love for the divinity of beauty and hold an important place in the work of Michelangelo. It is to their inspiration that most of his love poems are due. For a long time this was either not known or a stupid and unfortunate attempt was made to conceal it."

Most of these poems were written for Tommaso dei Cavalieri, whom the historian Varchi describes "as a young Roman of very noble birth . . . [with] not only incomparable physical beauty, but . . . elegance of manners . . . excellent intelligence and . . . graceful behavior." The only portrait Michelangelo ever did was of Tommaso—a life-sized drawing. The poems were not published until some 60 years after Michelangelo's death, by his grandnephew and namesake, and in the severe counterreformation atmosphere he was so afraid they would damage his uncle's reputation that he pretended they had been written to a woman.

It is entirely possible, as some psychiatrically oriented scholars believe, that Michelangelo had emotions which he sublimated in his works of art. It is also possible, of course, that if he had such emotions they may at some time have become overt. But there is no real evidence that this was so. Symonds' analysis of the love poems still stands: "This one idea predominates: that physical beauty is a direct beam sent from the eternal source of all reality, in order to elevate the lover's soul. . . . Carnal passion he regards with the aversion of an ascetic." In short, the key to the poems, as to so much else in Michelangelo's art, is the Platonism he acquired in boyhood at the court of Lorenzo.

The foregoing comments help considerably in our understanding of the *Last Judgment,* a strange and difficult scene by any measure. Michelangelo's lifelong preoccupation with the nude—the body as the temple of the soul, the idealized male body as a Platonic symbol of man's innate nobility—had produced seeming mysteries and incongruities beginning even with his first painting, the *Doni Tondo.* Although the subject of that work is the Holy Family, five well-formed naked youths loll in the middle distance with the ease of Greek heroes in the Elysian Fields and—lacking the Platonic key—with shocking irrelevancy. Again, in the Sistine ceiling frescoes, there are the 20 puzzling *Ignudi:* muscular, godlike youths sitting at the corners of the "histories" in a variety of attitudes and moods. For centuries the consensus was that their function was simply decorative. But a newer theory is that they symbolize the thoughts of the prophets and the sibyls who sit below them contemplating the ways of God and men, and thus are an organic link between these seers and the histories. They are nude because, for Michelangelo, the human body was an instrument for expressing the *concetto* or "inner idea" of all experience from Genesis to the Last Judgment.

Michelangelo's portrayal of the latter scene teems with hundreds of

nude forms—so intervolved and conveying such a range of violent emotions that for all its immense size it seems suffocatingly crowded. In the time of Julius and Leo, probably few would have found anything morally objectionable in this swirl of naked saints and sinners, but by the late 1530s the mood was changing. Pope Paul's Master of Ceremonies, Biagio da Cesena, declared the work more fitting for a public house than for a temple of the Lord. Michelangelo retaliated by putting Biagio in the picture—in deepest hell, horned and wearing nothing but a venomous serpent around his body. Biagio complained to the Pope; but Paul thought the riposte a fine joke and replied, "Had the painter sent you to purgatory, I would use my best efforts to get you released; but I exercise no influence in hell; there you are beyond redemption."

Not many years later, the reformist Pope Paul IV (very unlike Paul III) sent an aide to Michelangelo to express his objections to the nudity in the *Last Judgment*. Michelangelo replied: "Tell His Holiness that this is a small matter, and can easily be set straight. Let him look to setting the world in order; to reform a picture costs no great trouble." As a result the Pope, with Michelangelo's consent, commissioned one of Michelangelo's assistants, Daniele da Volterra, to paint draperies over the intimate parts of a number of the figures—which won for Daniele the nickname of *Il Braghettone,* the breeches maker. Under later popes others continued this decorous work, to the gain of modesty but little else.

In the context of Michelangelo's life as a man and an artist, the *Last Judgment* is significant for two other matters, one being the "inner idea" that he brought to the subject from the depths of his own changing personality, the other being the different style he used to express this idea.

As noted earlier, Michelangelo's religious outlook was compounded of Christianity and Platonism. He was not an intellectual, and he never sorted the components of his beliefs into a systematic philosophy, but from his works it is apparent that for a long time the Platonist elements predominated. In the *Last Judgment* the Christian elements are strongly asserted. Here in all its poetic horror is Dante's Inferno; here is the Apocalypse in the Doomsday voice of Savonarola; and here are the consciousness of sin and the panicky dread of death that had sent him—at least a half dozen times—into headlong flight from real or imagined assailants. He had nursed these feelings most of his life. Now, in this final period of his life, they would increasingly rule his thoughts.

What brought the change? Age itself, of course, with its heightened awareness of the inevitable end; the lengthening list of deaths among relatives, friends and patrons; the tragedies that had overtaken Florence and Rome; and particularly his relationship with Vittoria Colonna.

With Tommaso dei Cavalieri, he had broken through the constraints of native shyness and habitual reserve and given himself heart and soul to a human relationship. Now the happy miracle of loving and love-requited happened also with her. So far as is known she was the only woman he ever loved, and hence in her he concentrated all his potential but unarticulated love for women—although again this is not to say that he was either "in love" or consciously felt a physical attraction. She herself was a poetess, and he in turn expressed himself to her in some of his finest son-

Although Michelangelo looks remarkably young for one so old in the medallion shown opposite, the artist apparently saw himself otherwise. In a poem written when he was still in his seventies, he provides a self-portrait, not untinged by a wry sense of humor:

"I have a voice like a hornet in an oil jar . . .
My eyes are purplish, spotted, and dark.
My teeth are like the keys of an instrument,
for by their moving the voice sounds or falls still.
My face has a shape which strikes terror.
My clothes are such as chase crows to the wind . . .
A spider-web lies hidden in my one ear,
while all night long a cricket chirrups in the other."

nets and madrigals. But being more visual artist than poet he expressed himself too by making some of his most eloquent drawings for her.

A woman of intellectual substance who also took pleasure in being a hostess, Vittoria liked to convene little gatherings of friends for informal conversations. She once arranged a series of such meetings on Sundays in the gardens of the convent of San Silvestro, inviting Michelangelo and a few others, including a visiting Portuguese miniature artist known as Francisco d'Ollanda. Francisco made notes and later reconstructed the conversations in his book, *Dialogues on Painting*—and to this we owe many of the frankest spontaneous opinions of Michelangelo recorded anywhere. A few samples will give the flavor.

On the public's uncomprehension of artists: Artists are reputed to be "eccentric in their habits, difficult to deal with, and unbearable; whereas, on the contrary, they are really most humane." However, "I dare affirm that any artist . . . who has nothing singular, eccentric, or at least reputed to be so, in his person, will never become a superior talent."

On "solitary habits": "What claim by right do you have [on a man who prefers solitude]? Why should you force him to take part in those vain pastimes which his love for a quiet life induces him to want to shun?"

On art: "The science of design, or of line-drawing, if you like to use this term, is the source and very essence of painting, sculpture, architecture. . . . Sometimes . . . it seems to me that . . . all the works of the human brain and hand are either design itself or a branch of that art."

On style: "A lofty style, grave and decorous, [is] essential to great work."

On being facile versus being good: "It is . . . useful to be able to work with promptitude. . . . [But] a good artist ought never to allow impatience to overcome his sense of the main end of art, perfection. . . . The one unpardonable fault is bad work."

Vittoria Colonna, the noblewoman with whom Michelangelo had one of his closest relationships, is shown in a woodcut from a book of her poems. Their closeness was based upon an appreciation of what each considered to be the other's worth. She saw Michelangelo as an individual to be valued more highly than his works, and compared him even to Christ. "You follow the example of the Savior," she wrote, "like Him, you cast down the proud and raise up the lowly." But Michelangelo saw her simply as "a man, a god rather, inside a woman."

Of all the products of their friendship, the most important was the effect that Vittoria had on Michelangelo's religious thinking. She was among the prominent liberal Catholic intellectuals who were influenced by Protestant ideas but who strove to reform the Church from within. Ever since her widowhood in 1525, when she was 35, she had spent much time in semiseclusion, latterly in convents; her poems on religious themes were admired throughout Italy. She and Michelangelo had met about 1536—when he became fully occupied with the *Last Judgment*—and there was opportunity for her influence to be reflected in that work. Manifestly it was. She believed ardently, and from now on, so did he: what had been simple Christian piety took fire. She had once written, "Christ comes twice: the first time . . . he only shows his great kindness, his clemency and his pity. . . . The second time he comes armed and shows his justice, his majesty, his grandeur and his almighty power, and there is no longer any time for pity or room for pardon." Among the millions of words that have been written about the *Last Judgment*, the emotions it conveys have never been better summarized.

Vittoria Colonna died in 1547. By then Michelangelo had begun to try to accustom himself to the idea of death. But while preparing for his own, he was not prepared for hers, and it came as a dreadful blow: after-

ward, Condivi noted, "recalling her death, he often remained dazed, as one bereft of senses."

The *Last Judgment,* a turning point in Michelangelo's philosophy, was a turning point in his artistic style as well and to a substantial degree in the style of the Cinquecento. Between it and the frescoes of the Sistine vault there is only a cousinly relationship: they seem almost to have been fathered by different artists. Spaciousness versus a cramped design, serenity versus agitation, richness without clutter versus confusing overabundance—the list of contrasts could go on, but perhaps it is enough to say that style had turned into stylization. Everything is exaggerated, including the basic tool of Michelangelo's art, the nude form, now idealized to the point of distortion. In all its complexities, the *Last Judgment* sounded a knell for the calm classicism of High Renaissance art and signaled the coming triumph of its stormy successor style, Mannerism.

B y the time Michelangelo finished Pope Paul's next assignment, the two Pauline frescoes, he was 75. They were his last pictures, and, as Vasari wrote, were "painted . . . as he told me himself, at cost of great fatigue. Painting, and especially in fresco, is not for old men." Nor is sculpture. Michelangelo continued always to have a piece of some sort in progress, but he no longer had the stamina to undertake commissions.

For more than a decade he worked on a marble Deposition from the Cross that he intended for his own tomb. Among the group of four figures, the one commonly called "Nicodemus" (properly, Joseph of Arimathea), whose "old sad face, surrounded by the heavy cowl, looks down forever with a tenderness beyond expression," probably is Michelangelo himself. Unfinished, this *Deposition* now stands behind the high altar of Florence's cathedral, under Brunelleschi's great dome—and fittingly so. For of course this vast dome had been the familiar sight of Michelangelo's apprentice years, when he had roamed the streets of Florence and drunk in the experience of art and dreamed of being himself someday a great artist. And it was while he was planning the dome of St. Peter's, for which the Brunelleschi dome was the inspiration and in part the structural model, that he was also carving his monument.

Michelangelo had tried to refuse Pope Paul's appointment as chief architect of St. Peter's, and had been summarily overruled. Even as decades earlier he had had to abandon the cartoon of the *Cascina* fresco at Julius II's summons, so he had had to suspend work on the second Pauline fresco to heed Paul III's command. And besides these coincidences of the interrupted frescoes and the similar temperaments and arbitrariness of the two Popes, there was, of course, another that will be remembered: it was because of Michelangelo's design for the tomb of Julius—on such a scale that there was no church to contain it—that Julius had decided the new St. Peter's should be built. Now Michelangelo was himself to be its builder: his work had come full circle.

In effect St. Peter's would be his to build because, during the intervening 40-odd years, construction had been sporadic, and amounted to little more than a good beginning. Thus the plan was open to change—and Michelangelo's first act, after inspecting the wooden scale model of the design by his predecessor, Antonio da Sangallo, was to change it back to

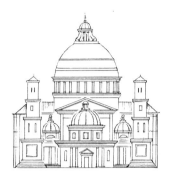

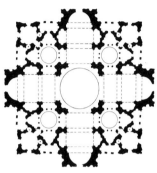

How two of Michelangelo's predecessors envisioned St. Peter's is shown by these ground plans and façades. Bramante's church *(above)* was to have been laid out as a Greek cross within a square, and the exterior would have been alike on all four sides. Sangallo's plan *(below)* swelled Bramante's plan beyond recognition—with ambulatories curving around three of the arms, a wide entrance hall appended to the fourth and an elaborate façade flanked by tall bell towers.

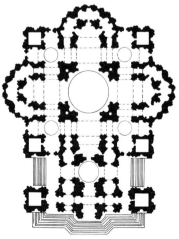

the design of his old enemy Bramante. His feelings toward Bramante had not mellowed; it was simply that he honestly recognized the superiority of this design—a Greek cross surmounted by a vast central dome—over all the ones that followed; and these had been as many as there had been chief architects, beginning with Bramante's kinsman and chosen successor Raphael. However, while keeping Bramante's concept, inevitably, once his interest was engaged, he treated it according to his own architectural ideas. And it is a measure of Michelangelo's inner coherence, despite his often erratic-seeming outward behavior, that these came from precisely the same source that had governed his painting and sculpture: his veneration and masterful understanding of the human body.

As he once wrote: "The members of an architectural structure follow the laws exemplified in the human body. He who . . . is not a good master of the nude . . . cannot understand the principles of architecture." The concept may seem strange; yet it was because he was so accustomed to thinking in terms of the human organism—not of arms and legs and separate members, but of the living form—that he was able to bring to his structures a unique sense of organic unity and true functionalism. As the architectural historian James S. Ackerman says, there is even "an implication of mobility; the building lives and breathes," and it was this that made him "one of the greatest creative geniuses in the history of architecture," and that was his all-important contribution to St. Peter's.

With a constantly deepening piety added to his usual obsessiveness, Michelangelo attacked his task with a holy zeal and disregard for obstacles that were truly awesome. And since his usual intolerance of imperfect workmanship, materials and artistic standards increased in the same ratio, he made many more enemies much more quickly than usual.

Sangallo, the late chief architect, had spent some 30 years on the planning and construction of the basilica. Consequently Michelangelo inherited a human apparatus made up of people who had a vested interest in the work in process and the many commercial and official relationships involved. They were offended when he discarded the Sangallo plan, shocked when he tore down the completed parts that interfered with his own design and outraged when he denounced a number of them as thieves, canceled contracts and fired supernumeraries. Cardinals and high Vatican officials had close ties to the "sect of Sangallo," as Vasari called it, and the Pope found himself deluged with complaints and malicious gossip about Michelangelo.

Paul's response, finally, was to issue a papal brief which began "Forasmuch as our beloved son, Michael Angelo Buonarroti, a Florentine citizen, a member of our household, and our regular dining-companion, has remade . . . in a better shape, a model or plan of the fabric of the Basilica of the Prince of the Apostles in Rome . . . we hereby approve and confirm the aforementioned new design. . . . Moreover, trusting in the good faith, experience and earnest care of Michael Angelo himself, but above all trusting in God, we appoint [him] . . . for as long as he shall live. And we grant him . . . authority to change, re-fashion, enlarge, and contract the . . . building as shall seem best to him . . . without seeking permission . . . from anyone else whatsoever."

Having affirmed his trust in God and Michelangelo, Paul died within the month. Michelangelo wrote: "I have suffered great sorrow, and not less loss. . . . God willed it so."

Michelangelo had served four popes; he would serve three others before he died—Julius III, Paul IV and Pius IV. The Sangallists continued to attack, forcing a new crisis with each of these papacies. Each time they were defeated: all three Popes reaffirmed "the diploma of Paul."

From these dramas one small scene provides a perfect vignette of The Artist as Divinity. In 1551, soon after Julius III became Pope, the Sangallists persuaded him to convene a meeting at St. Peter's, attended by Michelangelo, the supervisors and workmen, and the "Deputies of the Fabric," an administrative board made up of noble citizens and high churchmen. Cardinal Marcello Cervini, an influential deputy and a Sangallist sympathizer, charged that Michelangelo had made no provision for letting light into the church from the side apses and that without this the structure would be a gloomy cavern. Michelangelo, according to Vasari, "explained that there would be windows in the vaulting of the apses. 'You never told us anything about that,' said the Cardinal. Michelangelo responded: 'I am not obliged to tell Your Lordship or anyone else what I do or intend to do. Your business is to provide the money and to see that it is not stolen. The building is my affair.'

"Michelangelo's spirited self-defense increased the Pope's love," Vasari finishes, "and he invited him to the Villa Giulia [his personal villa] where they held long discourses upon art."

There was a sequel to the story. When Julius III died four years later he was succeeded by none other than Cardinal Cervini—Pope Marcellus II. The Sangallists rejoiced, but—Providentially—Marcellus II was gathered to heaven after only 23 days and was succeeded by Paul IV, who (despite his objections to the nudities of the *Last Judgment*) "received Michelangelo most amiably" and left him in full charge of St. Peter's.

During the brief, unfriendly interregnum of Marcellus II he had very nearly decided to go back to Florence. The monstrous Alessandro was long since dead, stabbed in his bed one night by a young member of the "junior branch" of the Medici whose name—save the mark—was Lorenzo de' Medici. Known as Lorenzino—"little Lorenzo"—he was the grandson of the Lorenzo Popolano who supposedly had put the young Michelangelo up to making the false antique *Sleeping Cupid*. In honor of Lorenzino's tyrannicide, Michelangelo took time off from the *Last Judgment* to carve his only portrait-bust, the powerful, symbolic *Brutus*. Alessandro died without issue. The other bastard Medici, his cousin and possible rival Ippolito, who had been made a Cardinal by Clement, had died 18 months before—poisoned by Alessandro, it was assumed. There were no more males left of the senior branch of the Medici, and the succession passed automatically to the junior branch. Lorenzino himself was the eldest male of this line, but fearing the vengeance of Alessandro's henchmen he had fled to Venice. Shortly, his 17-year-old cousin Cosimo arrived in Florence to claim the vacant ducal throne for himself.

The Florentines regarded him in pleased wonderment. His name reminded them of Cosimo *pater patriae* of sainted legend. He was tall and

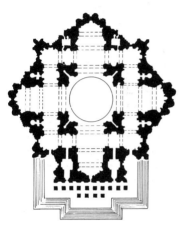

Michelangelo's plan for St. Peter's (*above*) reverted to Bramante's concept of a Greek cross, but simplified it. His exterior, however, represented a complete departure from Bramante's scheme. Instead of being symmetrical on all four sides, it was to have had, as in Sangallo's plan, a distinct façade, a portico. As the focus for the overall design, the dome rising above the portico would have dominated St. Peter's Square—which is not the case today, since a long nave was later added behind which the dome gradually disappears as visitors approach from the front.

handsome and a fine athlete. He had a fascinating ancestry: his father had been a celebrated *condottiere,* Giovanni (de' Medici) delle Bande Nere ("John of the Black Bands"); his mother was the daughter of Lucrezia de' Medici, the eldest daughter of Lorenzo the Magnificent. Thus young Cosimo was the product of *both* branches of the family. The Council of State installed him at the age of not quite 18 as Duke Cosimo I.

Cosimo astonished everyone by becoming a young tiger, quickly establishing one-man, or rather one-boy, rule. Then he settled down to being a dictator—sometimes harsh but, as he proved, motivated by a single-minded patriotism on behalf of the Florentine state, which he made the Grand Duchy of Tuscany. Under his regime, which lasted 37 years, from 1537 to 1574, there came that lesser artistic blooming already mentioned: the work of Cellini, Bronzino, Pontormo, Giambologna and others. To restore Florence to its place of artistic eminence, Cosimo was eager to have Michelangelo back. The invitations began in the 1540s; during the 1550s both Vasari and Cellini were repeatedly the Duke's emissaries to him, and there were direct letters from Cosimo himself.

Cosimo was particularly anxious to finish the Laurentian Library and the New Sacristy and Medici tombs; but when it became clear that Michelangelo was too old and too preoccupied with St. Peter's to come and supervise the work in person, the Duke urged that he send his plans and designs so that others could carry out the projects. Michelangelo replied sadly that the plans did not exist. Indeed it became fairly evident, through the correspondence, that for the most part they never had existed, except as ideas in his head or as tentative explorations. Eventually, a few years before he died, he sent an entirely new design for the grand staircase of the library; from this, the architect Bartolommeo Ammanati executed the staircase, a monumental but strange, voluted, spreading form which, as de Tolnay says, "seems to flow downward like a cascade of lava." But little else was forthcoming from Michelangelo; for as he wrote, "My mind and memory have gone ahead to await me elsewhere."

Realizing now how much and habitually Michelangelo worked by letting an idea develop under his hands, his friends began to press him to prepare models and drawings of St. Peter's and of the other large architectural project he had undertaken for Paul III, the Campidoglio, neither of which could possibly be finished by the time he died. He did finally create a complete wooden scale model of the dome for St. Peter's—although he failed to leave any detailed plans as to the rest of the church. The reason, evidently, was that he had determined to live long enough to complete so much of the construction that no successor could destroy his work or even violate his intention. And it was because of this that he could not leave Rome, much as he might have liked to spend his last years in peace and honor in his native place. To leave Rome, he wrote Vasari, would be to "rejoice many a scoundrel" and "to ruin the whole work, a great shame to me and for my soul a great sin."

By the time he died he thought that he had achieved his aim, for the main structure of St. Peter's was within sight of completion, and he was already preoccupied with the problems of building the dome. He was mistaken, however. Later architects changed the proportions of the

building and even the silhouette of the dome. Yet his personality pervades the structure, and in its essentials the dome is his: the great dome, the landmark of Rome and of all Christendom, the grandest monument of the Renaissance and of the life and World of Michelangelo.

Slowly, almost imperceptibly, his physical capacities declined. But he never underwent the indignity of senility or invalidism. At 85 he could still inspect the construction work at St. Peter's on horseback. Even as he approached 90 he rode every evening in good weather and regardless of the weather he went out walking.

On February 12, 1564, he spent all day with his chisel on another *pietà,* the *Rondanini Pietà* now in Milan. On February 14, although it was a cold, rainy day, he went riding in the countryside. That afternoon his friend and pupil Tiberio Calcagni heard that he had become ill and went to visit him. "When I saw him," Tiberio wrote, "I said that I did not think it right and seemly for him to be going about in such weather. 'What do you want?' he answered, 'I am ill, and cannot find rest anywhere.' The uncertainty of his speech, together with the look and color of his face, made me feel extremely uneasy about his life." Even so, he insisted on trying to ride again the following day; but, as another devoted friend, Diomede Leoni, related, "The coldness of the weather and the weakness of his head and legs prevented him; so he returned to the fireside, and settled down into an easy chair, which he greatly prefers to the bed." His fever worsened, and he sensed that his end was near. And so, as Vasari relates, "Still in perfect self-possession, the master at length made his will in three clauses. He left his soul to God, his body to the earth, and his goods to his nearest relatives. He recommended his attendants [Cavalieri, Leoni, and Daniele da Volterra] to think upon the sufferings of Christ, and departed to a better life. . . ." It was a little before five in the afternoon of February 18, 1564.

As he wanted, his body was taken home to Florence. Vasari writes: "The next day all the painters, sculptors and architects assembled quietly, bearing only a pall of velvet rich with gold embroidery. This they placed over the coffin and the bier. At nightfall they gathered silently . . . The oldest and most distinguished masters each took a torch, while the younger artists at the same moment raised the bier. Blessed was he who could get a shoulder under it! All desired the glory of having borne to earth the remains of the greatest man ever known to the arts."

He died disappointed in himself and his life, feeling that he had lost his way striving for less than eternal values. He did not believe in his "divinity": he never doubted that he was a frail and all-too-human being, far from his own ideal of beauty, full of inconsistencies, a mystery to others and often a perplexity to himself. He felt himself a failure because, of course, he was bound to fail, his goal being the perfection that is beyond the attainment of any mortal. And yet, even in failing, by that very effort he partook of divinity.

"True art," he once wrote, "is made noble and religious by the mind producing it." And the mind, the soul, becomes ennobled by "the endeavor to create something perfect, for God is perfection, and whoever strives after perfection is striving for something divine."

A sketch of the interior of St. Peter's, done a few years before Michelangelo's death in 1564, records the slow progress made on the crossing. The great dome has not yet been started, and even its base, the drum, is only partially constructed. There is a gaping hole in the roof, and the walls and piers below lack finishing touches, although they have been in place for years. Sitting incongruously in the middle is a temporary shelter, erected over the altar of the old basilica of St. Peter's —but which was not razed until 1592.

The Search for God

One of the wonders of Michelangelo's long career is that although he saw himself in his last years as being all but broken by his labors, he was nearly as productive as in his youth—and his work reverberated with richer and deeper meanings. Even at a time when he could write that his memory and brain had gone off to wait for him elsewhere and that his hand was already on the plow of the other life, his imagination remained intact, as fertile as it had ever been. Why?

A part of the answer lies certainly in religion, in Michelangelo's spiritual conversion. Whereas before he had been preoccupied with death, now he actively sought grace, the key, he felt, to salvation; and he offered such grand projects as St. Peter's and the Pauline frescoes almost as personal prayers to God. But as hard as he worked, repentant as he tried to be, there were times when he felt abandoned. "Despite Thy promises, O Lord," he wrote, "'twould seem too much to hope that even love like Thine can overlook my countless wanderings. . . ." Still, his faith did not waver, and at "the very end of art and life" he gave signs of having found what he was looking for. In the *Rondanini Pietà,* on which he was working six days before he died, he forsook all he had learned about the body and listened only to his soul. And out of this harkening came a beatific vision of spirits fused by the embrace of divine love.

St. Peter's, the major project of Michelangelo's last years, on which he worked "solely for the love of God," is seen in this view from the back. This is the portion that best preserves his intentions; the dome, which was to have been his crowning architectural achievement, was built after his death.

180

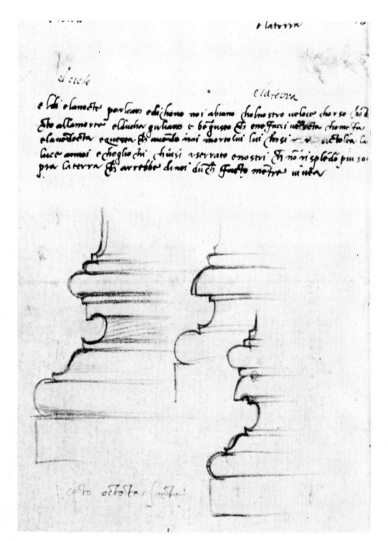

Medici Chapel, Study of Column Bases

St. Peter's, Detail of Pilasters

Michelangelo, the sculptor-painter turned architect, found his supreme
spiritual challenge in St. Peter's: for him the new church was to be nothing less
than a symbol of the Kingdom of Christianity and of the papacy's temporal
and spiritual power. How this biggest of all churches might have looked
if he had completed it himself is suggested in part by the close-up of the apse
(*opposite*), where once again a sculptor's imagination has left its mark on
building stone. Michelangelo conceived of the exterior as a vibrant surface
molded by light. He staggered the colossal pilasters in such a way (*above,
right*) as to create strong shadows—an idea he had apparently begun to
develop as early as the Medici Chapel, for which the sketch (*above, left*)
was made. As the building progressed, he was not content to rely solely on
his plans: to gauge the effect of a detail, such as a cornice, he would actually
have a wooden mock-up hoisted into place.

But the outside of St. Peter's, in Michelangelo's conception, has more than
texture; he gave it a sculptor's rhythm and movement. The wall bends and
curves, almost seeming to undulate, as the gigantic pilasters, a full 167 feet high,
ascend forcefully toward the cornice. Squeezing windows and niches
between them, they cancel out any unwanted horizontal effect these might
have had. In their inexorable sweep upward they point to the dome, the crown
of the basilica, shown in all its triumphant glory on the following pages.

St. Peter's, View of Apse

St. Peter's, Lantern

The only part of the dome Michelangelo saw built was its drum, whose windows and paired columns are seen in the view of the interior opposite. His first design for the dome had been a steeply rising structure, continuing the lifting movement of the walls below; but in his final concept he changed this to a hemispheric dome, heavy and calm, reflecting the growing peacefulness of his last years. This change required him not only to compensate for the decreased height of the new dome but also to resolve the upward movement of the building's lines. He planned therefore to extend the lantern at the peak of the dome, making it the climax of the overall design for the church, and to taper the broad ribs of the dome for an illusion of height. These would in effect transfer the upward movement to the lantern, there to be resolved in a series of architectural grace notes in the form of columns and cornices. But Michelangelo died before he had worked out a plan for the lantern. Della Porta, his successor, reverted to a dome with a steep profile, retaining enough of Michelangelo's vigor in his own version to make it one of the world's most copied structures.

St. Peter's, Interior of Dome

Conversion of St. Paul, 1542-1545

The Light of Revelation

One year after the mighty *Last Judgment*, Michelangelo began what were to be his final works as a painter—two frescoes for Pope Paul III's personal chapel in the Vatican. The first of these, the *Conversion of St. Paul*, is reproduced above: it shows the saint on the road to Damascus at the moment the light shone down upon him from heaven and the voice of Christ asked, "Saul, Saul, why persecutest thou me?" In the face of the blinded Paul *(opposite)*, many

have seen a spiritual portrait of the aged Michelangelo.

Despite their comparatively small size—some 20 by 21 feet—the frescoes took Michelangelo longer to do than the Sistine ceiling, in part because of pressures imposed by St. Peter's and other projects, in part because of ill health. But as the frescoes themselves demonstrate, there is no loss of vigor in the old man's style. His figures are even broader and heavier than before, and his colors have become brighter.

Conversion of St. Paul, detail

Crucifixion of St. Peter, 1546-1550

The second of the Pauline frescoes depicts the martyrdom of St. Peter. Although nailed to the cross, the saint is not shown writhing in pain; rather he is turning deliberately toward the viewer as though to involve him in his martyrdom with an anguished and accusing gaze. The awestruck, frightened figures that surround the saint, and the naked, almost spaceless landscape in which they stand are the culmination of Michelangelo's expressive tendencies in painting. The poses of many, with arms and legs crisscrossing, as in the detail, the crush of bodies almost parallel to the picture plane, the flat light, the lack of any real depth—all these are typical of the new Mannerist style in art for which Michelangelo's work was a major impetus. A dominant force in Italian painting, Mannerism soon spread far beyond Italy's borders to find in Spain, in the late 16th Century, its last and greatest adherent—El Greco.

Crucifixion of St. Peter, detail

Rondanini Pietà, 1555-1564

The Twenty-fourth Hour

I have reached," wrote the aged
Michelangelo to Vasari, his faithful friend of
many years, "the twenty-fourth hour of my
day, and . . . no project arises in my brain
which hath not the figure of death graven
upon it." His last two sculptures, the
Florentine *Deposition* and the *Rondanini Pietà*,
express this view—and show the old man's
intense yearning for oneness with God. In the
Deposition, a work he carved for his
sarcophagus, he gave the cowled face of
Nicodemus *(opposite)* features reminiscent of
his own, relaxed with compassion for the
dead Christ. In the *Rondanini Pietà (left)*, he
came even closer to a fusion of his spirit with
that of the divine. The tall, thin,
dematerialized figures of Christ and Mary,
carved in part from what at first was the
single body of the Virgin in an earlier
version, are literally blended by love into
each other.

Whether works like these can really be
considered finished, as some critics contend,
will always be open to discussion. On the
basis of Michelangelo's late style and his
spiritual conversion, it would seem that their
rough surface, glowing softly with light and
shadow, fulfilled his purposes in a way that
no polished and perfected statues could
possibly have. Michelangelo himself said on
his deathbed: "I regret that I have not done
enough for the salvation of my soul and that
I am dying just as I am beginning to learn
the alphabet of my profession."

Florentine *Deposition*, detail, c. 1550-1555

APPENDIX

Chronology: Painters of the 15th and 16th Centuries

Michelangelo's predecessors and contemporaries are grouped here
in chronological order according to school (Florence, Venice, etc.) or country.

The colored bands correspond to the life spans of the painters, or,
where this information is unknown, to the periods when they flourished (fl.).

Left column

1400 — 1500 — 1600

FLORENCE
UCCELLO 1397-1475
FRA ANGELICO c. 1400-1455
MASACCIO c. 1401-1428
FRA FILIPPO LIPPI 1406-1469
CASTAGNO c. 1410-1457
DOM. VENEZIANO c. 1410-1461
BENOZZO GOZZOLI c. 1420-1497
BALDOVINETTI 1425-1499
POLLAIUOLO, A. c. 1431-1498
VERROCCHIO 1435-1488
BOTTICELLI c. 1444-1510
GHIRLANDAIO 1449-1494
LEONARDO DA VINCI 1452-1519
FILIPPINO LIPPI 1457-1504
PIERO DI COSIMO 1462-1521
FRA BARTOLOMMEO 1472-1517
MICHELANGELO 1475-1564
ANDREA DEL SARTO 1486-1531
ROSSO FIORENTINO 1494-1540
PONTORMO c. 1494-1557
BRONZINO c. 1503-1572

VENICE
JACOPO BELLINI c. 1400-1470
ANTONIO VIVARINI c. 1415-1484
BARTOLOMMEO VIVARINI fl. 1450-1498
GENTILE BELLINI c. 1429-1507
GIOVANNI BELLINI c. 1430-1516
ANTONELLO DA MESSINA c. 1430-1479
CRIVELLI c. 1435-1495
ALVISE VIVARINI c. 1446-1502
CARPACCIO c. 1455-1526
TITIAN 1477-1576
GIORGIONE c. 1478-1510
PALMA VECCHIO 1480-1528
LORENZO LOTTO 1480-1556
SEBASTIANO DEL PIOMBO 1485-1547
JACOPO BASSANO 1510-1592
TINTORETTO 1518-1594

SIENA
SASSETTA c. 1392-1450
GIOVANNI DI PAOLO 1403-1482
VECCHIETTA 1412-1480
MATTEO DI GIOVANNI c. 1430-1495
FRANCESCO DI GIORGIO 1439-1502
NEROCCIO DI LANDI 1447-1500
SODOMA 1477-1549
BECCAFUMI c. 1486-1551

CENTRAL ITALY
PIERO DELLA FRANCESCA c. 1416-1492
MELOZZO DA FORLI 1438-1494
SIGNORELLI c. 1441-1523
PERUGINO 1445-1523
PINTURICCHIO 1454-1513
RAPHAEL 1483-1520
GIULIO ROMANO 1492-1546

1400 — 1500 — 1600

Right column

1400 — 1500 — 1600

NORTHERN ITALY
PISANELLO 1395-1455
FOPPA c. 1427-1516
COSIMO TURA 1430-1495
MANTEGNA 1431-1506
COSSA c. 1435-1477
DOSSO DOSSI c. 1479-1542
LUINI c. 1480-1532
CORREGGIO 1494-1534
MORETTO c. 1498-1555
PARMIGIANINO 1503-1540
MORONI c. 1525-1578

FRANCE
FOUQUET c. 1420-1481
FROMENT fl. 1450-1490
MAÎTRE DE MOULINS fl. 1480
JEAN CLOUET c. 1475-1547

GERMANY
MEISTER FRANCKE fl. c. 1424-1435
LOCHNER fl. 1410-1451
LUCAS MOSER fl. 1431-1440
KONRAD WITZ (SWISS) fl. 1433-1447
MULTSCHER c. 1400-1467
SCHONGAUER c. 1430-1491
PACHER c. 1435-1498
HOLBEIN, THE ELDER 1460-1524
GRÜNEWALD c. 1470-1530
DÜRER 1471-1528
CRANACH 1472-1553
BURGKMAIR 1473-1531
ALTDORFER c. 1480-1538
BALDUNG GRIEN 1480-1545
HOLBEIN, THE YOUNGER 1497-1543

FLANDERS
CAMPIN 1375-1444
VAN DER WEYDEN c. 1399-1464
PETRUS CHRISTUS c. 1410-1472
DIRCK BOUTS c. 1420-1475
MEMLING c. 1430-1494
VAN DER GOES c. 1440-1482
BOSCH c. 1450-1516
GERARD DAVID c. 1450-1523
MASSYS c. 1466-1530
MABUSE (GOSSAERT) c. 1470-1533
PATINIR c. 1475-1524
VAN SCOREL 1495-1562
PIETER BRUEGHEL c. 1525-1569

HOLLAND
VAN LEYDEN 1494-1533
HEEMSKERCK 1498-1574
AERTSEN 1508-1575
ANTONIS MOR (MORO) c. 1519-1576

SPAIN
MARTORELL fl. 1433-1453
BERMEJO fl. 1474-1495
MORALES 1509-1586
COELLO c. 1515-1590
EL GRECO c. 1542-1614

1400 — 1500 — 1600

Michelangelo: A Last Look

The catalogue that begins here and continues on the following pages shows those of Michelangelo's sculptures which, simply because his output was so enormous, could not be shown elsewhere in this book. Arranged in chronological order, they provide an overall view of Michelangelo's development not only as a sculptor but as a human being and—as he touchingly put it— a father: "My children," he wrote, "will be the works I leave behind. For even if they will be of little value, they will last for a while."

Kneeling Angel, 1494-1495. While a refugee in Bologna, Michelangelo carved this 20-inch-high candlestick.

St. Proculus, 1494-1495. Also done in Bologna. In its intense, angry gaze it anticipates the *David.*

St. Petronius, 1494-1495. Another work of Michelangelo's exile; the saint holds a model of Bologna.

Bacchus, c. 1497. The drunken god shows Michelangelo under the influence of classical sculpture.

St. Matthew, c. 1501-1506. This early unfinished work shows the artist's method of attacking stone.

"There are in marbles
rich or base images,
So far as our genius
can draw them out."

—1534

St. Peter and St. Paul, 1501-1504. Of the four
statuettes supposedly carved by Michelangelo for the
Piccolomini altar in Siena, only these two can be
safely attributed to the master.

Risen Christ, 1519-1520. This work
was finished by a pupil who bungled
the toes, fingers and beard.

The Victory, c. 1532-1534. Planned
apparently for the Julius tomb, it
was later eliminated.

Rachel and Leah, c. 1542. These Biblical figures flank *Moses* in
the final version of the Julius tomb.

Crouching Boy, c. 1524. This
figure was intended for the tomb
of Lorenzo de' Medici.

Madonna and Child, begun 1521.
Although left unfinished, this work
occupies a prominent place today
in the Medici Chapel.

Apollo, begun 1525-1526. Another
unfinished work, this may have
been conceived as a *David*.

Brutus, c. 1542. Michelangelo
did everything but supply
the finishing touches to this work.

Deposition, c. 1550-1555 (shown in a detail on page 192).
Out of impatience, Michelangelo smashed this work,
but let an assistant piece it together again.

Catalogue of Illustrations

ANGELICO, FRA: c. 1400-1455, Florentine. p. 50: *The Annunciation*, tempera on panel, 15" x 15", Museo di San Marco, Florence.

BOTTICELLI, SANDRO: c. 1444-1510, Florentine. p. 25: *Adoration of the Magi*, panel, 43¾" x 52¾", Uffizi Gallery, Florence. p. 52-53: *Primavera*, panel, 79⅞" x 123⅝", Uffizi Gallery, Florence.

BRONZINO, ANGELO: 1503-1572, Florentine. p. 141: *Alessandro, First Duke of Florence*, oil, 5" x 6½", Palazzo Medici-Riccardi, Florence. *Lorenzo, Duke of Urbino*, oil, 5" x 6½", Palazzo Medici-Riccardi, Florence.

BRUNELLESCHI, FILIPPO: 1377-1446, Florentine. p. 59: Old Sacristy, San Lorenzo, Florence.

CASTAGNO, ANDREA DEL: c. 1410-1457, Florentine. p. 55: *Youthful David*, leather, height 45½", width (top) 30¼", width (bottom) 16⅛", National Gallery of Art, Widener Collection, Washington, D.C.

DONATELLO: 1386-1466, Florentine. p. 60: *Judith and Holofernes*, bronze, height with base 7'9", Piazza della Signoria, Florence. *David*, bronze, height 62¼", Museo Nazionale del Bargello, Florence. p. 61: *St. Mark*, marble, height 7'9", Or San Michele, Florence.

GHIBERTI, LORENZO: 1378-1455, Florentine. p. 58: *Gates of Paradise*, gilt bronze, 15' x 8'3" (each plaque 31" x 31"), Baptistery, Florence.

GHIRLANDAIO, DOMENICO: 1449-1494, Florentine. p. 56: *Pope Honorius III Confirming the Rule of the Order of St. Francis* (detail), fresco, Sassetti Chapel, Santa Trinita, Florence.

GIOTTO: c. 1266-1337, Florentine. p. 28: *The Ascension of John the Evangelist*, fresco, 23'4" x 8'10", Peruzzi Chapel, Santa Croce, Florence.

GOZZOLI, BENOZZO: 1420-1497, Florentine. p. 26-27: *Journey of the Magi* (detail), fresco, Chapel, Palazzo Medici-Riccardi, Florence.

LIPPI, FRA FILIPPO: 1406-1469, Florentine. p. 49: *Madonna and Child*, panel, 36" x 25", Uffizi Gallery, Florence.

MASACCIO: 1401-1428, Florentine. p. 29: *The Tribute Money* (detail), fresco, Brancacci Chapel, Santa Maria del Carmine, Florence. p. 34: *St. Peter Distributing Goods to the Poor and Death of Ananias* (detail), fresco, Brancacci Chapel, Santa Maria del Carmine, Florence.

MICHELANGELO: 1475-1564, Florentine. p. 28: Drawing after Giotto, *The Ascension of John the Evangelist*, pen and ink, 12½" x 8", Musée du Louvre, Paris. p. 29: Drawing after Masaccio, *The Tribute Money*, pen and ink on red chalk, 15⅝" x 7¾", Staatliche Graphische Sammlung, Munich. p. 30: *Battle of the Centaurs*, marble relief, 33¼" x 33⅝", Casa Buonarroti, Florence. p. 31: *Madonna of the Stairs*, marble relief, 22" x 15¾", Casa Buonarroti, Florence. p. 32: *Pitti Madonna*, marble relief, diameter 33½", Museo Nazionale del Bargello, Florence. p. 33: *Taddei Madonna*, marble relief, diameter 43", Royal Academy of Arts, London. p. 62: *Doni Tondo*, wood, resin and tempera, diameter 47¼", Uffizi Gallery, Florence. p. 75: *Pietà*, marble, height 69", St. Peter's, Rome. p. 76-81: *Pietà* (details). p. 82: *Bruges Madonna*, marble, height 50½", Church of Notre Dame, Bruges. p. 83: *Bruges Madonna* (detail). p. 84: *David*, marble, height with base 16'10½", Accademia, Florence. p. 97: *The Fall of Phaëton*, black chalk, 16½" x 9¼", Royal Collection, Windsor Castle. p. 98: *Sketches for Sistine Ceiling and the Tomb of Pope Julius II*, red chalk, pen and ink, 11¼" x 7⅝", Ashmolean Museum, Oxford. p. 99: *Sketches for two Davids*, pen and ink, 10½" x 7⅜", Musée du Louvre, Paris. *Sketches for a River God*, pen and ink, 5¼" x 8¼", British Museum, London. p. 100: *Study of a Profile*, black chalk, 17⅛" x 11", Uffizi Gallery, Florence. p. 101: *The Virgin and Child*, black chalk, 10½" x 4¾", British Museum, London. p. 115: *Sketches for the Libyan Sibyl*, red chalk, 11⅜" x 8⅜", The Metropolitan Museum of Art, New York. p. 118, 119, 120: Ceiling of the Sistine Chapel, fresco, 45' x 132', Vatican, Rome. slipcase: *Isaiah* (detail), front end paper: *Temptation* (detail). p. 121-123: *The Creation of Adam* (detail). p. 124-125: *Deluge* (detail). back end paper: *Expulsion from the Garden of Eden* (detail). p. 126-127: *Last Judgment*, fresco, 48' x 44', Sistine Chapel, Vatican, Rome. p. 128-129: *Last Judgment* (details). p. 139: *Tomb of Lorenzo de' Medici* (detail), marble, Medici Chapel, San Lorenzo, Florence. p. 142: *Tomb of Giuliano de' Medici*, marble, height of central figure 5'8", Medici Chapel, San Lorenzo, Florence. p. 143: *Tomb of Lorenzo de' Medici*, marble, height of central figure 5'10", Medici Chapel, San Lorenzo, Florence. p. 144: *Night*, marble, length of block, 6'4¾", Medici Chapel, San Lorenzo, Florence. p. 145: *Dawn*, marble, length of block, 6'8", Medici Chapel, San Lorenzo, Florence. p. 146-147: *Tomb of Giuliano de' Medici* (details). p. 150: *Dying Slave*, marble, height 7'6½", Musée du Louvre, Paris. *Rebellious Slave*, marble, height 7'1", Musée du Louvre, Paris. p. 163: *Moses*, marble, height 8'4", San Pietro in Vincoli, Rome. p. 164-165: *Moses* (details). p. 166: *Youthful Captive*, marble, height 8'7", Accademia, Florence. *Atlas*, marble, height 9'2", Accademia, Florence. p. 167: *Bearded Captive*, marble, height 8'8", Accademia, Florence. *Awakening Captive*, marble, height 9', Accademia, Florence. p. 188: *Conversion of St. Paul*, fresco, 20'6" x 21'8", Cappella Paolina, Vatican, Rome. p. 189: *Conversion of St. Paul* (detail). p. 190: *Crucifixion of St. Peter*, fresco, 20'6" x 21'8", Cappella Paolina, Vatican, Rome. p. 191: *Crucifixion of St. Peter* (detail). p. 192: *Rondanini Pietà*, marble, height 6'4", Castello Sforzesco, Milan. p. 193: *Deposition* (detail), marble, Duomo, Florence. p. 195: *Kneeling Angel*, marble, height with base 20", San Domenico, Bologna. *St. Proculus*, marble, height 22", San Domenico, Bologna. *St. Petronius*, marble, height 25", San Domenico, Bologna. *Bacchus*, marble, height with base 80", Museo Nazionale del Bargello, Florence. *St. Matthew*, marble, height 8'11", Accademia, Florence. p. 196: *St. Peter*, marble, height 50", Piccolomini Altar, Siena Cathedral. *St. Paul*, marble, height 50", Piccolomini Altar, Siena Cathedral. *The Risen Christ*, marble, height 6'10", Santa Maria sopra Minerva, Rome. *The Victory*, marble, height 8'7½", Palazzo Vecchio, Florence. *Rachel*, marble, height 6'7½", San Pietro in Vincoli, Rome. *Leah*, marble, height 6'10", San Pietro in Vincoli, Rome. p. 197: *Madonna and Child*, marble, height 7'5", Medici Chapel, San Lorenzo, Florence. *The Crouching Boy*, marble, height 22", Hermitage, Leningrad. *Apollo*, marble, height with base 4'10", Museo Nazionale del Bargello, Florence. *The Brutus Bust*, marble, height 29½", Museo Nazionale del Bargello, Florence. *Deposition*, marble, height 7'8", Duomo, Florence.

RAPHAEL: 1483-1520, Umbrian. p. 102: *Mass of Bolsena* (detail), fresco, Stanza dell' Eliodoro, Vatican, Rome. p. 140: *Pope Leo X with Cardinal Giulio de' Medici and Luigi de' Rossi*, panel, 60⅝" x 46⅞", Uffizi Gallery, Florence. p. 141: *Giuliano de' Medici, Duke of Nemours*, tempera and oil on canvas, 32¾" x 26", The Metropolitan Museum of Art, Jules Bache Collection, New York.

SIGNORELLI, LUCA: c. 1441-1523, Umbrian. p. 57: *The Damned Cast into Hell* (detail), fresco, San Brizio Chapel, Duomo, Orvieto.

TOGNETTI, GUSTAVO: 1864-1955, Rome. p. 116: Reconstruction of Sistine Chapel before July, 1508. pen and ink drawing, 11" x 16", Archivio Fotog., Musei Vaticani.

UCCELLO, PAOLO: 1397-1475, Florentine. p. 54-55: *Battle of San Romano* (detail), panel, 72" x 127", Uffizi Gallery, Florence.

VENEZIANO, DOMENICO: c. 1410-1461, Florentine. p. 51: *St. Lucy Altarpiece*, panel, 82⅛" x 84", Uffizi Gallery, Florence.

VERROCCHIO, ANDREA DEL: 1435-1488, Florentine. p. 24: *Lorenzo de' Medici* (detail), painted terra cotta, height 25⅛", National Gallery of Art, Samuel H. Kress Collection, Washington, D.C.

VOLTERRA, DANIELE DA: 1509-1566, Tuscan. p. 8: *Michelangelo Buonarroti*, bronze bust, height 32", Museo Nazionale del Bargello, Florence.

Bibliography

*Paperback.

MICHELANGELO—ART

Ackerman, James, *The Architecture of Michelangelo* (2 vols.). Viking, 1961.

Carli, Enzo (ed.), *All the Paintings of Michelangelo*. Translated by Marion Fitzallan. Hawthorn Books, 1963.

De Tolnay, Charles, *The Art and Thought of Michelangelo*. Translated by Nan Buranelli. Pantheon Books, 1964.

Michelangelo (5 vols.). Princeton University Press, 1943-1960.

De Tolnay, Charles (ed.), and others, *The Complete Works of Michelangelo*. Reynal, 1965.

Goldscheider, Ludwig, *Michelangelo: Drawings*. Phaidon, 1951.

A Survey of Michelangelo's Models in Wax and Clay. Phaidon, 1962.

Michelangelo: Paintings, Sculptures, Architecture. Phaidon, 1953.

Hartt, Frederick, *Michelangelo*. (The Library of Great Painters) Harry N. Abrams, 1965.

Russoli, Franco (ed.), *All the Sculpture of Michelangelo*. Translated by Paul Colacicchi. Hawthorn Books, 1963.

Wilde, Johannes, *Italian Drawings in the Department of Prints and Drawings in the British Museum: Michelangelo and His Studio* (2 vols.). Trustees of British Museum, 1953.

MICHELANGELO—LIFE

Condivi, Ascanio, *The Life of Michelangelo Buonarroti*. Translated by Herbert P. Horne. Marymount Press, 1904.

The Divine Michelangelo: The Florentine Academy's Homage on his Death in 1564. Translated by Rudolf and Margot Wittkower. Phaidon, 1964.

*Rolland, Romain, *Michelangelo*. Translated by Frederick Street. Collier Books, 1962.

Symonds, John Addington, *The Life of Michelangelo Buonarroti*. The Modern Library, 1936. (Also paperback, Capricorn, 1961.)

Vasari, Giorgio, *Lives of the Painters, Sculptors and Architects* (4 vols.). Translated by A. B. Hinds. E. P. Dutton (Everyman's Library), 1963. (Also paperback, abridged and edited by Betty Burroughs, Simon and Schuster, 1946.)

MICHELANGELO—WRITINGS

Clements, Robert J., *The Poetry of Michelangelo*. New York University Press, 1965.

**Michelangelo: A Self Portrait*. Prentice-Hall, 1963.

Michelangelo's Theory of Art. New York University Press, 1961.

Complete Poems and Selected Letters of Michelangelo. Edited by Robert N. Linscott. Translated by Creighton Gilbert. Random House, 1963.

Letters of Michelangelo, The (2 vols.). Edited and translated by E. H. Ramsden. Stanford University Press, 1963.

RENAISSANCE ART

*Berenson, Bernard, *The Italian Painters of the Renaissance*. Meridian Books, 1964.
Italian Pictures of the Renaissance: Florentine School (2 vols.). Phaidon, 1963.
*Blunt, Anthony, *Artistic Theory in Italy: 1450-1600*. Oxford University Press, 1962.
Briganti, G., *Italian Mannerism*. S. Van Nostrand, 1962.
*Clark, Sir Kenneth, *The Nude: A Study in Ideal Form*. Anchor Books, 1959.
Freedberg, Sydney J., *Painting of the High Renaissance in Rome and Florence* (2 vols.). Harvard University Press, 1961.
Friedlaender, W., *Mannerism and Anti-Mannerism in Italian Painting*. Schocken, 1965.
Gould, C., *An Introduction to Italian Renaissance Painting*. Oxford University Press, 1957.
Klein, R. and H. Zermer, *Italian Art 1500-1600: Sources and Documents in the History of Art*. Edited by H. W. Janson. Prentice-Hall, 1966.
Lowry, B., *Renaissance Architecture*. Braziller, 1962.
Murray, Peter, *The Architecture of the Italian Renaissance*. Schocken, 1963.
Panofsky, Erwin, *Renaissance and Renascences in Western Art*. Almqvist & Wiksell, 1960.
Pope-Hennessy, John, *Italian Renaissance Sculpture*. Phaidon, 1958.
Italian Renaissance and Baroque Sculpture (3 vols.). Phaidon, 1963.
*Vasari, Giorgio, *Vasari on Technique*. Edited by G. Baldwin Brown. Translated by Louisa S. Maclehose. Dover, 1960.

THE RENAISSANCE

*Ady, Cecilia M., *Lorenzo dei Medici and Renaissance Italy*. Collier Books, 1962.
Baron, Hans, *The Crisis of the Early Italian Renaissance* (2 vols.). Princeton University Press, 1955.
De La Bedoyere, Michael, *The Meddlesome Friar and the Wayward Pope*. Hanover House, 1958.

Burckhardt, Jacob, *The Civilization of the Renaissance in Italy: An Essay* (2 vols.). Phaidon. (Also paperback, 2 vols. Harper Torchbooks, 1958.)
Chastel, André, *The Age of Humanism: Europe 1480-1530*. McGraw-Hill, 1963.
Elton, G. R. (ed.), *The Reformation 1520-1559*. (*The New Cambridge Modern History*, Vol. II.) Cambridge University Press, 1958.
Ferguson, Wallace K., *The Renaissance in Historical Thought: Five Centuries of Interpretation*. Houghton Mifflin, 1948.
*Gilmore, Myron P., *The World of Humanism 1453-1517*. Harper Torchbooks, 1952.
*Hale, J. R. (ed.), *Guicciardini*. Translated by Cecil Grayson. (The Great Histories) Washington Square Press, 1964.
*Kristeller, Paul Oskar, *Renaissance Thought: The Classic, Scholastic and Humanistic Strains*. Harper Torchbooks, 1961.
Lucas-Dubreton, J., *Daily Life in Florence In the Time of the Medici*. Translated by A. Lytton Sells. Macmillan, 1960.
McCarthy, Mary, *The Stones of Florence*. Harcourt, Brace & World, 1963. (Also paperback.)
Pastor, Ludwig von, *The History of the Popes from the Close of the Middle Ages* (Vols. III-XIV). Kegan Paul, Trench, Trubner & Co., 1900-1924.
Plumb, J. H., *The Horizon Book of the Renaissance*. American Heritage, 1961.
Potter, G. R. (ed.), *The Renaissance: 1493-1520*. (*The New Cambridge Modern History*, Vol. I.) Cambridge University Press, 1964.
Ridolfi, Roberto, *The Life of Girolamo Savonarola*. Knopf, 1959.
De Roover, Raymond, *The Rise and Decline of the Medici Bank: 1397-1494*. Harvard University Press, 1963.
*Schevill, Ferdinand, *The Medici*. Harper Torchbooks, 1949.
Medieval and Renaissance Florence (2 vols.). Harper Torchbooks, 1963.
*Trevelyan, Janet Penrose, *A Short History of the Italian People*. Pitman, 1956.
*Vespasiano, *Renaissance Princes, Popes, and Prelates: The Vespasiano Memoirs: Lives of Illustrious Men of the XV Century*. Translated by William George and Emily Waters. Harper Torchbooks, 1963.

Acknowledgments

The editors of this book are particularly indebted to Janet Cox Rearick, Assistant Professor of Art History, Hunter College, New York, who read the book in its entirety. They are also indebted to the Department of Western Art, Ashmolean Museum, Oxford; Umberto Baldini, Director, Gabinetto dei Restauri, Uffizi Gallery, Florence; Paola Barocchi, Florence; Eleanor E. Barry, Librarian, School of Museum of Fine Arts, Boston; Filippo de Benedetto, Biblioteca Medicea-Laurenziana, Florence; Luciano Berti, Director, Museo Nazionale del Bargello, Florence; Coins and Medals Department and Department of Prints and Drawings, British Museum, London; Deoclecio Redig de Campos, Direzione Generale ai Monumenti, Musei e Gallerie Pontificie, Vatican, Rome; Casa Editrice Giulio Einaudi, Turin; Renzo Chiarelli, Director, Galleria dell' Accademia, Florence; Colonel John R. Elting, General Staff, United States Army; Anna-Maria Forlani, Director, Gabinetto dei Disegni, Uffizi Gallery, Florence; Rodolfo Francioni, President, Opera del Duomo, Florence; David L. Hicks, Associate Professor of History, New York University; Christopher Kiernan, Administrator, Vatican Pavilion, New York World's Fair; Curator and staff of the Cabinet des Dessins, Musée du Louvre, Paris; Mario Pirolli, Fabbrica di San Pietro, Vatican, Rome; Ugo Procacci, Soprintendente ai Monumenti, Florence; Paolo Portoghesi, Rome; Raymond de Roover, Professor of History, Brooklyn College, City University of New York; The Royal Library, Windsor Castle; Vincent Scully Jr., Col. John Trumbull Professor of Art History, Yale University; Silio Sensi, Soprintendenza, Florence; Charles de Tolnay, Director, Casa Buonarroti, Florence; Irma Tondi-Merolle, Director, Biblioteca Medicea-Laurenziana, Florence; Francesco Vacchini, Fabbrica di San Pietro, Vatican, Rome; Bruno Zevi, Rome.

Picture Credits

The sources for the illustrations in this book appear below. Credits for pictures from left to right are separated by semicolons, from top to bottom by dashes.

Slip case cover and end papers—Frank Lerner.
CHAPTER 1: 8—Emmett Bright. 10—Vivarelli (Biblioteca Nazionale Centrale, Rome). 13—Tosi (German Institute, Florence). 15—David Greenspan. 19—Photograph by Evelyn Hofer from *The Stones of Florence* (Mary McCarthy) Harcourt, Brace & World. 20, 21—N. R. Farbman (copy of 15th Century woodcut, Museo di Firenze Com'Era, Florence). 22, 23—Gjon Mili. 24—National Gallery of Art, Washington, D.C., Samuel H. Kress Collection. 25—Scala. 26, 27—Fernand Bourges. 28—Scala—Eddy Van der Veen. 29—Fernand Bourges—Walter Sanders. 30—Emmett Bright. 31—Alinari. 32, 33—Anderson; Leonard Taylor.
CHAPTER 2: 34—Tosi. 37—Alinari (San Petronio, Bologna). 42—Tosi (German Institute, Florence). 44—Staatliche Museum, Berlin. 45—Tosi (Museo Nazionale del Bargello, Florence)—Staatliche Museum, Berlin. 46—Vivarelli (Biblioteca Nazionale, Florence). 47—Alinari (Palazzo Medici-Riccardi, Florence). 49—W. Curtin. 50—Fernand Bourges. 51, 52, 53—Scala. 54, 55—Scala; National Gallery of Art, Washington, D.C., Widener Collection. 56—Scala. 57—Bullaty-Lomeo. 58—Fernand Bourges. 59—Emmett Bright. 60—Alinari; David Lees. 61—Alinari.
CHAPTER 3: 62—Scala. 64—Heinz Zinram (British Museum). 68—Alinari (Museo di San Marco, Florence). 75 through 81—Arnold Newman. 82, 83—Gjon Mili.
CHAPTER 4: 84—Mark Kauffman. 87—Walter Sanders (Biblioteca Medicea-Laurenziana, Florence). 90—Culver Pictures, Inc. (Museo di San Marco, Florence). 92—

New York Public Library. 93—Paul Jensen—Walter Sanders (Accademia, Florence). 97—G. Spearman (Royal Collection, Windsor Castle, copyright reserved). 98—Ashmolean Museum, Oxford. 99—Eddy Van der Veen—John R. Freeman. 100—Emmett Bright. 101—John R. Freeman.
CHAPTER 5: 102—Marzari. 104—Publifoto-Keystone (Vatican Collections, Rome). 109—Biblioteca Medicea-Laurenziana. 113—Biblioteca Medicea-Laurenziana—translation of sonnet from *Sonnets of Michelangelo* by S. Elizabeth Hall, published 1905, Routledge & Kegan Paul Ltd., London. 115—Henry Groskinsky. 116—Vatican Museum Photo Archive. 117—Carlo Bavagnoli. 118, 119, 120—Frank Lerner. 121, 122, 123—Scala. 124 through 129—Frank Lerner.
CHAPTER 6: 130—Gjon Mili. 134, 135—Designed according to Charles de Tolnay's instructions by Denise Fossard, drawn by Peter Spier. 137—Alinari (Casa Buonarroti, Florence)—Alinari. 139—Emmett Bright. 140—Scala. 141—Henry Groskinsky; Scala—Marzari. 142 through 147—Emmett Bright. 148, 149—Biblioteca Medicea-Laurenziana; Scala.
CHAPTER 7: 150—Eddy Van der Veen. 157—Alinari (Casa Buonarroti, Florence). 163, 164—Walter Sanders. 165—Mark Kauffman. 166, 167—Walter Sanders.
CHAPTER 8: 168—Oscar Savio. 172—Alinari (Museo Nazionale del Bargello, Florence). 174—Biblioteca Nazionale, Florence. 179—Hamburger Kunsthalle. 181—Alinari. 182—Tosi (Archivio Buonarroti, Florence); Oscar Savio. 183, 184, 185—Oscar Savio. 186—Alifoto. 187 through 191—Scala. 192—Mark Kauffman. 193—Walter Sanders.
APPENDIX: 195—Alinari; Brogi—Alinari; Anderson; Brogi. 196—Brogi (2); Anderson—Anderson (3). 197—Anderson; Accademia Belle Arti, Bologna; Brogi—Brogi; Walter Sanders.
DRAWINGS AND CHARTS: 17, 66, 134, 135, 152, 154, 176, 177—Peter Spier. 108—Enid Kotschnig. 194—George V. Kelvin.

Index

Numerals in italics indicate a picture of the subject mentioned. Unless otherwise identified, all listed art works are by Michelangelo.

The text for this book was set in photocomposed Bembo. First cut in Europe in 1930, Bembo is named for the Italian humanist Pietro Bembo (1470-1547), an arbiter of literary taste. While it has some resemblance to letters designed in 1470 by Nicolas Jenson, it is largely based on characters cut by Francesco Griffo around 1490.

PRODUCTION STAFF FOR TIME INCORPORATED

John L. Hallenbeck (Vice President and Director of Production), Robert E. Foy, Caroline Ferri and Robert E. Fraser
Text photocomposed under the direction of Albert J. Dunn and Arthur J. Dunn

AUGUSTANA UNIVERSITY COLLEGE
LIBRARY

AUGUSTANA UNIVERSITY COLLEGE
LIBRARY

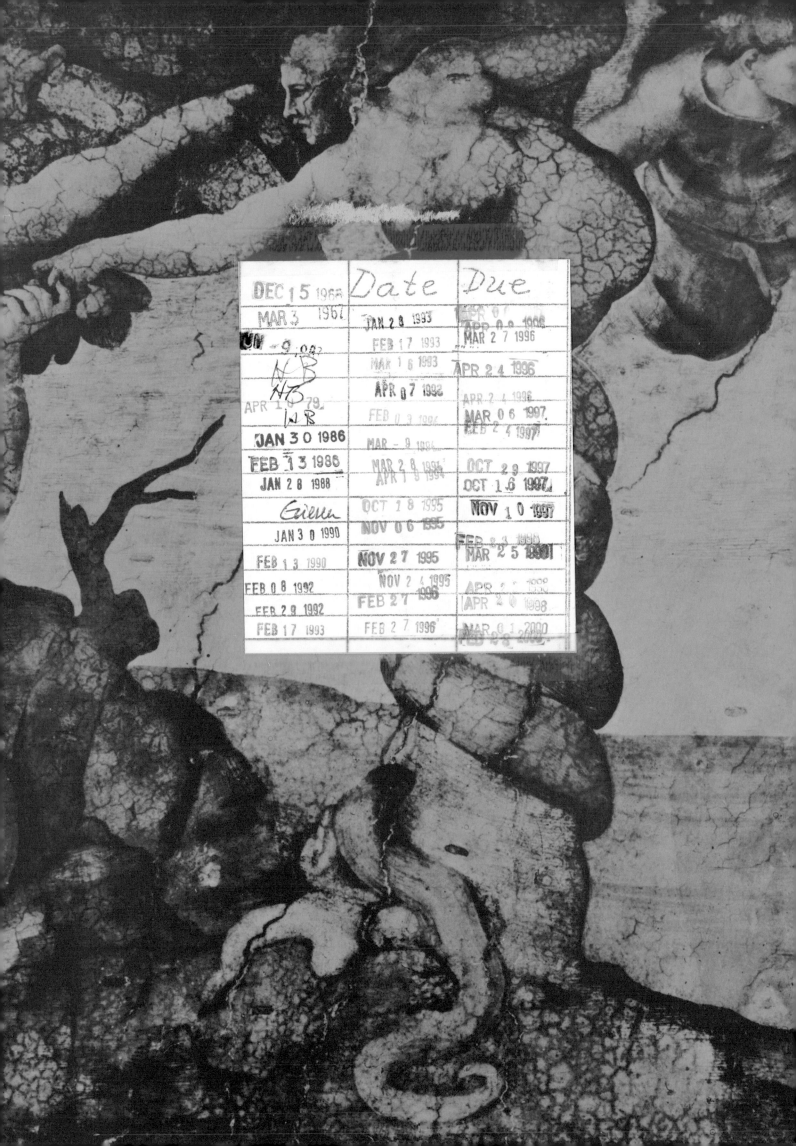